Jim Keogh
Cracking the Nursing Interview

Jim Keogh, DNP, RN-BC

Cracking the Nursing Interview

—

WITHDRAWN

ISBN 978-1-5015-1504-0
e-ISBN (PDF) 978-1-5015-0610-9
e-ISBN (EPUB) 978-1-5015-0625-3

Library of Congress Cataloging-in-Publication Data
A CIP catalog record for this book has been applied for at the Library of Congress.

Bibliographic information published by the Deutsche Nationalbibliothek
The Deutsche Nationalbibliothek lists this publication in the Deutsche Nationalbibliografie;
detailed bibliographic data are available on the Internet at http://dnb.dnb.de.

© 2017 Walter de Gruyter Inc., Boston/Berlin
Printing and binding: CPI book GmbH, Leck
♾ Printed on acid-free paper
Printed in Germany

www.degruyter.com

This book is dedicated to Anne, Sandy, Joanne, Amber-Leigh Christine, Shawn, Eric, and Amy, without whose help and support this book could not have been written.

Contents

Introduction —— vii

Part One: Understanding the Interview Process —— 1

Chapter 1: The Nursing Interview Process —— 3
How Nursing Jobs Are Created —— 4
The Nurse Job Description —— 4
Full-Time, Part-Time, Per Diem —— 5
Benefits and No-Benefits —— 6
Union vs. Non-Union —— 7
Job Postings —— 8
Applying In-house for a Position —— 9
Applying from the Outside —— 10
Networking Helps —— 10
Human Resources Interview —— 11
Nurse Manager Interview —— 12
Pre-employment Technical Tests —— 13
Job Offer —— 14
Pre-employment Health Exam —— 15
Background Check —— 16
Orientation —— 17
Probation —— 19

Chapter 2: Behind the Scenes of the Nursing Interview Process —— 21
The Challenges of Recruiting Nurses —— 21
The Ideal Nurse —— 22
How Decisions Are Made —— 25
The Flow of Interviews —— 25
Getting Lost in the Shuffle —— 26
The Dreaded Application Tracking System —— 27
Job Fairs —— 31
The Background Check Anxiety —— 32
Why You Didn't Get Hired —— 36

Chapter 3: The New Grad Nursing Interview —— 39
Before Graduation —— 39

What Type of Nursing Do You Want to Do? —— 41
You Don't Have Nursing Experience but You Have Experience —— 42
The Search Begins —— 43
Use Your Network —— 45
What Nurse Recruiters Look For —— 46
Selling Yourself in Your Resume and Job Application —— 47
Cover Letter —— 51
What to Expect During the Interview —— 52
After the Interview —— 55
Nursing as a Second ... or Third ... or Fourth Career —— 56

Chapter 4: The Experienced Nurse Interview —— 59
Are You an Experienced Nurse? —— 59
Risks of Changing Jobs —— 61
Transfer or Seek a New Employer —— 62
Per Diem Alternative —— 62
Resign or be Terminated —— 63
Hospital Mergers and Jobs —— 65
Returning to Nursing —— 66
    Returning to Nursing Under Disciplinary Action —— 68
Networking Helps —— 69
Applying for a Transfer —— 70
Applying for an Outside Position —— 72
Cover Letter or No Cover Letter —— 76
Reapplying to a Former Employer —— 77
What to Expect During the Interview —— 78
After the Interview —— 80
Meeting the Hiring Nurse Manager —— 82

Chapter 5: Choosing a Nursing Specialty —— 85
Developing a Career Path —— 85
    Obstacles to Change —— 86
    Assess Your Current Nursing Career —— 87
Changing Nursing Specialty —— 88
Is Management for You? —— 90
Agency Nursing —— 92
Travel Nursing —— 94
Home Healthcare Nursing —— 96
Case Management —— 97

Nurse Practitioner —— 99
Flight Transport Nurse —— 100
Nursing Informatics —— 101
Hospice Nurse —— 103
Infection Control Nurse —— 104
Military Nursing —— 105
Nurse Educator —— 106
Legal Nursing —— 108
Forensic Nurse —— 109
Utilization Review Nurse —— 110
Telehealth Nursing —— 111
School Nursing —— 112
Cruise Ship Nursing —— 113
Medical Sales Representative —— 114

Chapter 6: Preparing for the Interview —— 117
Preparing Your "Script" —— 118
The Game Plan —— 120
It's a Wrap —— 121
Some Thorny Questions —— 123
Bring a List of Questions to Ask —— 124
If the Interview Doesn't Go Well —— 126
Be Prepared to Walk Away —— 127
Prepare for the Online Pre-Employment Tests —— 128
Prep for the Technical Interview —— 131

Part Two: Key Facts Every Candidate Should Know —— 133

Chapter 7: Preparing for Medication Questions —— 135
You Don't Need to Be a Genius —— 135
Online Medication Tests —— 137
Prepping for Dose Calculation Questions —— 138
How Medications Work —— 139
Facts to Remember —— 141
Revisiting the Basics —— 142
Oral Medications —— 142
Liquid Medication —— 142
Sublingual and Buccal Medication —— 143

Transdermal Medication —— 143
Topical Medication —— 144
Eye Drop Medication —— 144
Eye Ointment Medication —— 144
Ear Drop Medication —— 145
Nose Drop Medication —— 145
Nose Spray Medication —— 145
Inhalation Medication —— 145
Nasogastric and Gastrostomy Tube Medication —— 146
Suppository Medication —— 146
Intradermal Injection —— 147
Subcutaneous Injection —— 147
Intramuscular Injection —— 148
Z-Track Injection —— 148
Intravenous Injections —— 148
Before Administering Medications —— 149
Things to Remember —— 150
Common Medications That Are Helpful to Know —— 152
Hypertension Medication —— 152
Diuretics —— 152
Medications That Interfere with Hypertensive Medications —— 154
Some Facts to Remember —— 155
Diabetic Medications —— 155
Insulin —— 156
Type 2 Diabetic Medication —— 156
Some Facts to Remember —— 157
Antibiotics —— 159
Facts to Remember —— 159
Pain Medications —— 161
Facts to Remember —— 163
Facts to Remember —— 164

Chapter 8: Preparing for Nursing Questions —— 167
Physiological Compensation —— 167
Estimating the Physiological Reserves —— 168
The Call for Help —— 169
The Cascading Effect —— 171
Assessments —— 172
Quick Assessment —— 172

Risk of Mortality —— 174
Baseline Assessment —— 177
Level of Consciousness —— 179
Reverse Triage —— 183
Dealing with Common Stressors —— 184
Prepping for the "Quiz" —— 185
Pre- and Post-Operative Care —— 186
Pre-Operative Care —— 186
Post-Operative Care —— 186
Cardiovascular Assessment, Disorders, Interventions —— 187
Angina Pectoris —— 189
Myocardial Infarction (MI) —— 190
Cardiac Tamponade —— 192
Cardiogenic Shock —— 192
Endocarditis —— 193
Congestive Heart Failure (CHF) —— 194
Hypertensive Crisis —— 196
Hypovolemic Shock —— 196
Myocarditis —— 198
Pericarditis —— 198
Pulmonary Edema —— 199
Thrombophlebitis —— 200
Respiratory Assessment, Disorders, Interventions —— 201
Acute Respiratory Distress Syndrome (ARDS) —— 205
Asthma —— 206
Atelectasis —— 207
Bronchiectasis —— 208
Bronchitis —— 209
Cor Pulmonale —— 210
Emphysema —— 211
Pleural Effusion —— 212
Pneumonia —— 213
Pneumothorax —— 214
Respiratory Acidosis —— 215
Tuberculosis —— 216
Acute Respiratory Failure —— 217
Pulmonary Embolism —— 218
Neurological Assessment, Disorders, Interventions —— 219
Cerebral Hemorrhage —— 223

Bell's Palsy —— 225
Brain Abscess —— 226
Brain Tumor —— 226
Cerebral Aneurysm —— 228
Encephalitis —— 228
Guillain-Barré syndrome —— 229
Meningitis —— 230
Spinal cord injury —— 231
Cerebrovascular Accident (CVA) —— 232
Seizure disorder —— 233
Concussion —— 234
Contusion —— 235
Subdural Hematoma —— 236
Diffuse Axonal Injury —— 237
Skull Fracture —— 237
Intracerebral Hematoma —— 239
Subarachnoid Hemorrhage —— 240
Gastrointestinal Assessment, Disorders, Interventions —— 241
Appendicitis —— 247
Cholecystitis —— 247
Cirrhosis —— 248
Crohn's Disease —— 250
Diverticulitis —— 251
Gastroenteritis —— 252
Gastroesophageal reflux disease (GERD) —— 253
Gastrointestinal bleed —— 254
Gastritis —— 254
Hepatitis —— 255
Hiatal hernia (diaphragmatic hernia) —— 257
Intestinal obstruction and paralytic ileus —— 258
Pancreatitis —— 259
Peritonitis —— 261
Peptic Ulcer Disease (PUD) —— 262
Ulcerative colitis —— 263
Musculoskeletal Assessment, Disorders, Interventions —— 264
Carpal Tunnel Syndrome —— 272
Dislocations —— 272
Fractures —— 273
Contusion —— 274

Gout —— **275**
Compartment Syndrome —— **276**
Osteoarthritis —— **276**
Osteomyelitis —— **277**
Osteoporosis —— **277**
Sprain and Strain —— **278**
Genitourinary and Gynecologic Assessment, Disorders, Interventions —— **279**
Testicular Torsion —— **284**
Acute Glomerulonephritis (acute nephritic syndrome) —— **285**
Kidney stones (Renal Calculi, nephrolithiasis) —— **286**
Pyelonephritis —— **286**
Renal Failure —— **287**
Urinary tract infection —— **288**
Ectopic Pregnancy —— **289**
Ovarian Cysts —— **289**
Pelvic Inflammatory Disease —— **290**
Preeclampsia and Eclampsia —— **290**

Index —— **293**

Introduction

Wavebreakmedia/iStock/Getty Images

Not yet! There's a long pathway (some feel it is a minefield) to navigate from applying for a position to starting work. Challenges begin when applying for the job and trying to be selected by the dreaded application tracking system - the computer program that "tells" the nurse recruiter which candidates to look at first. Then there are interviews where your background and nursing knowledge come under close scrutiny. Then there's the interview: a game of strategies where you anticipate the interviewer's moves and motivations, then try to respond appropriately knowing that the wrong word or gesture might injure your chances of being hired. And don't forget the pre-employment online tests that send a chill through even the most experienced nurses who probably haven't been formally tested in years. Worse, some healthcare facilities report that more nurses fail than pass pre-employment online nursing tests. The way to the nursing job of your dreams has more than a few hurdles.

Welcome to the new world of nursing! *Cracking the Nursing Interview* is here to help by providing you with information you need to know about the interview process, sample questions and tips that will likely appear in the interview, detailed review "cheat sheets" so that you will be prepared and confident, and more.

This book won't get you a nursing job...but the book provides insights and strategies that help you:

- Leverage your experience, whether a novice or seasoned professional.
- Beat the application tracking system at its own game with strategies that work.
- Successfully surmount what might seem insurmountable interview hurdles.
- Review material designed to help you pass pre-employment nursing tests.

This book was written to help you get the job you want. Much of what is written here may seem simple or even self-evident, but it is better to be prepared, confident and succeed than to lose a job because of something that could have easily been avoided. This applies to any existing nurse, nurses who may be looking for a job broader in scope than their current one, to candidates looking for their first job, for those still in school, looking forward to becoming a nurse or even those considering nursing as a profession.

Part One: **Understanding the Interview Process**

Part One provides the knowledge of what the hiring manager is looking for, expectations, suggestions for interviews, getting selected by the application tracking system, and more. This will make you more confident and successful in selecting and deciding on the right job for you. You will gain an understanding of the motivations, or how to determine the motivations, of the hiring manager.

Chapter 1
The Nursing Interview Process

Looking for a job as a nurse is challenging whether you are a new graduate looking for your entry into nursing or an experienced nurse seeking to move on to a better opportunity. Healthcare facilities – including private practices – are looking for competent nurses to join their teams and care for their patients. You are a competent nurse – even new graduates are considered basically competent – wanting to care for patients. However, there are hurdles you must jump over to tell a healthcare facility that you are a candidate for the job. There is no magic wand that can be waved that will lead you over these hurdles. There is no crystal ball that will tell you the words and the right moves to get you the job. However, understanding the nursing interview process gives you insights into developing your own strategies for getting noticed and jumping over the interviewing hurdles.

This book was written to help you get the job you want. Much of what is written here may seem simple or even self-evident, but it is better to have over-studied and succeed than to lose a job because of something that could have easily been avoided. So, bear with me if you know much of what is presented here; it is those bits that you may not have considered, or are reminded of, that you will find most helpful.

In the first part of this book, I hope that an understanding of the process, the knowledge of what the hiring manager is looking for, expectations, suggestions for interviews, getting selected by the dreaded application tracking system, and more will make you more confident and successful in selecting and deciding on the right job for you. You will gain an understanding of the motivations, or how to determine the motivations, of the hiring manager. The second part of this book is meant to supply you with an overview of what you may be expected to know in the interviews. It is a somewhat dense, but simple review of topics that will likely come up and, for ease of use, is broken down by medication types and body systems. You might think of this part as a big cheat sheet or memory jogger. Together, this book should give you what you need to know to successfully navigate through the interview process. We will start with the basics of the nursing job, personal human resource issues, job opportunities, and processes generally used to make a hiring decision. The processes for interviewing for nursing jobs are unique and as you will see, there are lots of options.

DOI 10.1515/9781501506109-001

How Nursing Jobs Are Created

Traditionally, there are three reasons nurse managers create a nursing position. The most common reason is the need to care for current patients as a result of a nurse leaving the healthcare facility or transferring to another position within the organization. Another reason is growth of the healthcare facility into patient care areas that are not currently provided by the organization. A healthcare facility increases the number of nurses to care for patients who are expected to use the healthcare facility in the near future. A third reason is to hire new graduate nurses to ensure there is a pool of qualified nurses to draw from in the future. Although nurse executives typically focus on current staffing needs and needs for staffing in the near future, they realize there is a sizeable group of senior nurses who are nearing or beyond retirement age that may leave a large gap in the workforce when they retire. Nurse executives know they must invest in new graduate nurses to fill that gap.

You may not care how the nursing job opportunity came about – you may simply need a job. However, you should care because the reason the position was created may provide a clue as to whether or not you should accept a position if offered to you. If a position opened because the previous nurse transferred or was promoted, then there are opportunities for advancement within the organization. That's a good thing. If the current nurse left the organization, then you probably want to explore the reason for the departure. The work environment may have been unbearable or there were few or no opportunities to move around the organization.

The Nurse Job Description

The breadth of categories of nursing jobs is too extensive to list. It is safe to say that not all nursing jobs are the same, which makes it challenging for nurse managers and nurses to find the right match for a nursing position. The initial challenge is to describe the position in writing. The job description typically has at least two divisions: general boilerplate requirements and specific requirements for the actual position. Boilerplate items appear in all job descriptions for the healthcare facility and covers general requirements expected of candidates who apply for the position. Specific job requirements describe what the nurse manager needs of the candidate. You need to focus on both the boilerplate and the specific job requirements.

The nurse manager describes the ideal candidate for a position knowing that the ideal candidate may not exist . . . but if one does exist, this person would be hired on the spot. The job description may list some requirements as "required" and other requirements as "preferred." Some healthcare facilities "require a BSN" while others "prefer a BSN." Healthcare facilities that require a BSN usually do so because they hold *Magnet* status by the American Nurses' Credentials Center (ANCC) or have similar obligations. Working toward a BSN usually applies only if you are currently employed by the healthcare facility, although they may consider a nurse who is a candidate for a BSN (all requirements are met and you are waiting for graduation). Typically, the only way a candidate without a BSN is considered is if the candidate has a unique skillset that is needed by the healthcare facility.

There are times when "required" requirements maybe waived by the nurse manager. This may happen when no candidate meets all the requirements for the position as described in the job description and the nurse manager is pressured to fill the position. Unfortunately, applicants and potential applicants rarely know about the waivers. Some applicants apply even if they don't meet all the "required" requirements hoping that "required" requirements may be waived.

Preferred requirements are sometimes referred to as "tie-breakers." If two candidates are equally qualified and one has the preferred requirement, then the candidate with the preferred requirement is offered the position. Don't assume that a preferred requirement is "required." Some nurse managers categorize a requirement as preferred because few candidates who apply for the position meet the requirement and the nurse manager doesn't want to discourage other candidates from applying. This allows them to specify "preferred" requirements and "required" requirements.

Full-Time, Part-Time, Per Diem

Nursing jobs are also described by the number of hours that the nurse manager allocates to the position. A full-time position is a position that is guaranteed 40 hours per week (the actual number of hours may vary depending on what the healthcare facility considers full time). There are busy periods when the nurse manager needs extra help for a few hours per day. For example, the patient care unit may have a high volume of discharges between 9 a.m. and 1 p.m. on weekdays. The nurse manager may create a part-time nursing position of 20 hours per week (4 hours per day) to handle the high volume of discharges. The part-time nurse is guaranteed 20 hours of work per week. Per diem is another description of a position based on the number of hours worked per week. Per diem is a Latin phrase meaning 'by the day.' Technically, the per diem nurse is guaranteed one eight-hour day of work based on the availability of the nurse and staffing needs of the healthcare facility. Some healthcare facilities require per diem nurses to work one or two holidays per year.

Internally, nursing positions are identified as full-time equivalent (FTE) positions. The nurse manager is allocated a specific number of FTEs. For example, the nurse manager of the patient care unit that has a high period of discharges during the day may be allocated 3.5 FTEs for each weekday day shift. This corresponds to three and a half full-time positions comprised of three full-time nurses and one part-time nurse. There can be smaller fractions than half a full-time position that results in a nurse working a few hours on the patient care unit per day or for a few days per week.

The healthcare facility may combine fractions of FTE into a full-time position based on the needs of the healthcare facility and the needs of patient care units. For example, the healthcare facility may find it difficult to find a nurse who wants to work 20 hours each weekday from 9 a.m. to 1 p.m. However, two part-time positions can be combined to create a full-time position that is split between two or more patient care units.

Benefits and No-Benefits

Employment benefits vary greatly. Don't assume all benefit packages are the same throughout the healthcare industry. It is wise to carefully assess the benefits package when you are offered the nursing position and compare the benefits package to those offered by your current employer. A substantial decrease in benefits may be costly and negate any increase in pay that you receive when changing jobs.

Not all nursing positions come with full benefits. Healthcare facilities offer benefits to full-time nurses. Part-time nurses may be offered prorated benefits that are offered to full-time nurses – or no benefits at all. Benefits are usually not offered to per diem nurses primarily because per diem nurses usually have full-time jobs that offer them benefits.

Make sure you find out when benefits begin – and when they are terminated. Benefits may not kick in until you are off your probationary period, which can last three months, depending on the healthcare facility. During that period, you are expected to find your own coverage – or hope you don't become ill. The Consolidated Omnibus Budget Reconciliation Act of 1985 (COBRA) may enable you to temporarily continue your current employer's health insurance when you terminate employment. Under COBRA, you'll be expected to pay the health insurance premium plus an administrative fee of two percent. Also, make sure you find out when benefits end. Some healthcare facilities stop providing benefits the day the employee is terminated. If you leave today, your benefits stop at midnight.

Union vs. Non-Union

Nurses in some healthcare facilities are represented by a union. A union is an organization of employees (called a bargaining unit) that negotiates terms of employment (called a collective bargaining agreement) for its members. The bargaining unit is usually affiliated with a state or national organization that has similar affiliations with bargaining units in other healthcare facilities. The state or national organization provides professional labor and legal services that guide local affiliates through the bargaining process and management of the collective bargaining agreement.

Terms of employment for covered positions are specified in the collective bargaining agreement. If you apply for a position covered by the collective bargaining agreement, then you must abide by terms of employment specified in the agreement. You will not be able to negotiate other terms of employment on your own, nor will the healthcare facility be able to do so.

During the first few days of orientation you will meet with a union representative who will explain the benefits of joining the union. If you agree to join, then you'll complete paperwork that permits the healthcare facility to deduct union dues from your pay and give the dues to the union. You'll have rights to participate in union activities without retribution from management. Under the National Labor Relations Act (NLRA), you have the right to refuse to join the union without any repercussions from the healthcare facility or the union. However, the NLRA permits the healthcare facility and the bargaining unit to enter into a union security agreement. The union security agreement requires employees who hold positions covered by the bargaining agreement and who are not union members to pay an agency fee to the union as a condition of employment. The agency fee is usually a substantial percentage of the union dues paid per pay period to the union for services in negotiating terms of your employment. You are bound by the collective bargaining agreement but you don't have any rights to participate in union activities since you are not a member of the union.

Some states have passed right-to-work laws that prohibit a bargaining unit from collecting an agency fee from non-union members who hold positions covered by the bargaining agreement. This means that the healthcare facility is an open shop where nurses are free to choose whether or not to join the bargaining unit. You'll probably be told by the healthcare facility if the healthcare facility is an open shop. You can also use online resources to find out if the state where you intend to work is a right-to-work state.

Job Postings

Once the nurse manager receives approval for the nurse position, Human Resources follows the healthcare facility's policies and procedures – and the collective bargaining agreement – to search for candidates. The initial search usually begins internally by posting the position on the healthcare facility's internal website and posting the position at designated sites throughout the facility. Current employees can contact Human Resources directly or apply online through the facility's internal website. Internal applicants must meet the same criteria as external applicants. After a period of time specified in the facility's policy and by the collective bargaining agreement, the internal posting is removed and the position is made available to both internal candidates and candidates who are not associated with the facility.

Healthcare facilities tend to be more favorable to current employees who want to transfer into a position than to outside candidates for a number of reasons. Current employees develop a reputation – hopefully a positive one – that nurse managers can use as an indicator of future performance in the new position. The current employee is already vetted – no background check is required – and is available to begin work once the transfer process is completed. Healthcare facilities tend to encourage current employees to grow within the organization. Current employees do have the inside track. This is especially true for new graduates who are employed in other positions in the healthcare facility. A certified nursing assistant (CNA) who becomes a graduate nurse may find it easier to transfer into a nursing position within their current healthcare facility than to find a new graduate position outside the healthcare facility.

However, being a current employee may work against the employee being offered a position. The employee's perceived skillset and work ethic may not be seen as favorable. Unofficial judgements are made based on perception by nurse managers rather than objectively made on facts. Furthermore, management may feel that filling the job of the employee's current position is difficult and thus deny the transfer. In some situations, the nurse manager has an outside candidate who is ideal for the position. The nurse manager will then find reasons to disqualify current employees.

Applying In-house for a Position

Be prepared to go through the interviewing process if you apply for a position within your current healthcare facility. You'll probably be asked to complete an abbreviated application form and submit your resume – again. The application is likely called a transfer request and probably requires notification of your present manager. Printed transfer forms typically require your manager's signature. Online transfer forms probably are sent to your manager at some point during the process. Human Resources tends to want the transfer process to be transparent so there are no surprises.

There will be requirements that you must meet before your transfer application is processed. Typically, your job evaluations must be acceptable and any disciplinary action will likely kill your transfer opportunities for the near future. You will also be expected to complete annual requirements for your current position such as online courses, passing skill competencies, and keeping your license and cardiopulmonary resuscitation certificates current.

There is always the dilemma of sharing your desire to transfer with your current manager before you are offered the new position. If you do so, your manager may feel that you are disloyal and treat you differently if you don't get the position. If you don't, your manager may feel slighted especially when the manager hears of your transfer application from Human Resources. Transparency is usually the better choice because in many cases your manager can provide you with insights into the other position that may affect your decision. Your manager may very well informally give you a great recommendation to the hiring manager.

If you are a new graduate, it is important that you keep the Human Resources manager abreast of your progress towards your license. Some healthcare facilities have a policy that prohibits a nurse from working in a non-licensed position such as a registered nurse working as a CNA. The issue is with the level of care that you are expected to give the patient. If a CNA recognizes a problem with a patient, the CNA is expected to tell the registered nurse who then assesses the patient and takes appropriate action to treat the patient. There is a potential problem if the CNA is a registered nurse and does not further assess the problem and take appropriate actions that the registered nurse is legally obligated to perform. A good approach is to have an open discussion with Human Resources months before graduation. This enables Human Resources to help you time when you get your license – when a nursing position opens.

Applying from the Outside

Applying for a position in a healthcare facility is challenging and requires patience because the human factor is removed from the beginning of the process. Whether or not you visit the Human Resources department personally, you will probably be told that applications are accepted only online. If you try dropping off a resume, you may be politely pointed to a computer where you can access the healthcare facility's website and begin the application process.

Human Resources departments typically receive thousands of resumes and the only practical way of processing them is through the use of an application tracking system (ATS). The ATS is the computer program that displays job postings on the healthcare facility's website and collects applications from candidates. There is actually much more to an ATS, which will be explored in Chapter 2, "Behind the Scenes of the Nursing Interview Process."

Applying online for a position is less personal than submitting your resume to a person, but it does have advantages – at least for Human Resources. The nurse recruiter must quickly review at least a few hundred resumes of candidates who apply for a nursing position. Paper resumes are not uniform, requiring the nurse recruiter to hunt through the resume for information about the candidate that indicates if the candidate meets the minimum qualifications for the position. The ATS sifts through resumes and applications, then displays qualified candidates to the nurse recruiter. Furthermore, the online application process flags missing critical information from the application before the application is accepted by the ATS. The candidate must supply the missing information in order to submit the application.

ATS also enables Human Resources to track the application throughout the hiring process. Paper resumes always have the chance of getting lost in the process, especially if the resume is passed along to several hiring managers. Some ATS systems alert Human Resources when a resume hasn't been reviewed by the hiring manager. Furthermore, the hiring manager can view resumes online and respond electronically to Human Resources.

Networking Helps

Does knowing someone who works at the healthcare facility help the you get the job? This is arguably one of the most asked questions by candidates. The answer is maybe; however, the candidate must still be qualified for the position. If you know the hiring manager and the manager wants to offer you the position, then knowing the manager can help you get the job.

More often than not, you don't know the hiring manager – at least not enough for the manager to give you the job. There is a better chance that you know someone else who works at the healthcare facility who can recommend you to either Human Resources or the hiring manager. You'll probably be told to apply online like everyone else. Let your contact know when the application is filed so your contact can alert Human Resources or the hiring manager. It is at this point when the recruiter or the hiring manager will use the ATS to display your resume – bypassing the normal search — basically placing your resume on top of the pile.

And this is about all the help you'll get. Your resume will be compared with the job requirements and possibly with other candidates. If you qualify for the job – even marginally – then you'll probably be called in for the first round of interviews. If your qualifications don't match the requirements of the job, you may receive a courtesy phone call from the recruiter who will explain your situation.

Human Resources Interview

Once your application has caught the eye of the nurse recruiter and you seem qualified for the position, the interview process begins. The first stop is usually Human Resources to meet the nurse recruiter. Some nurse recruiters may hold a telephone interview before inviting you for a face-to-face interview. The telephone interview may be informal where the recruiter asks "show stopper" questions. These are areas where there is no room for negotiations. For example, working every other weekend may be mandatory, so the nurse recruiter makes sure that you can fulfill those obligations during the phone interview. If you can't, then going further with the interviewing process is a waste of time.

The in-person interview with the nurse recruiter is a get-together where the nurse recruiter gets a feeling of how you are as a person. Are you pleasant? Can you communicate well? Can you think on your feet? Responses to these and many more questions help the nurse recruiter know if you may be a good fit within the healthcare facility culture. The nurse recruiter also reviews with you the requirements of the position giving you the opportunity to explain how you meet those requirements. This is where both you and the nurse recruiter determine if you should continue with the interview process. You'll find a lot more about the interviewing in Chapter 3, "The New Grad Nursing Interview," and Chapter 4, "The Experienced Nurse Interview."

The interview with the nurse recruiter may last 30 minutes or less. Don't read too much into the length of the interview. Some candidates believe a longer interview means that they are being seen as a good candidate and short interviews means they are not. Each nurse recruiter has his or her own style of interviewing.

A short interview might mean that you are a good candidate and there is no need to extend the interview. A long interview might indicate that the nurse recruiter is giving you more time to sell yourself – to show that you meet the job requirements. And in some healthcare facilities, the nurse recruiter is more of a facilitator than a decision maker, so the initial interview is relatively short. The candidate is then brought to the nurse manager for the longer more formal interview. The nurse manager decides whether or not to hire the candidate. The nurse recruiter can veto the decision if the candidate fails to meet the pre-employment requirements of the healthcare facility.

Nurse Manager Interview

The interview with the nurse manager is where you get to shine. The nurse manager is usually the person who decides who is offered the position, with some exceptions. The nurse manager probably can't overrule Human Resources' objections of failure to meet requirements established by the healthcare facility. Furthermore, the nurse manager may have little choice if the position is covered by the bargaining agreement. The bargaining agreement may contain rules for selecting a candidate especially if an in-house staff member wants to transfer into the position. If the staff member meets the qualifications for the position; has no disciplinary actions; and has seniority among other in-house candidates, then the position must be offered to the candidate.

Dress for success – remember this is your only chance to make a first impression. Business attire is appropriate unless you made other arrangements with the nurse recruiter. No scrubs unless you mention ahead of time that you're coming from work. Keep accessories (that is, makeup and jewelry) to a minimum. The nurse recruiter and the hiring nurse manager are checking even if it doesn't seem obvious during the interview. For example, they want to see nails that conform to general infection control policies (short, no artificial nails, clear nail polish). Greet the interviewer with a firm handshake then stand until you're invited to sit. A straight posture, solid eye contact, active listening (really listen to what is being said), and keeping your hands on your lap (don't touch your face) are hallmarks of a good impression. Bring your resume! Be prepared to quickly retrieve your copy of the resume (now is not the time to shuffle through papers in your bag) if you find the nurse recruiter or hiring nurse manager are having difficulty finding their copy. Give the nurse recruiter or hiring nurse manager time to ask the first question, but have your first question on hand if the opportunity presents itself. A good question to ask is: What are your expectations of the candidate who is offered the position? This helps to focus on details that become important if you are offered the position and should support a meaningful conversation.

Expect anything to happen during the interview with the nurse manager. That's the only thing that can be said with confidence about the interview. Although Human Resources may give guidance, the nurse manager determines how the interview will be conducted. Experienced nurse managers may have their own formal process. Inexperienced nurse managers may be learning how to interview prospective employees. In the end, the nurse manager must decide if you are a fit for the position. Fit doesn't necessarily mean that you are a super nurse, but usually answers the question: will you fit into the team of nurses on the patient care unit? If the answer is yes, then the nurse manager typically focuses on your nursing judgment. If the answer is no, then the nurse manager may forgo exploring your nursing skills because the nurse manager's foremost responsibility is to build a cohesive team who work together to provide quality patient care on the patient care unit. Unfortunately, you need to show that you fit without knowing much about the team. You'll find out how to deal with that situation in Chapter 3 and Chapter 4.

Getting a call back from Human Resources following the nurse manager interview is obviously a good sign that you are still in the running for the position. However, there are more hurdles ahead of you, some of which may quickly knock you out of contention with little or no recourse. These hurdles are:
1. Pre-employment Technical Tests
2. Job Offer
3. Pre-employment Health Exam
4. Background Check
5. Orientation
6. Probation

Pre-employment Technical Tests

One of those hurdles is pre-employment technical tests that some – not all – healthcare facilities require of candidates who have performed well during the interview process. These formal tests are usually conducted online in Human Resources. Tests are created and maintained by an outside organization that specializes in testing nurses. And yes, expect these tests to be more like NCLEX questions, where at least two answers are correct and you are expected to select the more appropriate answer.

Pre-employment technical tests focus on the basics for the nursing position. If you are applying for a medical-surgical nurse position, then there might be a test on med-surg. You'll need to brush up on signs, symptoms, assessments, procedures, treatments, and medications that are commonly used by med-surg nurses. The same is true about other nursing specialties. Candidates for any nursing position will likely be asked to take a test that covers medication administration and common medications. Human Resources may offer a reference guide to the areas you'll be tested on. Chapter 6, "Prepping for the Interview," and Chapter 7, "Prepping for Medication Questions," along with other chapters in this book will help you prepare for technical questions that may appear on a formal test or asked during interviews.

Why should you be tested on skills that you've been successfully using for years as a nurse? This question is asked often. Although the nurse recruiter and the nurse manager recognize your achievements, both need a clear way to document your knowledge and prove to regulatory authorities that you are a competent nurse. The relatively standardized test is an objective way to measure your knowledge compared to other candidates and nurses. The healthcare facility establishes the passing grade based on whatever criteria they deem appropriate. For example, the nurse executive may survey regional nursing schools to assess its criteria for passing and then use the same criteria. Passing the test determines if you continue to be considered as a viable candidate for the position. Human Resources may give you several opportunities to retake the test. If you fail to pass, then you are no longer a candidate.

It is not unusual for a healthcare facility to test only candidates for per diem nursing positions. Per diem nurses are expected to be experienced nurses who work in the field for another healthcare facility. Their orientation to the healthcare facility is typically one week and a few days. Pre-employment testing gives Human Resources and the nurse manager a way to further assess the candidate. This assessment would normally be conducted for full-time and part-time nurses during a full orientation period. Some healthcare facilities do little or no pre-employment technical testing, leaving additional assessment of the candidate to a formal orientation process.

Job Offer

With interviews and pre-employment technical testing out of the way, Human Resources and the nurse manager decide who to hire. All hope that there is one obvious choice among the remaining candidates. Sometimes there is a toss-up, and in a few cases, there will literally be a coin toss. The goal is to offer the position to the candidate who has good nursing judgment and who is likely to work well with the current team on the patient care unit. Achieving a perfect score on pre-employment technical tests is less important than fitting into the culture on the patient care unit and in the healthcare facility. You still have to pass those pre-employment technical tests.

The job offer is typically informally made over the phone by the nurse recruiter. The nurse recruiter will clearly emphasize requirements that might become problematic such as working every other weekend and no benefits – including health insurance – until the probationary period is completed. Job offers are conditional, which will be explained by the nurse recruiter. You still have to pass a pre-employment health exam and pass a background check. The pre-employment health exam will usually be scheduled while you are on the phone with the nurse recruiter. You should know the results of the pre-employment health exam before you resign from your current position. However, the background check may take a while before the nurse recruiter receives the result. You may have started orientation by that time.

Your official offer is sent in the form of a letter that contains your date of employment, position title, compensation, and any conditions of employment such as passing the pre-employment health exam, passing the drug test, and passing the background check. Furthermore, the offer letter will tell you how to arrange for the pre-employment health exam and drug testing if it wasn't already scheduled by the nurse recruiter. And of course, the letter states the date and time of employment, and where to report to work. You are expected to accept the offer in writing within a reasonable time period.

Pre-employment Health Exam

Before you begin orientation, you'll need clearance from Employee Health. The depth of the physical examination depends on policies of the healthcare facility. Typically, the goal of a pre-employment physical is to determine if you are healthy enough to do the job, with tasks like lifting 50 pounds and being flexible enough to bend and reach. Expect to be asked to take the Mantoux tuberculin skin test, better known as a TST or PPD, to determine if you've been exposed to the mycobacterium tuberculosis bacteria. You have the right to refuse; however, you'll probably be required to have a chest X-ray to rule out that you have tuberculosis. Alternatively, you can provide documentation from your practitioner or from your current employer that you have had a PPD and that the test results were negative. Many foreign born persons received the Bacillus Calmette-Guerin (BCG) vaccine and have antibodies to mycobacterium tuberculosis bacteria that will lead to a positive TST results. Make this known to Employee Health. A number of healthcare facilities require a more intense pre-employment physical including a baseline blood test.

Expect to be given a drug toxicology test, which is commonly in the form of a urine toxicology screening. This is a carefully orchestrated test that may be performed shortly after the job offer and before the pre-employment health examination. You are usually asked for a list of medications that you are taking. Be sure to include all natural supplements since natural supplements may have trace substances that may lead to a positive test result. No doubt you'll have to empty your pockets before being led into a designated bathroom for the test. Usually there is no running water. You'll be expected to fill a specimen container with fresh urine – and you're not permitted to flush the toilet. The sample will be taken by the nurse or medical assistant for testing. You'll be given hand sanitizers to wash your hands after you submit the sample. You'll be notified if the result is positive. If so, you'll be given an opportunity to explain what may have caused a positive result – assuming that you are not taking non-prescribed medications that would set off a positive result. Healthcare facilities are usually reasonable and may give you the benefit of the doubt – however, you still must either pass the toxicology screening or provide convincing evidence from a practitioner explaining why the result is positive.

Background Check

A healthcare facility runs background checks on all employees regardless of their position within the organization. The actual background check is typically conducted by a vendor that searches public records, online sources, and previous employers to verify information that you provided on the application and on your resume. No background check is conducted without your written permission, which is normally obtained either at the time you apply for the position or when you accept the offer. You don't have to give permission for a background check; however, the employer may reject your application as a result. Some healthcare facilities also request that you give them permission to view to your Facebook and other online accounts.

The background check usually involves a review of your credit rating, your history of debt and repayment of debt, and other financial information that may give the healthcare facility an indication of how well you honor your obligations. There is also a criminal background check to see if you have ever been convicted of a crime. Any legal action against you such as being sued will usually be reported in the background check.

It is typically legal for an employer to ask for background information during the hiring process. An employer is not permitted to ask medical information until you receive a job offer. Even after the job offer they can't ask you information about family medical history or genetic information except in very limited circumstances. The background check must be conducted on everyone who is hired for the same position. The employer is not permitted to select you for a background check based on race, national origin, color, sex, religion, disability, genetic information or age.

Human Resources receive a background report usually made available online by the vendor. You will receive a copy of the background report if something in the report causes the healthcare facility to withdraw your offer. You will also receive a notice of rights at that time that contains information on how you can contact the vendor who made the report to challenge the findings. Sometimes there are errors. Point out any error to the vendor and ask the vendor to fix the background report and send a corrected copy of the background report to the healthcare facility. Notify the nurse recruiter about the error and steps you are taking to have the error corrected. If there is something in the background report that concerns the nurse recruiter, you will likely be given an opportunity to explain the situation and why it will not affect your ability to perform the job.

There can be concerns about what a previous employer might say about you. There are few laws that prohibit a former employer to voice an honest opinion about you or state documented facts such as your time and attendance record. However, healthcare facilities and other organizations typically have policies that limit the information they share about you. Typically, a former employer will share your dates of employment. Other information such as reason for termination and performance evaluations may not be shared. More on background checks can be found in Chapter 2.

Orientation

Your next hurdle is orientation. Orientation is the process by which you become familiar with the operations of the healthcare facility and your position. Actually, more is taking place. You and your performance are constantly being assessed by staff of the nursing education department and the nursing staff who are precepting you to your new job. The orientation process varies by healthcare facility. There is a growing tendency to use more online courses than classroom courses, since less staff is required. At times, you'll be asked to take online courses on your own time, shortening the orientation period and saving money for the healthcare facility. You probably won't get paid for taking online courses on your own time.

There might be a full week of classes and presentations where you'll be introduced to policies and procedures of the healthcare facility, human resource rules and benefits, computer documentation, and nursing skills. You'll be expected to have nursing skills; however, you'll be shown how those skills are applied to the healthcare facility, such as how to use their clinical equipment. Expect to see a demo presented by a clinical nurse educator and then be required to return demo. The clinical nurse educator will determine if you demo the skill adequately to be considered competent. Each nursing skill demo and each course usually ends with a test that was created by the clinical education department. Usually these are simple tests – no NCLEX-type questions. Corrected tests and competency checklists become part of your clinical education file and is used to prove to The Joint Commission and other regulatory authorities that you are competent to practice nursing in the healthcare facility. And yes, regulatory authorities frequently examine the nursing staff's clinical educational files during audits.

Each healthcare facility has its own orientation process. Nurses usually begin clinical orientation by the second week of orientation – assuming they successfully completed the first week of orientation. Any concerns about the competency of an orientee by the clinical nurse educator is raised to the director of the clinical education department, Human Resources, and the hiring nurse manager. The orientee may then be given a performance improvement plan. Termination occurs if the orientee's performance does not improve.

Clinical orientation is the heart of nursing orientation. This is where you are teamed with a preceptor – another nurse – and you provide direct nursing care to patients. The preceptor is typically counted as part of staffing for the shift – but the orientee isn't part of the count. Each preceptor will have her own style of precepting. Some healthcare facilities place preceptors through formal training while others provide no training to the preceptor. Expect that the preceptor will have a "see one-do one" style where the preceptor performs the nursing task and you observe, then you perform the same task under the observation of the preceptor. Your goal is to eventually perform all tasks without assistance from the preceptor. You are expected to ask many questions until you can perform tasks independently. Don't hesitate to do so because you probably won't have this opportunity once orientation is completed.

The clinical nurse educator may be your preceptor for the first day or two of clinical orientation. For example, the clinical educator may want to supervise your first few medication administrations before letting you independently pass meds. The clinical nurse educator and all your preceptors want you to succeed but won't hesitate to raise concerns if they see that you are unable to perform the job after attempts to correct you have failed.

There will be lists of tasks that you must successfully perform in order to complete orientation. The clinical nurse educator or your preceptor(s) will sign off on each task. The orientation can last four to six weeks, more or less depending on the healthcare facility and your position. Per diem nurses are usually give a week and a few days of orientation because they are experienced – and usually work another full-time job. New nurse graduates have an extended orientation of six weeks or more. Orientation may be cut short or extended based on performance of the orientee and the needs of the healthcare facility. For example, orientation may be shortened a week if the orientee is an experienced nurse, has completed all orientation tasks, and has been working relatively independently for a week. Orientation may be extended if the orientee has promise but needs more time to feel comfortable in the position. The orientee does not need to agree to a reduced orientation. Don't agree unless you are confident that you can perform the job independently. You are guaranteed full orientation.

You may be oriented to one patient care unit if you are permanently assigned to that unit. You will be oriented to different patient care units if you are assigned to the float pool where each day you can work on any patient care unit in the facility. Float pool nurses are usually oriented to one of each class of patient care units that they may be assigned to during a shift. For example, you might be oriented to one step-down unit – not all step-down units in the facility. Orientation may occur on different shifts – day, evening, nights – depending on your position. Healthcare facilities tend to begin orientation on the day shift since this is usually the most active shift and gives you the opportunity to learn how the patient care unit really works. Once the clinical nurse educator and preceptors are satisfied with your performance, you are usually moved to your shift.

Probation

And your last hurdle is getting through the probationary period. The probationary period is the time period during which you can be terminated with or without cause with little or no recourse. Many positions in a healthcare facility are technically day-to-day positions even if no one really considers the position as such. Some executives receive an employment contract when hired that contains expectations of both the healthcare facility and the employee. The contract has a date when the contract begins and when the contract terminates. The executive is guaranteed the job as long as the executive doesn't violate terms of the contract.

Nurses who have bargaining unit positions also have a contract with the healthcare facility, which is better known as the bargaining agreement. The bargaining agreement is between the bargaining unit (the union) and the healthcare facility and contains terms of employment for the length of the contract. The bargaining agreement typically specifies procedures for disciplining nurses who underperform and procedures for terminating employment. However, the bargaining agreement usually states that those procedures do not come into play until after the probationary period is completed. In essence, the union can do little for you until the probationary period is over.

You work at the discretion of the healthcare facility if you are not covered under a contract or bargaining agreement. You are most vulnerable during the probationary period when you can be terminated at will with little notice. Once the probationary period concludes, then there are policies and procedures in place that specify how management must deal with underperforming nurses. Sometimes managers are required to give a verbal warning, then written warning, and possibly develop a performance improvement plan to rectify the issue. Termination usually follows failure of the performance improvement plan to improve the situation.

The nurse recruiter and nurse managers want you to be successful. They need you and spend an appreciable amount of time and money to recruit you and get you through orientation. The last thing they want is to terminate you and start the recruitment process over. However, they will terminate and cut their losses if there isn't promise that you will succeed. Some nurse managers are quick to terminate and not throw good money after bad by continuing your employment. Other nurse managers will give you time to assimilate to your position and the culture of the healthcare facility. They may ask the nurse manager to help find you another position in the organization if you are not a good fit for the current position.

Be proactive if you feel the position is overly challenging. You'll quickly know that the fit isn't a good one. The nurse manager and your colleagues will know too. Open a dialog with your nurse manager and your colleagues soon after you complete orientation. Share your challenges and encourage them to help you meet them. This shows that you are well aware of the situation and you are willing to ask for help. The goal is to incorporate advice into your practice so that you can work relatively independently.

Chapter 2
Behind the Scenes of the Nursing Interview Process

Finding the right job is challenging for you. In many ways, it is more challenging for the nurse recruiter to find the right nurse for the job. You may apply to a few healthcare facilities within commuting distance from your home for a nurse position. However, on the other end, the nurse recruiter for each healthcare facility receives hundreds of applications for multiple nursing positions and must identify and contact each potential candidate, arrange for interviews, coordinate interviews with nurse managers, and work through each step of the recruiting process. In this chapter, we'll take a brief look at what goes on behind the scenes after you submit your application to a healthcare facility. This behind-the-scenes look will give you insight into developing strategies for interacting with the nurse recruiter and hiring nurse manager.

The Challenges of Recruiting Nurses

Applying for a nursing position can become frustrating. You submit your application and then wait, sometimes with no response at all and other times receiving an automatic response generated by the application tracking system. You call Human Resources only to be told that your application was received and is being processed. And you continue to wait. Weeks or even months go by before you hear back. The response might be a general thank you for applying but the position has been filled. If you get lucky, you might get a call from the nurse recruiter – the beginning of a long onboarding process that can stop at any point along the way.

Let's take a moment to see what might be happening with Human Resources. Typically, there is one nurse recruiter who might also be recruiting for nursing assistants and technicians. The nurse recruiter's job is to find, vet, and hire qualified candidates after the nurse manager receives approval to fill a position. There are likely many positions that the nurse recruiter must fill – not just your position. At times the nurse recruiter may feel caught between a rock and a hard place. Qualified and unqualified candidates are knocking on the door trying to get a few minutes to pitch a resume. Nurse managers are knocking on the door wanting to know why the nurse recruiter hasn't filled positions for the nurse manager. In addition to locating the right candidate, the nurse recruiter must coordinate the onboarding process – collecting paperwork, background checks, scheduling pre-

DOI 10.1515/9781501506109-002

employment physicals, and scheduling orientation for applicants who received job offers.

The application tracking system is a computer program that handles the chore of sifting through the hundreds of resumes and applications (more on the application tracking system later in this chapter), assisting the recruiter in identifying seemingly qualified applicants who will be invited for interviews. The decision of whom to invite is coordinated with the hiring nurse manager who also reviews resumes and applications. The nurse recruiter does this for all open positions. Coordinating applications can be a nightmare. The nurse recruiter plays endless email tag and phone tag getting the hiring nurse manager to agree on which candidates will be called for interviews. Then it is finding time to schedule those interviews. Juggling these tasks is likely the reason for the many delays you encounter after you submit the application online.

Once the first round of interviews are completed, the nurse recruiter and the hiring nurse manager decide who to eliminate and who should be brought back for another round of interviews (sometimes there is one round) and for pre-employment testing (i.e., skills testing). A few days or weeks may go by before a decision is made. At this point the nurse recruiter schedules follow-up activities. All this goes on while applicants and nurse managers are knocking on the nurse recruiter's door asking for a status on their applications and when the nurse manager will fill the opening. This is why you receive an abrupt and cold response from the nurse recruiter when you finally get through to her.

Finding a qualified nurse isn't easy. The nurse recruiter works with the hiring nurse manager to define the qualifications for the position, salary, shift, full- or part-time, and other information the nurse recruiter needs to advertise the position. The position may have to be posted internally for ten days before the position is available to nurses outside the healthcare facility. The nurse recruiter must field inquiries from current employees who tend to stop by unannounced or call. Others in the organization suggest candidates – informal recommendations – and not just for one position, but for all open positions. Current employees expect to be treated as a colleague and as a friend – a level above someone from outside the organization. The nurse recruiter tries her best to meet these expectations while trying to respond efficiently. This is a nightmare.

The Ideal Nurse

Nurse managers and nurse recruiters all look for the perfect nurse. Who is the perfect nurse? Probably the nurse who the nurse manager felt was doing a great job – and who transferred or resigned from the position. The nurse manager and the nurse recruiter must define the characteristics of the perfect nurse in words and use them in the job description as a guide for interviewing potential candidates.

Although each nursing job is unique to the patient care unit, there is a tendency for the nurse manager and the nurse recruiter to develop a general description of the ideal nurse and use it to describe every nurse position. You'll find this at the beginning of the job description. Unique requirements for the position are found toward the end of the job description.

So what are the nurse manager and nurse recruiter looking for? Intuitively you may think "nursing skills," but often that's not at the top of the list. Team player and stable work history lead the list. If you are not a team player then you probably won't fit with the culture in the healthcare facility. Unless you have a unique skill not widely found in the market place, you'll probably be knocked out of the running by a nurse who fits in.

Stable work history is critical even if you are a team player. A stable work history implies that other organizations found your work acceptable– you showed up for work and performed a decent job. Each of us has our own definition of a stable work history and you'll see indications of the nurse manager's and nurse recruiter's definition in the job description. Your goal is to show that you don't jump around from job to job – including within the organization. For example, spending a year in med-surg then moving to the O.R. for another year and then working in the E.R. for the past year may seem like you widened your experience, but this may also imply that the med-surg job didn't work out. Instead of terminating you, they sent you to the O.R. – and when that didn't work out you ended up in the E.R. – which does not seem to be working out either because you are looking for a job outside the hospital. On the other hand, you might be a great talent who was urgently needed to fill hard-to-fill jobs. Now you are tired of jumping around and you want to settle down in one position, but that opportunity doesn't present itself within your current organization. Each of these scenarios is supported by your work history; however, the nurse recruiter is likely to assume the worst without a clear rational explanation in your application.

Next, do you have the skills to do the job? This does not necessarily mean that you can give medications, insert an IV catheter, or assess a patient. The nurse manager and nurse recruiter are looking for a candidate who has critical thinking skills, can solve problems, deal with conflicts and work independently. They want you to be patient-centered and an advocate for the patient. You see nursing as a profession and not simply a job. These are just as important as being competent in administering medications to patients.

Strong communication skills are high on the list of requirements. The nurse manager and nurse recruiter want a nurse who can express him- or herself logically, actively listen to patients and colleagues, and respond appropriately using both written and oral communication. Your resume, application, and cover letter are the first clues of your communication skills. Each conversation with the nurse recruiter and the nurse manager demonstrates your oral communication skills as you follow directions they give you throughout the recruiting process. Each encounter with the nurse manager, nurse recruiter, and other staff helps them learn who you are.

As you move down the requirements list you'll find basic requirements such as current nursing license and current CPR card. Education requirements may appear as basic requirements or "nice to have" depending on the healthcare facility and position. Healthcare facilities who have or strive for Magnet designation have specific educational requirements such as possessing a BSN degree for all nurses, MSN degree for all managers, and DNP degree for the executive nurse. Magnet status is recognition from the American Nurses Credentialing Center (ANCC) for hospitals who have quality nursing programs as established by the ANCC criteria. A healthcare facility that does not seek or is not qualified for Magnet designation may accept less than the ANCC criteria for education. They may prefer that the candidate has a BSN, but candidates with an associate's degree or diploma are also encouraged to apply.

The "nice to have" but not required items typically include bilingualism and computer literacy (functional knowledge of how to use a PC and the ability to use an electronic medical records system). At times these are basic requirements for the position. Other "nice to have" items might include use of specialized equipment, flexibility of schedule, and leadership roles within your current or previous organizations. Leadership roles typically are memberships on committees such as nurse leadership, quality improvement, or employee safety and not necessarily management positions.

The nurse manager and the nurse recruiter are looking for a competent nurse who shows up to work, can work independently, think on his/her feet and is willing to help the team care for patients. The nurse should have realistic expectations of compensation, work schedule, and their role on the team. Your job is to convey these requirements in your resume, job application, and during each encounter with the nurse manager and nurse recruiter.

How Decisions Are Made

After breaking through the application tracking system; passing interviews with the nurse manager and the nurse recruiter; and passing pre-employment tests; a decision is made to offer you – or someone else – the position. It seems to be a simple decision. Pick the candidate who is most qualified. Sometimes it isn't that simple.

Human Resources makes sure that the candidate is qualified based on policies and regulatory requirements imposed on the healthcare facility. Employee Health decides if the candidate is physically capable of doing the job. The nurse manager decides if the candidate is a good fit for the team. Although the nurse manager makes the hiring decision, Human Resources and Employee Health can veto that decision.

The process of determining who is hired is similar across healthcare facilities; however, each healthcare facility has its own quirks in the process. For example, a nurse manager noticed that a new nurse hired for her patient care unit started orientation. She didn't remember hiring the nurse, although Human Resources said she did. The nurse manager had interviewed many candidates for the position and told human resources the candidates she wanted to hire: Yes candidates (plural). The nurse manager whet through this exercise a few times because not every candidate she selected could pass the pre-employment medication administration test. Months went by until a selected candidate passed the test. By that time, the nurse manager had lost track of who she had selected.

The Flow of Interviews

There is a lot of planning that goes into interviewing candidates. Interviews performed by the nurse recruiter are well-organized. Time is slotted for the interview and the nurse recruiter has a proven strategy for conducting the interview. The same may not be said about the hiring nurse manager. The hiring nurse manager may not be available for the interview at the scheduled time because of operational issues – or simply because of conflicts related to poor planning. You may be asked to reschedule the interview or, more likely, you are interviewed by another nurse manager who is not the hiring manager. The nurse manager steps in for the hiring manager. Whether this is a good or bad thing is debatable. Will a hiring nurse manager agree to hire a nurse she did not interview? It depends on the hiring nurse manager.

At times, you might be interviewed by two or more nurse managers in the same interview. This happens when the hiring manager is a relatively new manager and is not comfortable with interviewing nurses. At other times, it just so happens that the other nurse manager is in the room. For example, the interview may take place in the nursing office rather than the hiring nurse manager's office and other managers may happen to be there. This tends to be a good thing because you have a chance to impress multiple nurse managers. Hopefully one of them will advocate for you in discussions with the hiring nurse manager and with the nurse recruiter after the interview concludes.

A few healthcare facilities encourage the hiring nurse manager to arrange a group interview with staff on the patient care unit. You get to meet your potential colleagues and they get to meet you. On a positive note, you get to ask questions about how the patient care unit works and they have an opportunity to set realistic expectations. Focus on the patient care unit (i.e., types of patients, schedules, workflows of shifts). Your colleagues can't hire you. Instead they will let the hiring nurse manager know if they think you are a fit. The downside of a group interview with your possible future colleagues is that information contained on your resume may have been shared with them before the interview; information you may not want to have been shared.

Getting Lost in the Shuffle

One of the horrors of applying for a position is that your application may get lost – and it does happen. A nurse manager shared her frustrations with the hiring process: A nurse manager has a million and one things to do and hiring is just one of them. They must deal with staff schedules; conflicts on the patient care unit; rooms that are too hot or too cold; leaking pipes; complaints from patients that they're not being treating properly; practitioners complaining about nurses; nurses complaining about practitioners; going to meetings; auditing charts; budgeting; staff evaluations; and the list goes on.

And, yes, the nurse manager must find time to hire a nurse. Resumes and applications arrive electronically once the nurse manager arranges for Human Resources to post the position. In some healthcare facilities, Human Resources takes the lead by looking through applications and then suggesting a few candidates to the nurse manager. In other organizations, the nurse manager sifts through online applications to find likely candidates. In this case, the nurse manager can sometimes forget to check the application tracking system for applications. Weeks might go by without checking the system. He remembers when the staffing office complains that they are having trouble staffing the open position with float nurses.

He states that he doesn't arrange the interview. Instead, he sends an email to the nurse recruiter who contacts the candidate. The nurse manager's request gets placed somewhere on the nurse recruiter's to-do list – and the nurse manager focuses on other things until the nurse recruiter gets back to him. All this time, the candidate's frustration level increases to the point where the candidate stops sending emails and stops calling Human Resources – the candidate simply gives up, assuming that the position was filled and they had not yet taken the job posting down.

Things get worse when the nurse manager interviews several candidates over a few days, according to the nurse manager. The nurse manager admitted that sometimes he gets resumes and the candidates mixed up in the few days following the interviews. He is left with resumes and must try to remember his impression of each candidate. He can easily tell Human Resources to hire the wrong person and not realize it until the person begins orientation.

A nurse recruiter reported a mix up that left a new hire frustrated. The job was posted as a float pool nurse on a night-shift job (nurses worked eight-hour shifts) and a candidate was hired and onboarded. During orientation, the staffing coordinator realized there was no night-shift float pool position. That particular position had been filled several months ago. Withdrawing the job offer was problematic since the employee gave up his full-time nursing position to accept the night-shift float pool nurse position. The solution was to explain the situation and offer a hybrid schedule – two night shifts and three day shifts – until another night-shift float pool nurse position opened. It took a year before such as position was available.

Can you get lost in the hiring process shuffle – yes, and there is little you can do about it.

The Dreaded Application Tracking System

Yes, you must deal with the application tracking system (ATS). With hundreds of resumes and multiple nursing positions – not to mention other positions – open there is no practical way to manage applications without using the application tracking system. Nurse recruiters will admit that the application tracking system removes the human factor from the initial recruiting process; however, there is a benefit. The application tracking system helps to sift through hundreds of resumes and applications to find candidates that seem to qualify for a specific position. "Seem to qualify" is the key phrase. The application tracking system is likely to overlook qualified applicants primarily because their resumes and applications don't match the search criteria. Think of it this way: a nurse recruiter quickly scans resumes to filter unqualified applicants and so does the application tracking system. However, the application tracking system literally matches applications and resumes with the words in the job description. It usually doesn't recognize synonyms for those words, so qualified candidates can be overlooked.

The application tracking system also helps the nurse recruiter manage applications. The nurse recruiter can quickly display your resume on the computer when you call instead of having to sift through a large pile of resumes. The hiring nurse manager can also review resumes on the computer without having to obtain copies from human resources. Chances are slim that your resume will be lost. In addition, the application tracking system helps the healthcare facility comply with anti-discrimination laws in hiring and assist in compliance reporting.

The application tracking system works by searching resumes and applications for contextual keywords and phrases. Simply inserting keywords probably won't help get your resume selected. Keywords must be used in context. Each keyword and phrase is assigned a value sometimes referred to as a weight. Words and phrases considered more significant to the job qualification receive a higher weight. Sometimes the weight is based on the number of times the keyword or phrase is used in the resume.

For example, you may write in your resume...

"I care for up to eight patients a day in the medical surgical unit with oversight from the charge nurse."

The ATS is looking for the following words and phrases:

"Provides direct patient care by assessing, planning, implementing, and evaluating care of assigned patient." Your resume scores low because you've left out "provides direct patient care...assessing, planning, implementing and evaluating". The resume implies that you provide direct patient care with the assumption that you assess the patient, plan and implement interventions and evaluate the results of the interventions. However, the ATS may not recognize the implications in the resume.

The search result appears as a score based on relevancy to a specific open position. Applicants with the highest scores are sent to the nurse recruiter. Human Resources determines qualifying scores. It does not necessarily mean that applicants with lower scores are not qualified. It simply means that the application tracking system was unable to find a match for contextual keywords and phrases in the resume or application. The resume or application may have been poorly written or poorly formatted.

The nurse recruiter, with input from the hiring nurse manager, determines the contextual keywords and phrases used to identify resumes and applications of potentially qualified candidates. This information will not be shared with you. You must anticipate the search criteria and make sure those keywords and phrases appear clearly in your resume and application. Furthermore, you must avoid things that might confuse the application tracking system such as fancy formats on your resume. This may work well with humans but it can confuse the application tracking system. Here are some tips that may help you to catch the "eye" of the application tracking system.

Keep your resume simple – no graphs, tables, illustrations, no headers and footers, no columns, no special characters, no multiple fonts. Use standard resume formatting with sections such as Work Experience and Education. Use commonly used fonts such as Arial, Courier, or Times New Roman no smaller than 11-point size. Start your work experience with your employer's name then your title, and then dates – each can be on its own line, making it easy for the application tracking system to read.

Use bullet points to highlight key information. This helps when the nurse recruiter needs to call you in for an interview. Uploading your resume in a Word document or rich text document may work better than using a PDF file. Some application tracking systems may have difficulty parsing through a PDF file. Typically, the application tracking system will display your parsed resume in the application tracking system's format. Carefully review the parsed document and make any corrections. This is the document that will be searched and scored by the application tracking system – and this will probably be your last chance to tweak your information.

You'll need to guess at the contextual keywords and phrases that will be used in the search. Chances are pretty good that verbiage found in the job description on the healthcare facility's website will be incorporated into the search criteria. Therefore, use that exact verbiage in your resume and application. Use both acronyms and the full spelling of words that make up the acronym. The application tracking system may search for one and not the other. Make sure that your resume doesn't have typos and misspellings and that you use proper capitalization. The application tracking system doesn't use a spell checker and will give you a low score if it is unable to understand what you are trying to say. Furthermore, the nurse recruiter is likely to reject your misspelled resume should it get through the application tracking system.

Keep in mind that the resume parsed by the application tracking system will be read by the nurse recruiter should it be selected. Therefore, don't simply stuff contextual keywords and phrases from the job description into your resume. This will be too obvious. Sophisticated application tracking systems may pick up on this and give your resume a low score. Instead, use contextual keywords and phrases no more than three times. The length of your resume doesn't matter because the application tracking system will parse resumes of any length.

When the application tracking system identifies your resume as a good match, it brings your resume to the attention of the nurse recruiter. Depending on the application tracking system, the nurse recruiter may be presented with information that the application tracking system retrieved from the resume – and not the entire resume. Key information may be inadvertently excluded by the application tracking system, especially if you don't use a standard format for the resume. Some application tracking systems also automatically email the applicant if the application was rejected; however, this could be sent in error and the applicant may later receive an invitation to meet the nurse recruiter.

Application tracking systems typically are position-oriented in that it searches resumes of applicants for a specific open position. It doesn't search resumes of candidates who applied for a different position. Therefore, you need to indicate what positions you want to apply for.

Application tracking systems use optical character recognition (OCR) technology that scans your resume, and Statistical Natural Language Processing (SNLP) to score your resume. Here's how some application tracking systems work:

1. Removes all formatting from the resume
2. Locates contextual keywords and key phrases
3. Organizes the resume into specific categories based on contextual keywords and phrases:
   – Work Experience
   – Education
   – Contact Information
   – Skills
4. Matches contextual keywords and phrases to the healthcare facility's job requirements
5. Gives the resume a score based on matches
6. The nurse recruiter selects the highest scored resumes to review

Avoid gaming the system by using such gimmicks as white words – copying the job description to the bottom of your resume then changing the color of the type to white. The application tracking system will be able to read it but not the recruiter because words in white blend in with the white background of the screen and paper. Newer application tracking systems are aware of such tactics.

Your resume may receive a lower than expected score for trying to manipulate the system.

Job Fairs

Job fairs are gatherings of nurse recruiters who are looking for nurses and nurses who "might be" looking to change positions. Some nurse recruiters are there to support the sponsor of the job fair.

Here are some tips when you attend a job fair:

1. Arrive at the beginning of the job fair. Nurse recruiters are most enthusiastic about attending at the beginning of a job fair. Halfway through a job fair nurse recruiters are likely to lose interest. Standing in the booth, seeing an endless sea of potential candidates, and answering the same questions hundreds of times per hour takes a toll.

2. Make an impression. This can be challenging because you are one of a few hundred nurses trying to do the same thing. Dress professionally. Keep your pitch short, to the point and memorable. The nurse recruiter is probably going to forget you as soon as you walk away. Tell the nurse recruiter something about you that makes you different from the other candidates who visit the booth such as, "I used to write computer programs for Wall Street firms then switched to nursing." Later you can mention this in emails, phone calls, even on your application to jog the nurse recruiter's memory.

3. Set realistic goals. You may submit your resume to the nurse recruiter, but this is probably not the best time to do so. Your resume will be one of hundreds in a pile and chances are good that the pile will be the last thing the nurse recruiter wants to sift through when returning to the office. It is best to submit your resume and application using the application tracking system on the healthcare system's website. Spend your brief moments with nurse recruiters to discover the hot jobs they are trying to fill. The nurse recruiter will likely be anxious to talk about those jobs. You can also use this time to ask questions that you probably are hesitant to ask at an interview for fear of sending the wrong message. For example, is it possible to work every Sunday instead of every other weekend? Can your work schedule be accommodated around your school schedule? Questions like these may be interview stoppers. Chances are good that the recruiter wouldn't remember you asking those questions if they are asked at the job fair.

4. Keep your conversation brief and to the point. You won't be interviewed at the job fair.

5. You may want to contact the nurse recruiter, but the nurse recruiter may not want to be contacted. Don't take this personally. From reading this chapter, you should realize that the nurse recruiter has a very busy job and the last thing they want is to spend time responding to phone calls and emails from everyone they meet at a job fair. If they ask you to contact them, then do so, otherwise apply online.

In addition, perhaps the nurse recruiter is not looking to recruit nurses at the job fair. Instead, the healthcare facility may have sent the nurse recruiter to the job fair to support the organization sponsoring the job fair. The goal was not to recruit nurses but to keep the name of the healthcare facility in front of nurses, other healthcare facilities, and to support organizers of the job fair.

The Background Check Anxiety

It isn't over once you've beaten the application tracking system; impressed the nurse recruiter and the nurse manager during interviews; passed pre-employment tests; and received an offer – and possibly a start date. You still must pass the background check. The background check isn't a "from birth" background check that potential Federal agents must pass. Yet it can be more involved than those that candidates in other industries experience because healthcare facilities typically have stringent legal requirements – you care for patients and have direct involvement administering medication. The primary goal of the background check is to protect patients.

Human Resources typically does not conduct background checks except to verify your nursing license (which is verifiable online), and drug screening (which is performed by Employee Health). A vendor is hired to perform background checks. The vendor uses multiple sources to verify your background. For the most part, the background check verifies everything you have on your application, resume, and sometimes what you said during your interviews. The best advice can be summed up in a line from the award-winning movie Moonstruck: "Tell him the truth. They find out anyway."

The background check cannot be conducted without your written permission. One of the documents that you are asked to sign once you are offered the position is a consent form authorizing the healthcare facility to conduct the background check. You have the right to refuse to sign the consent form; however, the job offer will probably be rescinded. Your arm is not being twisted to sign. It is simply that the healthcare facility is protecting patients.

A background check typically includes searches of:
- Court records (criminal and civil)
- Credit reports
- Motor vehicle reports
- Verification of your education and employment record
- Actions against your license
- Employment eligibility verification (I-9, E-Verify)
- Identity verification
- Background checks cannot include:
- Any negative information that occurred from incidents after seven years, except for criminal convictions
- Bankruptcies that occurred more than 10 years prior
- Civil suits, civil judgments, and arrests that are more than seven years prior
- Tax liens (paid) after seven years
- Incidents of credit collections after seven years

Nearly all background checks are conducted electronically contingent on whether the data is electronically available to the vendor. Results are usually presented electronically to Human Resources within a week. The report typically identifies discrepancies between your application and resume and what the vendor found. The report also identifies derogatory results that came up during the background check. A derogatory result is when someone said something negative about you. Human Resources determines if any negative result from a background check warrants disqualification from working at the healthcare facility.

The nurse recruiter carefully follows the healthcare facility's policy before taking steps to rescind your job offer. The nurse recruiter doesn't want to start the recruiting process over if you are an acceptable candidate. The nurse recruiter verifies that the vendor's background check was reported on the correct candidate. The nurse recruiter typically uses a decision matrix to decide if negative items on the background check report are within hiring criteria for your position. The decision matrix ensures that the healthcare facility has consistent hiring practices.

If the job offer might be rescinded because of a negative background check, Human Resources will send you a pre-adverse action letter, a copy of the background report, and a copy of the summary of your rights under the Fair Credit Reporting Act. You will be given a reasonable time to explain elements of the background check report that could disqualify you from the position. The nurse recruiter realizes that a background check is not always 100% accurate. For example, you might be the victim of identity theft – and you don't know it yet. You will be given a reasonable amount of time to address discrepancies with the nurse recruiter and/or the vendor who conducted the background check.

If you don't make any attempt to explain discrepancies or your explanations do not satisfy Human Resources, then you will receive an adverse action letter. The adverse action letter states that the job offer is rescinded based either in whole or in part due to the information provided in the background report. The letter will contain the vendor's contact information so you can further explore the matter with the vendor.

A criminal conviction may or may not disqualify you depending on the nature of the crime. If you hold a valid nursing license and the criminal conviction occurred before you received your license, then the state licensing board apparently determined that the conviction would not impede you from receiving a nursing license. A criminal background check is usually performed as a requirement for getting your nursing license, therefore, Human Resources may also have such an opinion.

However, you may have a valid nursing license if you were convicted of a crime after receiving your nursing license and the state licensing board has yet to find out about the conviction. This is problematic. Even if you have a criminal conviction that would impede hiring, you may be able to have that conviction expunged depending on the nature of the crime and regulations within your state. Some states offer rehabilitation programs for nurses and other medical professionals who have an addiction problem. Their medical license is suspended until they complete the rehabilitation program, subsequently, their license is restored. Healthcare facilities are aware of such rehabilitation programs and may give nurses who attend a program a second chance.

Lying on your resume is a common finding on a background check. What is a lie versus an exaggeration? The nurse recruiter must determine this. Where you worked, your title, and dates of employment and compensation are hard to exaggerate. Likewise, schools you attended, dates you attended, and degrees earned are also factual. The actual work you did can be exaggerated to some extent. Lying reveals your character. The nurse recruiter and nurse manager expect a little exaggeration on your experience knowing that pre-employment testing will objectively measure your abilities. Outright lying implies that you are dishonest – and that you can't be trusted. Remember that the nurse recruiter and nurse manager decide the extent to which an exaggeration is a lie. What might seem minor to you could be major to them.

Will your current and former employers say something that will prevent you from getting another nursing job? Possibly, but not necessarily. Many healthcare facilities have a policy of verifying employment by confirming your job title, dates of employment, and salary. Characterizing your work performance may expose the healthcare facility to libel claims and lawsuits by trying to prevent you from finding work. Some nurse managers may still give an opinion about you when requested, regardless of policy.

References that you supply the nurse recruiter will be contacted and presumably will give you a good reference. However, the healthcare industry is a relatively small network where nurses know one another. It is not uncommon for the hiring nurse manager to call a friend who may know someone who works in your current healthcare facility and ask for an informal reference – "How is she?" The response – or lack of a response after acknowledgement that they know you – may weigh heavily on the hiring nurse manager's decision about you long before a decision is made on a candidate for the position.

Be aware that your Facebook account, tweets, blogs, videos, and other things you post on social media may end up in your background check. Some healthcare facilities find that your Facebook account and other online postings provide more insight into your character than other items in the background check. References to heavy drinking, violence, or sexually offensive material on your postings can quickly eliminate you from contention for a position. However, employers must be careful doing so because your online content might reveal political leanings, your religious views, your ethnicity, or your existing medical conditions and other things about you that legally cannot be revealed to your employer until after you are hired. Some employers pressure candidates to provide ID and passwords to their online accounts. There is legislation pending in several states to ban this practice. It is important to be aware of your on-line presence before your job search begins.

You are entitled to receive a free copy of your background check report even if there is no adverse action expected. It might be wise to ask your Human Resources for a copy of your present background check report to get an idea of what your employer sees. If you see any problems that weren't brought to your attention, you may still want to explore why they occurred – even if you don't share it with Human Resources, although once the background check is completed and you are offered the job, there is no real need to address anything negative in your background check because it did not stop you from getting the job.

Be prepared to honestly explain items in your background that are hazy during your initial interviews with the nurse recruiter – well before the background check. No one has a perfect background – and the nurse recruiter knows this. Being honest – not elusive – goes a long way to show your true character. If you worked for three months and left a position, point this out to the nurse recruiter and explain what occurred and why it probably won't occur again. For example, you may have had a negative experience at your first nursing job and so you left the job. You could say this was too much too soon and you and the nurse manager realized you were over your head. Since then you have been successful in more appropriate positions.

Why You Didn't Get Hired

You were perfect for the job. Interviews went well. Both the nurse recruiter and nurse manager gave you the feeling that you were a good fit for the job. So why didn't you get it? Let's begin with the interviews. A good interviewer will leave you with a positive feeling after an interview unless you are obviously not qualified for the job. If you are unqualified, the interviewer is likely to describe what the nurse will be doing by painting a mental picture that lets you discover for yourself that you are probably not well-suited to the particular position. If you might be qualified for the job, then the interviewer wants to keep you motivated to continue to explore the opportunity – even if the interviewer realizes you are, say, the fourth most qualified candidate for the position. The first three may not accept the job offer and they don't want to be too quick to discourage you.

So what are reasons for not getting the job? It might be something you said during the interview. You may have narrowed your requirements such as shift and clinical area that gave the perception that you are not flexible. Furthermore, you might have trashed your former employer and manager during the interview. No matter how true it might be, this is not a good idea, and the nurse recruiter and nurse manager may feel you are too negative. Be sure to keep the discussion on a professional level when speaking about your current job.

Failure to communicate effectively during your interview is another reason some nurse recruiters reject applications. Your background on the resume might be perfect but you are unable to effectively discuss your background with the nurse recruiter or nurse manager. The nurse recruiter is hiring a person – not your resume. Your goal is to tell your story within the first ten minutes of the interview. Hit the highlights only. Save the details for when the nurse recruiter or nurse manager asks questions. Don't focus on one factor of the job such as compensation or schedule. Prepare for the interview. Research the healthcare facility. Ask questions about issues that might affect the healthcare facility, such as potential takeovers.

Dressing inappropriately can scuttle you as soon as the nurse recruiter sees you. Explain in advance of the interview that you are coming from work and will be in your work attire, if that is the case. Ask if this will be a problem – and, if so, reschedule the interview. Your work attire is likely acceptable but it is always wise to make this known ahead of time – and restate this at the beginning of the interview – "Excuse my attire, I'm coming directly from work as I mentioned during our phone call."

Not having documentation is another reason why you may not have been offered the position. Always bring your nursing license, board certifications, valid CPR cards, and any other document that is required. Offer them to the nurse recruiter during the interview so copies can be placed in your application. Eventually you'll be asked for them if you don't bring the documents to the interview.

And sometimes the nurse recruiter or the nurse manager just didn't feel you were a fit for the job. What that means is they didn't like you well enough – not that you can't do the job. Something turned them off about you during the interviews. You might have said something inappropriate, lacked motivation or failed to express yourself. Some nurse managers place themselves in the position of a patient and ask, would I want you as my nurse? If the answer isn't a solid yes, then you probably won't get the job.

Chapter 3
The New Grad Nursing Interview

Successfully completing nurse school was probably more challenging than you anticipated. The faculty went out of their way to prepare you for each test, then it was up to you to pass. No curves. No extra credit. No sad stories. It was you and the test questions – most, if not all, multiple-choice questions. The correct answer was on the page along with a few misleading answers many of which could also be correct but weren't. You had to pick the correct one. The passing grade for courses was higher than for non-nursing courses. There was no wiggle room for the instructor to boost your grade if you got close to passing. The line was drawn in the sand (passing grade) and you had to cross the line (pass) yourself with no help. Fractions of a point mattered. 79.4% is failing if the passing grade is 80%. This was all done to get you ready to take the nursing board exams (NCLEX). Your next challenge is to get your first nursing job once you pass the nursing boards. You'll learn a few strategies in this chapter that can help you find and be offered your first nursing job.

Before Graduation

Be proactive. Start building a network of contacts while you are in nursing school. Each clinical rotation presents hands-on learning experiences and the opportunity to introduce yourself to the clinical staff at the healthcare facility. You can be just another nursing student to the staff or a nursing student that they'll remember after you complete your clinical rotation.

Each clinical rotation gives you a chance to meet the nurse manager of the unit. Briefly stop the nurse manager in the hallway or politely knock on the nurse manager's office door and introduce yourself. Don't be afraid to do so. Nurse managers tend to look forward to meeting nursing students who have a clinical rotation on their unit. They want to be a good host, share experiences – and nurse managers are always on the prowl for potential nursing candidates even if there are no current openings.

Don't stalk the nurse manager and don't ask for a job. Build a casual relationship during the rotation since you are likely to see the nurse manager each time you are on the unit. Make small talk. Find out something unique about the nurse manager – pets, hobbies – just like you would when you meet a new colleague. Give the impression that you are already part of the staff. Ask the nurse manager a few meaningful questions about the unit or the patient population a couple of

DOI 10.1515/9781501506109-003

times during the rotation. This demonstrates a sincere interest in the patients on the unit. Keep questions short. Listen carefully to the reply and give the nurse manager feedback that you understood the answer. Limit conversation. Politely interrupt if the conversation goes long. Say, "This is very interesting. I have to get back to my patients but I would love to continue this later." The interruption demonstrates that you can prioritize – patients first.

Stop by on the last day of your rotation to thank the nurse manager for having you on the unit. Mention that you had a positive experience and enjoyed working with the staff and the patient population. Close your comments with, "after graduation I'd like to work on a unit like this." Again don't ask for a job. You are simply planting a seed that may or may not grow into an opportunity in the future. Be sure to thank the staff for their congeniality. Encourage your class to bring in refreshments for the staff on the last day of clinical rotation as a thank you to the staff. Before leaving, make sure you ask the nurse manager for her business card and get the names of staff members. They become your network of contacts for employment opportunities or references.

You may return to a different unit in the same healthcare facility for another clinical rotation. If so, try to create an opportunity to stop by your previous unit nurse manager's office and say "hi." Don't stalk. Don't wander on that unit. You don't have any reason to be there. Stopping by the nurse manager's office briefly is acceptable. Simply say, "I'm on unit (name of unit) doing my cardiac rotation and I thought I would stop by on my break to say hi." Make small talk asking about the nurse manager's pets or something unique that you remember about the nurse manager. Keep the conversation short. Don't sit down in the office. Don't bring up anything about graduation or a job. The goal is simply to show your face and return to your unit – planting a seed for the future.

Stay in touch with the nurse manager after you finish your rotations at the healthcare facility. Don't be forward. The nurse manager doesn't want to be your best friend or a pen-pal via email. Every four months or so send a short email asking the nurse manager a question. For example, explain a situation that you encountered during clinical rotation and ask how a similar situation is handled at the nurse manager's facility. You may also inquire about externships that might be available at the healthcare facility. Some healthcare facilities offer an externship program for the summer prior to graduation. Senior nursing students are brought in to assist the nursing staff for the summer months, creating another important opportunity to make yourself known to nurse managers and the nursing staff. There is a tendency for nurse recruiters to hire their externs as new graduate nurses.

Consider volunteering at the healthcare facility where you may want to eventually work. You wouldn't be able to perform nursing duties. You will be performing normal volunteer duties such as running specimens to the lab and transporting patients. You'll get to know the staff and have an opportunity for the nurse manager to know you as a volunteer. Show your personality and a readiness to learn. You'll have many chances to demonstrate that you are a good worker. You won't have first dibs on open positions (working in an unlicensed staff position, such as a CNA, makes you an insider giving you a chance at an open position before the position is available to non-employees). Volunteering gives you a great opportunity to build your network – contacts that may help you get a new grad nursing job.

Local chapters of nursing associations also provide a good way to build your network of contacts. The faculty of your nursing school can probably identify local chapters – they might also be a member. Look online for the state chapter website. It usually lists information about local chapters along with contact information. Send the contact an email explaining that you're a nursing student and would like to join their group. Some chapters may limit membership to licensed nurses but may invite you as a guest to their meetings. Go to their meetings if invited. Your goal is to develop relationships and keep in touch with members – keep building your network.

What Type of Nursing Do You Want to Do?

Prepare yourself for questions that nurse recruiters, nurse managers, and members of your contact network will likely ask you. The first is: What type of nursing do you want to do? You may be thinking "any nursing job," but don't say it. They realize that finding your first nursing job is challenging and you likely will accept the first job that is offered. However, the real question is, have you given any thought to the kind of nursing practice that you might do in the future?

Clinical rotations exposed you to the most common nursing practice areas giving you some foundation to choose a clinical path. Decide on a practice environment such as a hospital, private practice, urgent care center, surgery center, rehabilitation center, or nursing home. There are also opportunities in non-clinical environments, such as health insurance organizations. Experienced nurses suggest you get a few years of clinical experience preferably in a hospital where you can develop your clinical skills.

And what type of nursing do you see in your future? ER, ICU, NICU, OR ... there is an endless list of specialties from which to choose. The nurse recruiters, nurse managers, and members of your contact network don't expect you to have your whole nursing career mapped right out of nursing school. Instead, they simple want to see what area piques your interest – so far – and that you are thinking ahead, planning how you are going to build your nursing career.

Answer questions honestly. Don't try to tailor your answers based on what you think the nurse recruiters, nurse managers, and members of your contact network want to hear. You don't have to pick any area of nursing at this point. A good response is to say you want to be a good nurse and you are looking for a position that will help you develop good nursing skills. Mention specialty areas that interest you. Try not to commit to one specialty unless you've worked in that practice area as an unlicensed staff member. A few weeks of clinical rotation in a specialty area doesn't give enough insight on how it is to work in that area as a nurse.

You Don't Have Nursing Experience but You Have Experience

Clinical rotations don't count as experience! Avoid listing your clinical rotations as your job experience on your resume and job application. There is a tendency to do this because clinical rotations are the closest thing you can offer as nursing experience. You get to list names of healthcare facilities and practice areas – and it can really beef up your resume. Nurse recruiters don't consider this work experience. All new grads have the same clinical rotations where they work under close observation of the clinical instructor. No one works independently caring for a full patient load while on clinical rotation.

The nurse recruiter knows you are a new grad without any nursing experience. Your new nursing license implies that you are basically competent as a nurse. Healthcare facility administrators see you as a liability and a relatively expensive nurse to hire. New grads make a lot of mistakes – it is all part of learning. Patients may be adversely affected by mistakes made by a new grad. Therefore, new grads typically receive more intensive orientation than that given to an experienced nurse – and it is expensive. The new grad is assigned a preceptor who is an experienced staff nurse. The preceptor is responsible for care given to patients who are assigned to the new grad during orientation. Both the preceptor and the new grad receive full salary during the new grad's orientation. In essence, the healthcare facility is paying for two nurses for care that is normally provided by one nurse. Orientation may last two months before the new grad is permitted to work independently.

The nurse executive knows that the healthcare facility must invest in onboarding new grads otherwise the pool of available nurses will shrink in the future as current nurses retire. However, the nurse executive and the nurse recruiter are very selective as to which new grads will be offered to join their new grad program. The selection process is challenging because the new grad lacks proven work experience as a nurse.

Your goal is to show the nurse recruiter that you are a good investment by demonstrating that your successful non-nursing experience can carry over to your nursing practice. What you did is less important than how you did it. The nurse recruiter is looking for a new grad that has a good work ethic. You show up for work and call in well in advance if you can't to give staffing time to replace you. You complete each assigned task. You demonstrate critical thinking. You follow procedures. There are times when procedures are not appropriate – and you identify these situations and ask for direction. You'll encounter similar situations as a new grad. Questioning whether something isn't right based on your limited nursing knowledge is important to the nurse recruiter because you asked for help rather than risking a mistake that may injure a patient. As you gain experience, your critical thinking becomes the basis for solving those problems independently. Tell the nurse recruiter how you incorporated good customer service in your previous experiences. Patients are your new customers and they expect – and should receive – compassionate care. Show how you went that extra mile for customers in your previous jobs.

Your work in a hospital environment is important to share with the nurse recruiter. Direct patient care experience such as that of a certified nursing assistant, medical assistant, or patient care assistant is a good foundation for nursing. Other jobs in a hospital such as a ward clerk or non-direct patient care positions also help to convince the nurse recruiter that you are a good investment. The nurse recruiter is not looking for you to have nursing skills but is looking for you to have a good work ethic, critical thinking skills, good customer service skills, and be willing to learn ... and learn ... and learn. There is a lot to learn as a new grad.

The Search Begins

Start your search a year or so before graduation. Some healthcare facilities that have new grad programs run those programs once a year. You want to find out about those programs well in advance of the application deadline. You might be able to apply at the end of your senior year or immediately after graduation while you wait to take your licensing boards. Yes, you can be hired without a nursing license. You are considered a graduate nurse. Your practice is limited until you get your license. One of the terms of employment is that you obtain your nursing licenses within a month or two of starting work.

Begin your search with your nursing school. Faculty may have contacts at local hospitals and may know which healthcare facilities offer a new grad program – and know who you can speak with at the healthcare facility to apply to the program. Be realistic. You are one of many new grads from your school all of whom are looking for their first nursing job and a facility will treat each of you equally.

You should look at online job postings at healthcare facilities within your area. Don't apply for advanced nursing positions. This is a waste of time. Sometimes a posting will say "new graduates invited to apply." Other times, the nurse recruiter may consider a new grad but not mention that fact in the job posting. How do you find out? There is no magic answer. Email the nurse recruiter and ask.

An online search or a call to Human Resources is the best way to identify the nurse recruiter. You may find the nurse recruiter's email that way too. Alternatively, you can probably deduce the nurse recruiter's email address by finding the email address of someone else who works at the healthcare facility. For example, looking at the press contact section of the healthcare facility's website, you'll find names of the Public Relations staff and their email addresses (mjones@myhospital.com). Chances are good that nurse recruiter Mary Smith's email address is msmith@myhospital.com.

Keep your email short and to the point. Your email is one of hundreds received by the nurse recruiter. The subject line is very important. Don't hide the fact that you are a new grad. State something such as, "Brief question from a new grad" or "Brief question from a new grad from (name of the local nursing school)." This helps the nurse recruiter prioritize your email – and yes, you'll have a relatively low priority but that doesn't mean that you won't receive a response. Naming your school in the subject line may help. Local healthcare facilities sometimes have a formal or informal connections with nursing schools in their area. Responding to your email might be viewed by the nurse recruiter as maintaining that connection.

Be patient for a response! It may take a few weeks and you may never receive a response – then again, the response may be immediate. The nurse recruiter can easily get your email out of the inbox by hitting reply and writing a few words. With luck the response is yes with instructions on how to apply.

Should you visit Human Resources personally? Yes, but not to apply for a job. Many healthcare facilities use an online application tracking system to handle applications (see Chapter 2 "The Dreaded Application Tracking System"). Instead, visit Human Resources to inquire whether the healthcare facility has a new grad program and if so, how you can get information about it. You'll probably be speaking with a receptionist although there is always a chance you'll get to chat with the nurse recruiter.

Be realistic on where you want to work. It would be great to find a job in your local hospital – you and new grads from all the local nursing schools have the same thought. There aren't enough positions for local healthcare facilities to hire all of you immediately following graduation. Consider broadening your search area. You may have to explore opportunities at healthcare facilities in a different part of your state or in other states.

Be honest with yourself. Working for a healthcare facility outside where you live may require you to move. Traveling three or four hours to work every day may not make sense. Your commuting expenses will be high; traffic may delay your trip; and it might be a nightmare commuting in inclement weather. Remember that nurses are expected to work their shift even during bad travel weather. Health care workers are generally exempt from weather-related travel restrictions. Relocating may be the only feasible option if you find a job outside your current area.

Another job option that is sometimes overlooked is the military. The military recruits nurses as commissioned officers. New nurses come in as junior officers. In exchange for commitment to military service, new nurses can continue their education financed by the military and can gain experience that can easily be transferred to civil life. Financial compensation is based on rank, although many branches offer financial incentives for board certifications and specialties. You must also complete a basic officer leader course where you learn to be an officer.

Use Your Network

Graduating and getting your nursing license does not guarantee you a nursing job. It is time to let the world know that you are a new nurse looking for your first nursing job. Don't keep it a secret. Friends, friends of friends, neighbors, family acquaintances, any of these contacts may know someone associated with a healthcare facility who can help you contact the nurse recruiter (they may even know the nurse recruiter). Chances may be slim but you never know who may help you open the door to your first nursing job. For example, a relative of your neighbor may be friends with a nurse manager. Your neighbor may speak about you to her friend...and her friend might mention you to the nurse manager...who may recommend that the nurse recruiter setup an appointment with you. Nurse recruiters usually like referrals because someone knows the candidate.

Your best opportunity is working the network you built during your clinical rotations. Email nurse managers and others on the nursing staff you met while on clinical rotation on their unit. Do this months before graduation. Don't think you can simply knock on their door and say, I got my nursing license when do I start? It doesn't work that way. Even if the nurse manager wants to hire you there first must be an open position – and that opening may not exist. Give members of your network time to help you.

Email your network – especially nurse managers – asking for advice, but not a job. Ask if they have any suggestions on how to find your first nursing job. They'll know you are looking for a job. You don't have to mention it. Make reference to your previous contacts with them. For example, "You may recall that we met when I was doing my clinical rotation on your unit." Be sure to include anything that may uniquely identify you from other nursing students who also had a clinical rotation on that unit. Hopefully, you planted that seed during your clinical rotation and now it is time for the seed to germinate.

Don't become a nuisance. Send the email and be patient. You can follow up in a couple of weeks with another short email updating them on your search. Keep it light and a little humorous. The goal is to remind them that you are still looking.

What Nurse Recruiters Look For

So what might a nurse recruiter look for in a new grad candidate? Each nurse recruiter has her own requirements – some set by policy, some set by requirements of the hiring nurse manager, and some are subjective. No one can tell you exactly what criteria the nurse recruiter is looking for, but there is a good chance they include the following characteristics:

– Be brief and to the point when communicating (i.e., emails, phone conversations) with the nurse recruiter
– Show respect for the nurse recruiter by not stalking her. Don't send follow up emails daily. Give her time to process you request.
– Read the job description and clearly relate something in your background that matches the job description – even if that experience isn't in nursing. Sometimes you'll find a job posting that states "new grads welcome" so drawing the link between your non-nursing background and the job descriptions helps the nurse recruiter justify bringing you in for an interview.
– Show a positive attitude. You know enough about nursing to make you minimally competent. You know you have a lot to learn and you are willing to learn.

- Display a good work ethic. You are punctual and arrive early anticipating that you may get lost or traffic may delay your arrival.
- Demonstrate that you are a team player. You are willing to do things outside your job description to care for patients.
- Be honest and accountable. You know your strengths and you know your weaknesses. You want to be a great nurse, but you have a long way to go and need everyone's help to get there. You will make mistakes. However, you acknowledge it and ask others to help you rectify the mistake. We learn from our mistakes. This shows that you are accountable for your actions.
- Understand the job requirements. You know that you'll be working weekends, holidays, and late shifts. Some shifts are eight hours and others are 12 hours. Eight-hour shifts are days, evenings, or nights. 12-hour shifts are days (7 a.m. to 7 p.m.) or nights (7 p.m. to 7 a.m.). You don't get to pick your shifts or your days off. You won't have personal days and vacation until you are off probation. Let the nurse recruiter know up front if you have plans already, such as a wedding or vacation. The nurse recruiter may or may not be able to accommodate you.

Notice that nothing is mentioned about nursing skills, grade point average, or your class rank. These are usually of less concern to the nurse recruiter. The state licensing board certifies that you have basic nursing skills. The healthcare facility's orientation program will teach you skills required to care for their patients. You won't pass orientation if your skills are not adequate to do the job.

Selling Yourself in Your Resume and Job Application

Your email opens the door and your resume is an advertisement that tells the nurse recruiter to stop looking – I'm your new grad. This may be wishful thinking; however, your resume should give a sales pitch that encourages the nurse recruiter to take a closer look at you and invite you in for an interview. Likewise, this is true about the job application you submit on the healthcare facility's website.

Take a tip from advertisers: Advertisers tailor each advertisement for a specific group of customers. The group has the same needs and the advertiser can fulfill those needs. The description of the open position identifies the needs of the nurse recruiter. You believe you can fulfill those needs, so your resume and job application should show how you can meet them.

Each resume and job application must be tailored to a specific job posting. Yes, this is time-consuming but you'll have a better chance of success than sending a general resume. The nurse recruiter has a list of job requirements for a position – and minimal time to review the qualifications of each applicant. The application tracking system (see Chapter 2 "The Dreaded Application Tracking System") will complete the first review of candidates.

Format your resume in common sections:
- Contact information
- Work Experience
- Employer's name, your title, dates
- Education
- Skills

Make a list of job requirements. Next to each job requirement enter something in your background that meets the requirement. Keep entries brief and to the point. Be honest. Leave it blank if you don't meet a specific job requirement. Rarely is there a candidate who meets all requirements of the job.

Next write those entries incorporating the exact words and phrases that are used in the job description. The goal is to use keywords found in the job description at least three times in your resume or job application. This makes it easier for the application tracking system to give your resume/application a high score.

The nurse recruiter matches the job description to information in the candidate's resume and application. You make the nurse recruiter's job easier if you do the matching for her in your resume/application. The nurse recruiter can scan your resume/application quickly without having to read long descriptions of your work history. Remember that non-nursing experience is important for the nurse recruiter. A new grad will probably not have nursing experience.

This is same strategy advertisers use to encourage potential customers to take a closer look at their product. Advertisers identify the customer's need (job description) and pointedly show how their product (you) meet each need (your resume/job application). Advertisers leave little room for the customer (nurse recruiter) to misinterpret the message.

Practice! Go online and find job postings at your local hospital's website even if you are not going to apply for the position. List job requirements and match your background to them using words and phrases contained in the job posting. Next, look at their job application. Jot down the information on the job application. Prepare your responses offline. Remember this is an exercise and you're not applying for the position. Few new grads do this and end up filling out the application online without much forethought.

Here is a sample job requirement for a new grad position.

Job Summary:

The graduate registered professional nurse (RN) is responsible for providing and supervising direct and indirect total nursing care responsibilities to patients. A training program will be under the direct supervision of a preceptor for all principal duties and responsibilities during the training program. Eventually the graduate nurse will transition to independent practice after successful training program completion. The graduate nurse will adhere to all rules and regulations of all applicable local, state, and Federal agencies and accrediting bodies.

Required Experience:
- Basic Life Support Certified (American Heart Association)
- Graduate of an accredited school of nursing
- Bachelor's degree in Nursing (Preferred)
- Current license as a registered professional nurse

Job Responsibilities:

Completes timely assessments of patients. Sets measurable and achievable short- and long-range goals for patients based on the patient assessment and diagnosis. Assists in developing and implementing a plan of care for the patient. Prioritizes interventions, assesses results, and evaluates and modifies the plan of care as needed. Demonstrates the ability to interpret diagnostic data related to the patient's assessment and diagnosis. Demonstrates knowledge of procedures, medications, and the use of equipment in the treatment of the patient based on the patient's diagnosis and care plan. Follows strict infection prevention processes. Demonstrates safe medication practices. Teaches the patient about safe medication administration and about adhering to prescribed treatment based on the patient's diagnosis. Successfully communicates with patients and family using therapeutic communication. Effectively communicates with the interdisciplinary team. Documents all patient encounters in the electronic medical record system based on institutional policy.

Here is an illustration of a simple resume that is designed to be "read" by an application tracking system. Noticed that words and phrases from the job posting are used in the description of work experience. Clinical rotations are not really considered job experience and will be discounted by the nurse recruiter; however, placing it in the work experience category provides the opportunity to include words and phrases contained in the job description. Remember that the initial goal is to have your resume selected by the application tracking system – and then read by a human. You can modify the format of the resume and elaborate on your experience as needed but make sure you include words and phrases that appear in the job posting.

Mary Jones
555 Any Street, Any City, Any State 55555
Phone: (555)-555-5555 Email: MaryJones@domain.com

Work Experience
My Hospital, Some City, Some State 55555
    Certified Nursing Assistant
    January Year to Present
    Provided direct nursing care to patients under the direct supervision of a registered professional nurse while adhering to all rules and regulations of applicable local, state, and Federal agencies and accrediting bodies. Completed timely assessment of patients. Achieved measurable short- and long-range goals for patients set by the patient's treatment team. I prioritized interventions and suggested to the registered nurse modifications to the patient's care plan based on my assessment and evaluations. I provided direct patient care following strict infection prevention processes and documented interactions with the patients in the electronic medical record system.

Some Hospital, Some City, Some State 55555
    Student Nurse
    Year to Year
    During clinical rotations, I demonstrated the ability to interpret diagnostic data related to the patient's assessment and diagnosis and demonstrated the knowledge of procedures, medications, and the use of equipment in the treatment of a patient based on the patient's diagnosis and care plan. I demonstrated safe medication practices while administering medications to patients during clinical rotations. I also taught patients and their families about safe medication administration and the importance of adhering to prescribed treatment based on

the patient's diagnosis. I effectively communicated with patients and the interdisciplinary team during clinical rotations.

Education
Bachelor of Science in Nursing (BSN)
    My Nursing School, Some City, Some State 55555

License
License Professional Registered Nurse (RN), Some State
    Basic Life Support Certified (BLS) (American Heart Association)

Special Skills
    Bilingual: Spanish

Cover Letter

Some candidates might feel that a cover letter is relevant if you are sending a paper resume to the nurse recruiter. Rarely is this done today with the introduction of the online application tracking system. The application tracking system streamlined the process by doing away with unnecessary paperwork.

An application tracking system may give you an opportunity to upload a cover letter. If it does, then create and upload a cover letter. The cover letter is an introduction to your resume – not a replacement for your resume – that encourages the nurse recruiter to read your resume. Tailor the cover letter to the job posting. Avoid generic cover letters. Keep the cover letter brief and to the point. The cover letter should be one page.

Use the nurse recruiter's name in the salutation, such as Dear Ms. Smith. Identify who you are and the position for which you are applying. Tell your story in one paragraph. Conclude with a paragraph stating that you applied online and you would like to meet in-person to discuss opportunities at the healthcare facility.

Here is a sample email cover letter that you can upload with your application and/or email directly to the nurse recruiter.

Dear Ms. Smith:
    As a new graduate registered nurse from *my school* with a current registered nurse license, I am confident that my talents make me an excellent candidate for your new graduate nursing program based on requirements stated in the job posting.

My online application is complete and I uploaded my resume. You will notice that I developed excellent nursing skills through my classroom and clinical rotations. Furthermore, I demonstrated the ability to provide exceptional whole patient care for the patient's physical, emotional, and psychosocial challenges. My references will attest to my work ethic and desire to treat patients with compassion.

My application provides a glimpse of my enthusiasm for nursing and quality patient care. I look forward to a time when we can further discuss how my background and qualifications complement the requirements for your new graduate nurse program. I can be reached at (555) 555-5555 or email: MaryJones@domain.com.

I look forward to hearing from you.

Sincerely,
Mary Jones, BSN, R.N.

What to Expect During the Interview

Get to the healthcare facility a half hour before the interview. This gives you time for you to find your way in case you get lost on the campus or in the facility. Arrive at Human Resources 15 minutes before your scheduled appointment. There is a chance you may get in to see the nurse recruiter earlier than scheduled. This benefits the nurse recruiter because it keeps her ahead of what can be a very busy schedule.

You get one chance at making a first impression so dress the part of a new nurse. Don't wear scrubs. Dress in business casual. Scrubs are fine if you are coming from your current job and you tell the nurse recruiter at the time you make the appointment. Every detail of your appearance counts. Keep nails short and nothing fancy. Infection control policies at the healthcare facility dictates grooming of nails and hair. It is a plus if the nurse recruiter doesn't have to tell you about grooming for infection control purposes.

Stand, extend your hand, make eye contact, put on a smile, and introduce yourself to the nurse recruiter. Consider the nurse recruiter a friend that you are meeting for the first time rather than the person who will decide to give you your first nursing job. A newly graduated nurse once commented that she didn't expect to be offered the job, so she relaxed and was herself during the interview.

The worst that could happen was that her expectations were met. Any other outcome surpassed her expectations. Ninety percent of how you are perceived is your appearance and how you handle yourself. Casual business attire and a relaxed respectful affect projects the type of person your really are to the nurse recruiter.

Open the conversation with small talk — short and to the point — such as how you found traveling to the healthcare facility. Speaking up first shows that you are comfortable communicating with strangers. Let the recruiter take the lead from there. There is a tendency for the nurse recruiter to find out about you before describing the position and the healthcare facility. Some nurse recruiters tell you about the position only if what you say makes you a good candidate for the position. Otherwise, you might be told that this position probably isn't a good fit.

After a minute or so of small talk, the nurse recruiter asks the first of many open-ended questions. The objective is to find out who you are but also to decide if you meet the job requirements and fit in with the healthcare facility's culture. The former is a checklist, the latter is a gut feeling. The nurse recruiter looks for gaps in your background too. For example, you might graduate in December but passed your licensing boards in March. The nurse recruiter might ask, "Did you fail your licensing boards the first time?" Be honest. If so, it isn't a show stopper. However, it might also be that you wanted to take time to study.

The first question might be, "Why did you become a nurse?" Answer honestly and logically. You may have volunteered on your community's ambulance service and found caring for others rewarding. Nursing seemed to be the next logical step. You may have relatives who are nurses who shared the rewards and trials of being a nurse. And you might have cared for a family member who needed home care. Whatever the reason, the nurse recruiter is very interested in how you communicate. Did you listen to the question and did your response make sense? Be sure to speak in complete sentences and use conversational words. Medical terms are fine but the nurse recruiter is more interested in hearing a complete story using words that others will understand.

The next question might be "What are your career goals?" New grads – and even some experienced nurses – find this question difficult to answer because you probably don't know. You haven't worked as a nurse yet. Again, be honest. Your clinical rotations exposed you to different specialties, but not all specialties. You may have had a walk-through ICU or the emergency department or stood in the corner of the OR during a procedure. This was insufficient to give you any clue as to what it is like being a nurse in those areas. You might respond by saying, I found my maternity clinical rotation interesting; however, once I get experience as a nurse I'll be in a better position to know which area of nursing is for me. Even if you are set on a specific area of nursing, tell the nurse manager that you want to develop a good foundation in nursing before moving into your dream nursing job.

Another commonly asked question is, "What are your strengths and weaknesses?" This is a tricky question to answer because you are being asked to identify weaknesses that you probably want to keep to yourself for fear of losing the opportunity for the job. No one is a perfectionist. Don't put a spin on your weaknesses. Nurse recruiters may feel you are being dishonest. You may answer by saying; during clinical rotations, I worked well in pressure situations paying great attention to details. When things are slow, though, I get bored. However, I learned to spend those moments talking with my patients. You gave both a strength and weakness. You also explained how you work towards strengthening your weakness.

Be prepared to answer this frequently asked question: "What makes you a good person for the job?" Don't mention that you have a nursing license. Tell the nurse recruiter why you think you'll be a good fit for the job. Base your response on the clinical rotations, if you had clinical rotations in that healthcare facility. You experienced the type of patients cared for by the healthcare facility and you've seen the level of quality care expected of the staff. You got to meet the staff and have seen how they worked as a team – and you feel you fit nicely. If your clinical rotations were at a different healthcare facility, then speak about the experience in the same manner. Mention there are differences in healthcare facilities but delivering quality patient care is expected by staff regardless of the healthcare facility. Restate that you have a strong work ethic and are eager to build on the basic nursing skills acquired at your school.

"What do you expect to learn from your colleagues once you join our nursing staff?" An objective of asking you this question is to determine if you understand that you have a lot to learn about nursing. The nurse recruiter is not looking for specifics such as inserting an I.V. into a patient. Instead, the nurse recruiter is looking for you to briefly describe what you don't know but want to learn. Speak about quality patient care and types of nursing skills that you haven't mastered. You might want to conclude by saying; I expect to learn how to be a good nurse. I know there are things I don't know – I want my colleagues to help me learn those things.

Still another commonly asked question is, "How did your education prepare you for your first nursing job?" This is your opportunity to credit the faculty of your school for doing a great job. You were inexperienced the first day of nursing school. You knew nothing about nursing. You were a minimally competent nurse when you graduated and passed your licensing boards. The faculty – and your hard work – helped you develop the nursing skills needed to begin your career as a nurse. Nurse educators and your future colleagues at the healthcare facility will help you build on your basic nursing knowledge to become a professional nurse.

Speak with confidence about your abilities and experiences. Be social and humorous at times, then serious when answering the core of questions. Avoid negative comments – even when you are being humorous. Negative remarks may be misinterpreted and you have no way of correcting the misinterpretation.

The direction of the interview may switch from you selling yourself to the nurse recruiter selling the healthcare facility and position to you. This may be a signal that you convinced the nurse recruiter that you are a viable candidate. However, the recruiter explaining things about the healthcare facility and the job might simply be a way of signaling that the interview is over.

Stand. Maintain eye contact. Extend your hand and thank the nurse recruiter for spending this time with you. State that you realize that other candidates are being interviewed. Ask the nurse recruiter what will be the next step in the process. The response gives you a hint of what you should do next. The nurse recruiter should tell you approximately when you should be hearing from them – so you don't harass the nurse recruiter with emails and phone calls. On occasion, the nurse recruiter may be honest about the process. You'll be told there is a stronger candidate but we haven't reached a decision yet. This helps you set realistic expectations about prospects of getting the job.

After the Interview

Be patient! It is unrealistic to expect a call from the nurse recruiter when you get home from the interview. Don't harass the nurse recruiter. Send a brief email the day following the interview thanking the nurse recruiter for the opportunity to meet and discuss the position. Include three brief examples of how your background compliments requirements for the position. Conclude by saying that you are looking forward to continuing the interview process in the near future.

You will be contacted if the nurse recruiter feels you are a viable candidate for the position. However, there is no set time period for when the nurse recruiter will get back to you. You are one of many candidates for the position – and there are many positions that the nurse recruiter needs to fill. There are a lot of things going on behind the scenes (see Chapter 2 "The Dreaded Application Tracking System") that may delay the nurse recruiter from responding to you.

Plan to send a follow up email a week to ten days after the interview. Ask a question relevant to the position in the email such as: "Is choice of working holidays based on seniority?" or "Is tuition reimbursement available during the probation period?" These are reasonable questions that require the nurse manager to respond. The response may include the status of your application.

A long delay in a response doesn't mean that another candidate was selected for the position – although that might be the case. Rejection emails are typically sent automatically by the application tracking system once a decision is made on your application. A delay for a couple of months might be normal for the healthcare facility. It takes time for the nurse recruiter to complete the first round of interviews and to arrange for interviews with the hiring nurse manager. You may be a viable candidate but not in the top three candidates who will get the first crack at interviewing with the hiring nurse manager. You'll be called if one of the three is rejected by the hiring nurse manager.

The best course of action is to keep looking for your first nursing job. Continue to look at job postings at healthcare facilities where you were interviewed. Send an email to the nurse recruiter – who likely remembers you from the interview – that you are qualified for the other position. Name the position in the email.

Continue to send a follow-up email every week to ten days inquiring about the status of your application. This is a reasonable request and won't be considered harassment by the nurse recruiter. At some point, you'll either be invited back for an interview with the hiring nurse manager or receive a rejection. Don't be discouraged by rejections. You are a new grad looking for a healthcare facility that is willing to invest in you. There are fewer new grad programs than there are positions for experienced nurses. Keep widening your search to include non-hospitals such as sub-acute facilities, nursing homes, and healthcare facilities out-of-state. You are looking for your first nursing job – not your perfect nursing job. And yes, there is a nursing job for you – you just have to find it.

Nursing as a Second ... or Third ... or Fourth Career

You are a new grad – much older than others in your graduating class because you already had a career or more in fields other than nursing. Your kids are grown and out of college, now it's your turn. The economic downturn wiped out any opportunity to continue in your previous career. You retired relatively young and you don't want to sit at home. Or it is just time for a change? Whatever the reason, you're trying nursing.

Nursing school was tougher than you imagined. That two-year program at your community college was more like four years. Two years of prerequisite courses and two years of nursing courses. The real challenge was going back to school – and being the oldest in the class. Nursing school is an equalizer. Young or old, everyone had to take the same courses, pass the same tests, and complete the same clinical rotations. Age probably seemed to disappear as everyone in the class looked for ways to increase the chances of passing.

Nursing schools tend to have an up or out policy. You pass the course and move on to the next course or you fail and you're out of the program – although some nursing schools give you one chance to recover by retaking a course. And this applies to everyone regardless of age. At the beginning of each term, you and your younger colleagues probably counted heads to see who made the cut.

Passing each course wasn't as easy as it was passing courses for your previous career(s). Many college courses use the horseshoe method of passing- at least that is what some call it. Getting close to the peg (passing) usually means you pass. Instructors have a tendency to curve actual grades that give borderline students a boost to a passing grade. Not so in nursing school. That was probably an eye-opener. No curves.

Likewise, there are no curves when it comes to getting your first nursing job. You'll go through the sample application and interview process as all new grads. The nurse recruiter is prohibited by law to consider age as a qualification for the position. However, maturity is on your side in another way. You are probably very comfortable speaking with strangers (i.e., nurse recruiters, hiring nurse managers) because you've done so in your previous career. Furthermore, you can tap into experiences dealing with people in your other career that can carry over to nursing.

Although you may connect with the nurse recruiter on a mature level, you'll still need to answer questions that are asked of all new grads (see What to Expect During the Interview). Why did you leave your previous career? Why do you think nursing is better than continuing in your previous career? Do you plan to go back to your previous career? These are all questions that you must be prepared to answer.

Develop a one-minute response that explains your transition to nursing. For example, you might say that your previous career was developing computer applications. The economic downturn hit and companies offshored those jobs. You had been volunteering on the community ambulance service for many years and enjoyed helping people. Nursing seemed to be a great opportunity to continue caring for people so you decided to change careers. You really enjoyed nursing school and caring for patients during clinical rotations. You feel nursing is a perfect career choice.

Be sure to link experiences in your career to requirements of the nursing job. Experiences and skills honed in other industries are applicable to nursing. You need to make the connection in your cover letter, resume, and during the interview.

You are still a new nurse and are prone to all the same weaknesses of any new nurse. Don't be afraid to admit that you have a lot to learn about nursing. Briefly tell the nurse recruiter about how you had to adjust to returning to school and meeting the challenges of nursing school. This demonstrates that you recognize that you have to change – and that you successfully met those challenges by graduating nursing school and passing the licensing boards.

Being a new grad doesn't mean you have nothing to offer the healthcare facility. You are basically competent when you pass the licensing boards. You are a novice and the nurse recruiter knows it. You need to hone your nursing skills and move through the ranks of an advanced beginner, fully competent nurse, proficient nurse and an expert nurse. The nurse recruiter and the hiring nurse manager want to give you the opportunity to grow. You need to convince them that you're worth their investment of time and money to let you grow within their healthcare facility.

Chapter 4
The Experienced Nurse Interview

Are You an Experienced Nurse?

As strange as it may sound, there isn't a clear definition of an experienced nurse. Some say that after six months as a practicing nurse you are no longer a new grad, but six months is really not a lot of experience. And experience doing what? Is five years of experience as a nurse in a nursing home equivalent to five years of experience working on a medical surgical unit? Is five years of experience working in an urgent care center equivalent to five years working in an intensive care unit? Probably not.

Some healthcare facilities have adopted a clinical ladder that describes levels of nursing experience that associate each level with progressively higher compensation. Levels are identified as Nurse Clinician followed by the level number. Each level is usually described in a paragraph that describes the characteristics of the nurse. Here's a brief sample of a clinical ladder.

- **Nurse Clinician I:** A graduate nurse who is being oriented and has not completed the probation period.
- **Nurse Clinician II:** A nurse who has developed sound practice skills and assumes primary responsibility for a patient assignment. The nurse must have successfully completed the probation period. The nurse is prepared to learn the responsibility of being a charge nurse.
- **Nurse Clinician III:** A nurse who has demonstrated in-depth knowledge of nursing practice and is considered a proficient practitioner. The nurse has demonstrated good critical thinking skills and has developed good clinical judgment. This nurse can handle unanticipated problems and emergencies effectively.
- **Nurse Clinician IV:** A nurse who is considered an expert in nursing practice. The nurse has a comprehensive knowledge base. This nurse is innovative, self-directed, and can respond to complex and rapidly changing patient care situations. This nurse makes things happen.

This seems a logically structured approach to define nurse experience but there are challenges with the clinical ladder. Many characteristics are difficult to objectively define and measure. For example, it is a judgment call to consider a nurse a proficient practitioner, not something that can be measured. The clinical ladder also has the undesirable consequence of limiting nurses from exploring special

DOI 10.1515/9781501506109-004

areas beyond the nurse's current specialty. For example, a Nurse Clinician IV in an addiction treatment unit who wants to move to the intensive care unit may find herself moving to a lower level in the clinical ladder. The nurse must develop new skills and is technically at Nurse Clinician I – on orientation in this new unit – and hasn't completed a probation period. Technically, compensation should be adjusted for her new level.

Some say an experienced nurse should have worked as a medical surgical nurse for a period of time. Medical surgical nursing exposes the nurse to a breadth of patient care experiences and enables the nurse to develop a skillset that is transferable to all aspects of nursing. While true, the question remains: how many months of medical surgical nursing experience is necessary to consider you an experienced nurse?

And can nursing experience be summarized by months or years of experience? There are nurses who work the nightshift who have little experience admitting and discharging patients because patients are rarely admitted to the unit or discharged from the unit at night. Based on the patient population, a nurse may rarely insert a nasogastric (NG) tube. Both are medical-surgical nurses.

There are new grads who have better nursing skills – including critical thinking – than nurses with years of experience. New grads are taught the latest nursing skills and their knowledge is thoroughly tested. Experienced nurses may not have kept up with changes in nursing practice and rarely is their knowledge thoroughly tested. For example, there is an increased use of clinical simulators in nursing schools that require nursing students to respond to changing clinical situations. The experienced nurse may not have seen those clinical situations in practice.

Defining an experienced nurse is baffling and frustrating when you are looking for a nursing position. It is also baffling for the nurse recruiter and hiring nurse manager who look at experience from a practical – not academic – viewpoint. Both you and the nurse recruiter want to know if you have the experience to do the job. The hiring nurse manager knows the experience needed to do the job and has, with the help of the nurse recruiter, defined the required experience in the job description.

Decide if you can do most, if not all, tasks described in the job description. The perfect candidate can do all tasks but the perfect candidate may not apply for the position leaving the nurse recruiter to select the candidate who can do most of the required tasks. Your next task is to show (in your resume and job application) where your experience complements the required experience for the job.

Risks of Changing Jobs

If only you had a crystal ball to tell you if that new job is really a good fit for you. There is no crystal ball and you'll never know if the job is a good fit unless you try it on. What happens if it isn't a good fit? Can you return to your old job? This is a dilemma facing everyone who considers changing a nursing job. When you are unemployed or a new grad, you have nothing to lose by taking a new job – but you have everything to lose if you are giving up your job for the prospects of a new one.

Decide why you want to change jobs before applying for a new job. There are lifestyle reasons for moving on, such as a change in shift for childcare; working closer to home; or better compensation. There are also work environment reasons for a change. You dislike your boss or your colleagues; the work rules imposed by the healthcare facility are burdensome; or you are simply overwhelmed. Maybe it's just time for a change.

The primary risk of changing a job is that the job isn't a good fit and you are terminated – not only from the job but also from the healthcare facility. You and your new nurse manager want you to succeed when you change jobs, but you have to prove to yourself and to your nurse manager that you can do the job. There will be an orientation and a period of probation during which you can be terminated with or without cause. If that happens, you are unemployed, with no income and no benefits, prospects of finding a new job may be months away, and you have to prove yourself all over once you find a new job.

If you left for a new healthcare facility, then you'll probably be offered several opportunities to improve your performance as part of a performance improvement plan. The performance improvement plan will contain specific measurable objectives that are to be completed at specific milestones and a date when the nurse manager and you will review your performance. If milestones were met, then you're probably out of the woods, otherwise you'll probably be terminated. There is no guarantee that the new job is a fit. There is no gray area. Either the job is a fit or it isn't a fit. The nurse manager – not you – makes this decision.

Identify the reason you want to change jobs. Is the reason worth the risks associated with a change? Try addressing the reason that you want to leave your current position before you begin looking for a new job. Voicing your concerns to your nurse manager – assuming your nurse manager isn't the issue – may lead to solutions that can be implemented while you remain in your job. The nurse manager may welcome the conversation because finding your replacement is the last thing the nurse manager wants to do if you are doing a good job. You may avoid the risks associated with changing jobs by working out your issues with your nurse manager.

Transfer or Seek a New Employer

Transferring to nursing positions within an organization is a way to accommodate your personal needs, such as taking an evening position so you're available to take the children to school. Likewise, you'll probably have opportunities to learn new specialties while minimizing the risk of changing positions if you transfer within a healthcare facility.

The rumor mill usually announces availability of potential positions well before the position is posted by Human Resources because the nurse leaving the position is given a going away or retirement party. Open positions are usually posted internally ten days before the position is announced to the public.

If you transfer to the new position, you may be able to return to your old position if the new one doesn't work out – assuming the position remains available. Alternatively, you may be offered to apply to other open positions, some of which may not be desirable because of shift or specialty area. And you may be terminated although a good healthcare facility will try not to penalize a good nurse who fails at a new position – but don't count on that.

Next, looking for positions within your healthcare facility is usually a safer choice compared with seeking a nursing job elsewhere. You have a track record within your healthcare facility plus friends and colleagues, including your nurse manager, who may informally help introduce you to the hiring nurse manager. And the nurse recruiter and nurse managers may help you find another spot within the healthcare facility if the nursing job isn't a fit for you. Be prepared to take what may be considered a less desirable position (for example, float nurse) in this situation.

Lastly, look for a position in another healthcare facility. This is the riskiest option because your termination is a likely result if you are not a fit for the position – unless Human Resources encourages you to apply for a more appropriate open position if one is available.

Per Diem Alternative

A per diem position offers an alternative to transferring or leaving your present nursing position for another at a different healthcare facility. A per diem position offers you a chance to work at another healthcare facility while keeping your present nursing job. You and the staffing coordinator at the other healthcare facility determine when you work. Per diem employees fill in when regular employees are unavailable, such as on weekends and holidays and usually float throughout the healthcare facility.

As a per diem nurse, you get a chance to test whether or not you like working for the healthcare facility without having to give up you current nursing position. If you like it, then you also have the inside track on part-time or full-time positions there. Since you are a current employee, you can transfer from a per diem nurse position to a part-time or full-time nursing position. If you don't like working at the healthcare facility, you simply resign your per diem position and continue with your present nursing job.

The nurse recruiter hires only experienced nurses for per diem nurse positions and expects candidates to know how to do the job after being oriented to the healthcare facility. You will likely have to take pre-employment tests to demonstrate your nursing knowledge. Your orientation will be shorter than part-time and full-time employees because of your existing experience and availability. The nurse recruiter realizes that you have obligations associated with your full-time position. Orientation must work around those obligations.

The orientation schedule for a per diem nurse position varies by healthcare facility. Expect that you'll need to give up a week of your vacation. Orientation may be held for one week during the day and you will be expected to attend each day for the full day. Most days are spent in class, sitting through computer-based learning modules, and some clinical sessions. Clinical orientation may be only a few shifts based on your availability, which you arrange with the education department.

Resign or be Terminated

Your job is not forever. There may come a time when you are no longer a fit for the job – according to your nurse manager. A new nurse manager may have taken over your unit and set performance expectations that you are unable or unwilling to meet. You receive hints that your performance is lacking and suggestions on how to improve from the new manager before the nurse manager starts to officially document your performance deficits.

Next comes the official verbal warning followed by the written warning and then the dreaded performance improvement plan. Each healthcare facility has its own process giving time for a nurse to improve, but there is a clear decision point defined. If you meet performance goals specified in the performance improvement plan, then you'll be back on course. If not, you're terminated.

Even if you meet performance improvement goals, you may want to consider looking for another job outside of the healthcare facility because your reputation may be tarnished within the organization unless other nurse managers perceive that you were treated wrongfully. Time might diminish any prolonged effect of a disciplinary action if no additional disciplinary action occurs.

Should you resign before getting fired? This isn't an easy question to answer. Resigning may be easier to explain to a prospective employer than a termination. However, a resignation may prevent you from collecting unemployment insurance. You still have to pay your bills. Termination usually entitles you to collect unemployment insurance.

If you wait for termination, then you need to explain the termination to a prospective employer. Don't bad-mouth your former healthcare facility or your nurse manager. Instead, simply state that the job was no longer a fit and explain the reason. Mention there were no other suitable positions within the organization, if that was the case. The nurse recruiter may still be suspicious, so expect to focus on your successful work history especially if you had a long run at the healthcare facility.

The best approach is to acknowledge to your nurse manager and Human Resources that the job requirements of your present position seem to have changed and that it would be mutually beneficial if you look for another position within and/or outside the organization. Negotiate a time period for your job search. Be reasonable, but the longer time you have, the better off you'll be. The nurse manager and Human Resources will probably be open to negotiate. They don't have to pressure you to leave, which is just as uncomfortable for them as it is for you. There is an end date when their problem employee – you – will no longer be a problem. More important, it is a win-win for everyone. You have time to find another job and Human Resources and your nurse manager will support you in your endeavors.

Speak with Human Resources and ask a few important questions. First, will you be on the do-not-rehire list? Yes, there is such as list. Unless you have a bad track record with the organization, you probably won't be on the do-not-rehire list. The job was simply no longer a fit but something more suitable might open up in the future. Ask what Human Resources will release to a prospective employer. This is always good to know when writing your resume and applying for another job to ensure that what you say about your former position coincides with what your former employer reports. Human Resources usually releases dates of service, last job title, and confirmation of salary. Sometimes Human Resources may state if termination was voluntary or involuntary.

Hospital Mergers and Jobs

Healthcare providers, especially hospitals, have been in consolidation mode for some time now. Hospital mergers occur primarily for sustainability. Third-party payers developed reimbursement requirements that changed the business model of many hospitals in an effort to contain the runaway increases in medical expenses. Consolidation enables the hospital to offer a breadth of services under one roof giving hospital administrators an advantage when negotiating reimbursement terms with third-party payers. Furthermore, consolidation usually places the hospital in a stronger financial position when negotiating terms for loans with the financial community.

Consolidation of hospitals, however, may place the nursing staff at a disadvantage. The realignment of services by the hospital may result in layoffs. Staffing requirements are based on patient load, regulatory requirements, and contractual obligations with bargaining units. If consolidation results in a discontinuation of certain services, then positions that support these services are no longer required and staff who hold those positions may be laid off. Consolidation also may result in duplicate services. This may not result in layoffs if hospitals that form the new organization serve different communities or if there is no change in patient load. Layoffs may occur if hospitals are within a similar geographical area and each hospital has less than a full patient load for the service.

Realistically, layoffs may occur although hospital administrators make an effort to retain nursing jobs. The hospital is a business – even if it is designated as a not-for-profit organization. Nurses are hired to provide a service that the hospital sells to patients and third-party payers. Layoffs may be based on seniority depending on the hospital's policy and contract with the bargaining unit. However, there are limits to seniority. Nurses with seniority must also be qualified for the remaining nursing positions. Some hospitals will train a nurse for a position rather than laying-off the nurse, but don't count on it.

Alternatively, hospital administrators may offer nurses to transfer to positions in other hospitals that fall under the new consolidated organization rather than be laid off. There are challenges with this option. Commuting may be a concern if other hospitals within the organization are a substantial distance away. There may also be a culture difference and you'll find yourself having to prove yourself all over again.

One of the least mentioned and arguably most important factors about hospital consolidations is the impact it has on nursing opportunities. Consolidation tends to result in one cohesive organization with one culture and one set of policies. There are limited opportunities for a nurse who doesn't fit into the new organization. Where there may have been five independent hospitals in the area each having its own culture and policies, three hospitals may exist after consolidation – two independent hospitals and the consolidated organization. Choices of employers are reduced. This is further limiting if there are fewer independent hospitals in your area.

In addition, a nurse on the consolidated organization's "no hire list" may have to move out of the area to find a nursing position if all hospitals in the area are part of the consolidated organization. There are no alternatives to working for the consolidated hospital. Consolidation has created a de facto monopoly within the area.

Returning to Nursing

It's time to get back into nursing. You've cared for your kids – and maybe your parents – and now you want to re-start you nursing career. This can be a challenge if you haven't held a nursing job for years. You're not a new grad yet your nursing skills are not current. You are competing for nursing positions with nurses who have current nursing skills. Your primary job is convincing to the nurse recruiter that you still have good nursing skills and you can do the job.

Be realistic. You may not be the ideal candidate, especially if you've been away from nursing for years – but don't give up! Say you were the nurse recruiter who is required to find a full-time medical-surgical nurse position. You have a resume from a nurse who is currently working on a medical-surgical unit and has five years of experience as a medical-surgical nurse. You also have a resume from a nurse who has ten years of successful medical-surgical nursing but who hasn't worked as a nurse for the past five years. Who would you invite for an interview?

Finding your first nursing job after a hiatus is daunting, especially if you live in a small community with few healthcare facilities. Older nurses working through retirement age and more new grads than there are positions only further complicate your situation. But don't give up. You have value to offer the nurse recruiter especially if your specialty is in short supply. Your job is to convince the nurse recruiter and the hiring nurse manager to take a chance on you.

Study! Your personal goal is to regain the confidence as a nurse and hone your critical thinking abilities. You will likely be asked to take pre-employment nursing tests that demonstrate your nursing knowledge. It is critical that you keep your nursing knowledge current. A refresher course, even if not required, may be something you want to attend. Passing the pre-employment nursing tests on the first try shows the nurse recruiter that you still have your nursing knowledge.

Research the requirements for returning to nursing. There may be penalties if you were absent from nursing for more than five years. Your nursing license may have been inactivated by the state nursing board. Make sure that your nursing license is renewed and you have any required continuing education units and practice hours completed, if necessary. You may require refresher courses before you can return to nursing.

Make sure you are proficient with computers. Nearly every healthcare facility has adopted an electronic medical record (EMR) system that is used to document nursing activities. Ideally you will know how to interact with the EMR system used in the healthcare facility, but that's unrealistic. You'll be trained to use the EMR system; however, you'll need to be familiar with using a computer: open an application, click buttons, select check boxes, display pull-down lists, and so on. These are features that you probably use on your home computer.

Consider your personal practitioner as a starting point. Your practitioner may be looking for a nurse who can work a flexible schedule, which is a great way to get back into nursing. Furthermore, you may be able to use the practitioner's network of colleagues to get you an interview at a healthcare facility. You get to sit down with the nurse recruiter without the hassle of fighting the application tracking system to get your application to the top of the pile.

Contact your network of colleagues, especially the nurse recruiter from your last nursing job. You may be remembered. With luck, the nurse recruiter may try to find a position for you. Even if you are not remembered, there is a connection between you and the healthcare facility that may place your application at the top of the pile. Attend job fairs where you'll have an opportunity to ask nurse recruiters for advice – not a job. This is a great place to get advice from a person who hires nurses. You never know, the nurse recruiter might have a position that's right for you.

Keep in mind that you don't have to return to the same nursing specialty that you left. Look for a position that will give you time to dust off your nursing skills. Some healthcare facilities hire part-time nurses during peak periods to perform admission assessments and process admissions on a unit. This is a perfect position for a returning nurse. The routine of performing an admission assessment lets you practice basic nursing skills without having the primary nursing responsibility for the patient.

Returning to Nursing Under Disciplinary Action

A serious nursing error may cause a State Board of Nursing to take action against your nursing license. One of the most common actions is substance abuse that may lead to diverting narcotics and syringes. The nurse may administer an underdose to a patient or no dose but document that the patient received a full dose of medication. Nurse executives follow investigative procedures when there is probable cause to believe that a nurse is taking patient medication for personal use.

The nurse is terminated immediately when the investigation confirms suspicions. Police and the State Board of Nursing may be notified for follow-up action. The nurse may challenge the results of the investigation in court and before the Board of Nursing and usually requires the services of a lawyer. The nurse's license is temporarily suspended during the appeals process.

Substance abuse is considered a disease that can affect anyone, including nurses and practitioners. Many nursing boards offer a voluntary confidential recovery program as an alternative to disciplinary action. The program is sometimes called the Chemically Addicted Nurses Diversion Option Program. The nurse's license is suspended for the length of the program which may run for 12 months and the nurse's license may be reinstated after successful completion of the program. The program provides nurses with appropriate treatment and nurses are closely monitored during recovery. Disciplinary action is commenced if the nurse fails to complete the program.

Punishing a nurse who has a substance abuse disorder with loss of a nursing license has a chilling effect in the nursing community. Colleagues may hesitate to report suspicions fearing such a measure will result in a nurse losing her job. The healthcare facility may terminate the nurse but not report the nurse for fear of litigation. The nurse finds another nursing job and the problem persists. Punishing a nurse who has a substance abuse disorder is contrary to nursing ethics of compassion for the sick.

The challenge in returning to nursing after you have completed the program is convincing the nurse recruiter to give you a chance to prove that you can once again provide quality nursing care to patients. Some state nursing boards encourage healthcare facilities to hire nurses who successfully complete the recovery program. The success of the program depends on the incentive to return to work once the nurse completes the program. The nursing board may provide nurses with nurse recruiters who are willing to consider them for a nursing position. The nurse recruiter knows your background. You need to convince the nurse recruiter that you can do the job.

You will be assigned a workplace supervisor who monitors your work and reports your performance to the program director. You will work in an environment that is conducive to recovery – less stress and no access to controlled medications. Eventually you may be assigned to primary nursing care; however, another nurse will administer controlled medications to your patient. It is unlikely that you will be permitted to work for multiple employers, be self-employed, work as an agency or private duty nurse, work in home healthcare or float to units other than the unit where you are supervised. You may work out-of-state if your recovery program can be transferred to that state's Board of Nursing. Once you successfully complete the recovery program your suspension may not be reported by the State Board of Nursing to the public or to potential employers depending on the practice in your state.

There is usually a zero-tolerance policy for nurses who slip backward into substance abuse while in the recovery program. You are removed from the program and disciplinary proceedings begin immediately. The recovery program may not be offered if your action caused serious harm or death to a patient; if you were selling or giving drugs to others; or if you are deemed too great a risk.

Networking Helps

Network . . . network . . . network. . . You've probably heard this countless times when speaking to colleagues about finding another nursing job. Although many experienced nurses find nursing jobs by searching websites of healthcare facilities, many are referred to the nurse recruiter by a colleague or by a friend.

You probably have a network that can help you get your foot in the door of a new healthcare facility. Former or current classmates are part of your network. Even if you haven't contacted them in years, they still might remember you if you rekindle the relationship. Your former nursing instructors are also a good networking source. Current and former colleagues are part of your network. Don't overlook friends, family, and your own practitioner. They too might directly or indirectly have contacts at a healthcare facility.

Realistically, your network will not get you a nursing job unless a member of the network is in a position to arrange for you to be directly hired. This rarely occurs. However, your network may get your application – yes you still need to apply – in front of the nurse recruiter or hiring manager without having to overcome the challenges posed by the application tracking system.

The conversation may go something like this:

"Mary is an excellent nurse and is perfect for your spot," your network tells the hiring nurse manager.

"Tell her to apply online and email me when she completes the online application."

The hiring nurse manager then pulls up the application from the application tracking system circumventing the application tracking system selection process. Your application is placed at the top of the pile – and will be seen by the hiring nurse manager or nurse recruiter. You don't have to game the application tracking system.

But that's all you can expect. Your resume and application gets seen. You still must sell yourself to the hiring nurse manager and nurse recruiter. Your background will be compared with other applicants, then a decision is made as to who to invite for an interview. You may be called for an interview if your background is marginally acceptable because you've been recommended for the position. The hiring nurse manager or nurse recruiter may feel obligated to see you. Although the interview might be a courtesy, you still have the opportunity to give the hiring manager or nurse recruiter your sales pitch. You may change the courtesy interview into a nursing job by selling yourself.

The courtesy interview is also a time to explore other potential opportunities within the healthcare facility, and to develop a rapport with the hiring nurse manager or nurse recruiter. Acknowledge that the current position may not be a fit. This shows that you have realistic expectations. Ask the nurse recruiter what type of positions within the healthcare facility would be better for you and how frequently those positions are posted. The answers help to manage your expectations. Remember, the hiring nurse manager and the nurse recruiter just became new members of your network.

Applying for a Transfer

Transferring to a different position within your organization has many of the same requirements as applying from the outside. You'll need to check the internal posting board for open positions then typically complete a transfer application and send it with your resume to the nurse recruiter. This is all done electronically in many healthcare facilities; however, you probably won't have the hassle associated with an application tracking system since less than a handful of nurses apply internally for a position. All internal applications are likely reviewed by the nurse recruiter.

Transferring has its own challenges. There is a waiting period – typically 6 to 12 months – before you can apply for a transfer. The period begins when you are initially hired or when you last transferred. You must achieve a specific performance level in your last performance review. An acceptable performance level is usually the minimum criteria. This can pose what may seem to be an insurmountable obstacle if your present job isn't a fit. You want to transfer to a better "fitting" job, yet you can't if you're having trouble with your present job and receive less than an acceptable performance level on your review. Speak with your nurse manager and Human Resources if you find yourself in this predicament. Many times, the nurse manager and Human Resources want to find a mutually beneficial way of resolving the situation, so they may agree to help you transfer to a more appropriate position.

Another challenge is that your nurse manager may need to agree to the transfer. If you're doing a good job, chances are that the nurse manager may never want to lose you. Senior management of the healthcare facility is aware that this conflict may arise and has established policies and procedures to handle it. Some healthcare facilities require the nurse manager to make a compelling case to block the transfer, otherwise the transfer process continues. The nurse manager may have only one block, after that the nurse manager needs to develop a contingency plan that allows you to transfer in the future.

Seniority is another challenge when transferring within an organization. If two internal candidates meet the job requirements, then policy may dictate that the candidate with the higher seniority is offered the position. Seniority is usually defined in the policy. It might be length of employment in the healthcare facility. Alternatively, it might be the length of time as a nurse within the healthcare facility. For example, a nurse may have started as a unit clerk, and then worked as a CNA before becoming a licensed nurse. Seniority may begin from the time she was hired as a unit clerk. Seniority also might begin when she received her nursing licensed and worked as a nurse in the healthcare facility. Time worked as a unit clerk and CNA does not count towards seniority. Clarify the seniority policy with Human Resources when you apply for a transfer. Seniority plays a critical role when you want to transfer to a new position. The union contract and policies of the healthcare facility may give the transfer to an employee who has the higher seniority when two employees are equally qualified for the position.

Another possible tiebreaker when two equally-qualified applicants apply to transfer to the same position is the date and time of the transfer application. The applicant who applied first gets the position. Each transfer application is time-stamped when the computer application saves the application. The Human Resources staff usually hand-writes the date and time on paper transfer applications. Ask Human Resources if such a policy exists within your healthcare organization well before you consider applying for a transfer. This becomes important when the rumor mill speaks about a position coming open that is not yet posted.

You can easily forget to keep checking the internal posting board and someone else applies for the position before you apply.

Does someone have the inside track for the position? Could be. There are times when the nurse manager or higher level managers have a candidate in mind for a nursing position – and in some cases the position is created for that candidate. The challenge is to offer the position and stay within the healthcare facility's policies. This is even more difficult if the position comes under the bargaining unit where the bargaining agreement specifies the process for transferring employees. Not all positions must be posted but bargaining unit positions are likely required to be posted.

The nurse manager and Human Resources may keep the opening quiet if they have a candidate in mind for the position. The hope is that the position gets lost in all the open positions and no one on staff notices the posting. Requirements for the position may be based on the candidate's qualifications. Only that candidate meets the requirements for the position. Another strategy for limiting the applicant pool is for the nurse manager to talk other candidates out of applying for the position by overemphasizing the negative aspects of the position in interviews with candidates. There is only one candidate remaining at the end – the candidate that the nurse manager wanted before the position was posted.

Applying for an Outside Position

Applying for a position outside of your healthcare facility has its own challenges. In essence, you are starting over and have to convince the application tracking system, the nurse recruiter, and the nurse manager that you are a good candidate for the job – all in writing. You'll need to apply online using the application tracking system regardless of your experience and who referred you for the position. The application tracking system will match your application to job requirements set by the nurse recruiter (see Chapter 2 "The Dreaded Application Tracking System").

Your initial objective is to match elements in your background to each requirement specified in the job posting. Do this both in the application and in your resume. Take time and tailor your resume to complement the job posting. You leave matching your background to the job requirements to the application tracking system and the nurse recruiter by submitting a generic resume. You'll have better results if you do the matching to ensure that nothing is overlooked in the application process.

Create three columns. List each requirement for the job in the first column and how you meet the requirement in the second column. Realistically, you may not meet each job requirement – nor will other candidates – so be honest with yourself. If you don't meet the requirement then leave it blank. Write the exact wording that you'll use to describe your background in the third column. Incorporate words and phrases that you find in the job description at least three times. This helps the application tracking system give your application a high matching score when searching for quality applications.

Rewrite your resume using text that you've written in the third column. Format your resume in commonly used sections to make it easy for the application tracking system to parse your resume into sections of the application. Don't begin an entry with dates. Place dates at the end of the entry. Here is an example of sections of a resume.

- Contact information
- Work Experience
- Employer's name, your title, dates
- Education
- Skills

Here is a sample job requirement for an experienced nurse.

Job Summary:

The Clinical Level II Nurse functions as a caregiver for a specific patient population in order to achieve desired outcomes. This position directs and oversees the care provided by other caregivers. This position effectively coordinates patient care/unit activities among nursing peers, physicians, and support services.

Required Experienced:

- Consistently and independently prioritizes and delivers dependable and effective patient-centered care
- Performs ongoing patient assessment
- Plans and implements individualized patient care to meet immediate needs in collaboration with the interdisciplinary team
- Evaluates patients' response to interventions and adjusts the care plan accordingly
- Documents the components of the nursing process
- Communicates effectively
- Identifies and brings ethical issues to the attention of team members
- Utilizes clinical policy/procedures
- Incorporates evidence-based practice in patient care
- Responds to opportunities to enhance patient satisfaction

Education
– Graduate of a NLN/AACN accredited program in nursing
– BSN
– Minimum of 1 year prior nursing experience

Licenses and Certifications
– AHA BLS Certification
– NJ State Professional Registered Nurse License

Here is a sample resume designed to be parsed by an application tracking system. You'll notice that words and phrases are included from the description of the job in the job posting. Keep in mind that the initial goal is to have the application tracking system give your resume – once imported into the system – a high score. Elaborate on your experience, but make sure your resume contains the key words and phrases that appear in the job posting.

Mary Jones, BSN, R.N.
555 Some Street, Some City, Some State 55555
Phone: (555)-555-5555 Email: MarySmith@domain.com

Work Experience
My Hospital, My City, My State 55555
     Staff Nurse Clinical Level II
     January Year to Present
     Provided independent, dependable, and effective patient-centered care as a primary nurse to medical-surgical patients. Performed ongoing patient assessment as part of ongoing evidence-based practice. Worked with and communicated effectively with an interdisciplinary team to plan and implement individualized patient care that met the immediate needs of my patients. Evaluated the patient's response to intervention and recommended adjustments to the patient's care plan. Documented components of the nursing process based on clinical policy and procedures.

Some Hospital, Some City, Some State 55555
 Staff Nurse Clinical Level II
 Year to Year
 As a primary nurse to patients in a step-down unit, I provided independent, dependable, and effective patient-centered care and performed ongoing patient assessment. Based on ongoing evidence-based practice, I planned and implemented individualized patient care that met the immediate needs of my patients. My evaluation of the patient's response to intervention and other components of the nursing process based on clinical policy and procedures were documented and effectively communicated to the interdisciplinary team that care for the patient. Recommendations were made to the interdisciplinary team to adjust the patient's care plan.

Any Hospital, Some City, Some State 55555
 Staff Nurse Clinical Level II
 Year to Year
 In a medical-surgical unit, I provided independent, dependable, and effective patient-centered care based on ongoing evidence-based practices as a primary nurse to up to ten patients per shift. I performed ongoing patient assessment, planned and implemented individualized patient care, and evaluated patient responses, which were documented based on clinical policy and procedures. The patient's response to interventions were effectively communicated to the interdisciplinary team that cared for the patient and I recommended adjustments to the patient's care plan based on the patient's immediate needs.

Education
Bachelor of Science in Nursing (BSN)
 My Nursing School, Some City, Some State 55555

License
License Professional Registered Nurse (RN) Some State
 Basic Life Support Certified (BLS) (American Heart Association)

Special Skills
 Bilingual-Spanish

Cover Letter or No Cover Letter

In the days before submitting resumes electronically, resumes were sent on paper through the postal service. In those days, you greeted the nurse recruiter for the first time in a cover letter that briefly introduce yourself, told the nurse recruiter why you were contacting her, and asked the nurse recruiter to read your enclosed resume.

Today few candidates send resumes by mail because nurse recruiters prefer (demand) all inquiries about jobs to be made electronically using the application tracking system that is available on the healthcare facility's website. An email is accepted but the reply politely redirects you to the application tracking system. Keep in mind that you are one of hundreds who are applying for the many positions posted on the healthcare facility's website.

The application tracking system usually offers the option to upload a cover letter. It seems a waste of time to do so since the application tracking system parses your resume into the application form that is then searched for keywords and phrases to match your application against requirements for the job. For the most part, the application tracking system decides which applicants are presented to the nurse recruiter. The cover letter seems irrelevant.

Is the cover letter really irrelevant? Maybe not, considering a good number of applicants don't upload one in the application tracking system. You might standout if you include a cover letter. The cover letter must be brief and customized to the position. The salutation should use the nurse recruiter's name such as Dear Ms. Smith. State that you are an experienced nurse and specify the position for which you are applying. The next paragraph tells your story using some of the terms found in the job description. You want to make it easy for the nurse recruiter to match your background to the requirements of the job. The last paragraph encourages the nurse recruiter to invite you for an interview. Here is a sample email cover letter.

> Dear Ms. Smith:
>
> For the past seven years, I have been a Clinical Level II registered professional nurse working in the areas of medical-surgical and step-down unit nursing and would like to be considered for your medical-surgical nurse position.
>
> As you will note in my application, I provide independent, dependable, and effective patient-centered care based on ongoing evidence-based practices as a primary nurse to up to ten patients per shift. I am an effective member of an interdisciplinary

team that performs ongoing patient assessment, plans, and implements individualized patient care.

I look forward to meeting you in person to further explore your needs for a medical-surgical nurse. I can be reached at (555) 555-5555 or via email: MaryJones@domain.com.

Yours truly,
Mary Jones, BSN, R.N.

Reapplying to a Former Employer

Every sales person knows that it is easier to sell to a previous customer than to a new customer as long as the previous customer had a good experience with you. You are your own sales person and convincing the nurse recruiter to rehire you is less challenging than convincing a nurse recruiter from a different healthcare facility that you are the perfect candidate for a nursing position.

In some healthcare facilities, a terminated employee – resigning is a form of termination – may be placed on the do-not-rehire list depending on the employee's evaluation and reason for termination. Anyone not on this list might be considered for future positions within the healthcare facility. This typically means that the nurse recruiter considers your application along with other applicants.

Nurse recruiters and nurse managers realize that good nurses leave for new opportunities. As long as the parting was amicable, there is an excellent chance that the nurse can return to a previous employer. Did you leave on good terms? The answer depends on the nurse recruiter and the nurse manager(s) opinions. This may go beyond your last evaluations and not being on the do-not-hire list. It may be based on perception – and misperceptions – of your performance.

If you didn't have any time and attendance problems; you performed what was seen as quality patient care; and you didn't complain; then you are likely to be viewed as a good nurse and rehiring is a viable option. Likewise, if you were a team player; pitched in without being asked to do so and were a problem-solver, then you probably were seen as a super nurse. There is no question about rehiring you – in fact you might be actively recruited.

However, a negative perception by a nurse manager may present a barrier to being rehired. The hiring nurse manager may ask her colleague, "Did you know Mary Jones? She worked in med-surg three years ago and applied for my evening nurse position." Any negative response may cast doubt on the viability of her candidacy for the position – even if her colleague confused Mary Jones with Mary Adams, who was a terrible nurse.

Apply to your former employer using the application tracking system if you feel you fit the open position. Contact former colleagues who still work there and ask if they can recommend you to the nurse recruiter or the hiring nurse manager. The goal is to have the nurse recruiter or the hiring nurse manager retrieve your application from the application tracking system so you don't have to gamble with the application tracking system selecting your application.

You have a track record with the organization that the nurse recruiter can easily review. Even moderately successful experience may get you an interview with the nurse recruiter. Of course, you have to sell yourself during the interviewing process. Just because you worked there before and know the staff and nurse managers doesn't mean that you'll be hired. Sell yourself as if this was your first interview by following steps mentioned in this chapter. Don't assume they know you – they may have misperceptions about you that you can correct during the interviews.

What to Expect During the Interview

You get one chance on making a first impression, so treat your first interview with the nurse recruiter as something special. Let the nurse recruiter know if you are coming or going to work after or before the interview and that you'll be dressed in scrubs. This is understandable and giving the nurse recruiter a heads-up before the interview sets expectations on how you will dress for the interview. Dress professionally if the interview is scheduled for your off day. Make sure your grooming conforms to widely accepted infection control policies. They should if you are working in a healthcare facility.

Arrive early for the interview giving you time to find your way should you get lost or have difficulty finding a parking space. Arriving early may get your interview started early if the nurse recruiter is running ahead of schedule. This is usually a plus for the nurse recruiter. Be patient if the nurse recruiter is running late – and late may be over an hour. Sit calmly and avoid complaining. Ask the receptionist if you can reschedule your interview if you have a pressing appointment.

Put on a smile and introduce yourself to the nurse recruiter, being sure to make eye contact at all times. Be friendly and consider the nurse recruiter as a new colleague – you hope. Your body language and the tone in your voice projects your character more than what you say during the initial encounter with the nurse recruiter.

Start with small talk – your experience finding the facility, parking, and locating Human Resources. Don't be afraid to open the conversation. Speak in complete sentences. This shows that you are comfortable taking the lead when engaging a stranger. Nurses do this all the time. Small talk will smoothly trail into the substance of the interview when the nurse recruiter takes the lead in the conversation.

The nurse recruiter wants to know the person who is behind the application and might begin with an open-ended question, "So what makes you think our med-surg nursing job is right for you?" Keep in mind that the nurse recruiter already knows that your background is a fit based on your application. The nurse recruiter is really asking you to demonstrate your communications skills and how you think on your feet.

An open-ended question gives you the opportunity to sell yourself. And the best way to do this is to connect your experience to each job requirement. Be honest and let the nurse recruiter know which are a perfect fit, close fit, or no fit at all. Don't hide the fact that you don't meet every requirement of the job but do show how requirements you do meet overshadows those requirements that you do not meet.

This approach helps the nurse recruiter in a number of ways. First, you've read the job requirements. Next, you know you're qualified because you matched your background to each job requirement and you helped the nurse recruiter match your background to the job requirements. In essence you've done part of the nurse recruiter's job for her. Expect to be challenged on you comparisons to the job requirements especially those requirements that don't appear to match with your background. You'll know where these are and have a prepared response if you've done your homework prior to the interview. Speak with confidence about your abilities and experiences. Be social and humorous at times then serious when answering the core of questions.

Next, the nurse recruiter is likely to look for holes in your application by chronologically looking at your background. Let's say you graduated nursing school in May and your first nursing job was in February of the next year. This gap could have been spent looking for a new grad position or because you had to take the nursing board exams several times before you passed. The nurse recruiter is looking for what you've been doing for the past ten years or so. Gaps in employment or short periods of employment are fine as long as you have a rational explanation. However, a series of short period of employment is a red flag and is probably difficult to explain. Be prepared to provide a rational explanation of why your stay was short on each job.

The nurse recruiter would like to know why you want to leave your current position. Keep in mind that if you live within a region that has a few healthcare facilities, the nurse recruiter probably knows a lot about your current healthcare facility. Healthcare itself is a small community and employees move around the healthcare community several times during their careers.

Respond professionally. Avoid bad-mouthing your boss and your healthcare facility because the nurse recruiter will probably ask, "What makes you think things will be different here?" That's tough to answer since you haven't work there yet. Looking for a change is an acceptable response. Moving to a different area of nursing not presently available at your present employer is also a reasonable response. A change in schedule or shift makes sense for changing.

The nurse recruiter may ask you about your career goals. The nurse recruiter is trying to find out if you think of nursing as a job or a profession. Some experienced candidates simply want to do a great job caring for patients on a shift then go home. Other experienced candidates may do the same and look toward improving their professional skills through education and other professional activities away from the job. The nurse recruiter may find both of these experienced candidates qualified for the position. That is, there is no right or wrong answer.

At some point the interview changes directions from you selling yourself to the nurse recruiter telling you about the job. The nurse recruiter might tell you that this position probably isn't a good fit, thanks you for coming, and suggests that you keep looking at job postings for other positions. However, the nurse recruiter may start selling you on the job if you convinced the nurse recruiter that you are a viable candidate for the position. Don't read too much into the nurse recruiter's sales pitch. You still have a lot of hurdles to jump before you receive a job offer. And the nurse recruiter might be keeping your hopes up while she searches for the perfect candidate.

Always thank the nurse recruiter for spending time with you whether the interview ended on a positive note or not. Ask about the next step in the process and approximately how long before you hear back from her. If you weren't a fit for this position, ask the nurse recruiter if you should apply for more appropriate positions in the future. A positive response might indicate that you handled yourself professionally and there were no gaping holes in your resume that prevent you from applying for another position.

After the Interview

The hardest part of the interviewing process is waiting patiently for a response from the nurse recruiter especially if your interview ended on an upbeat note. Expecting a call from the nurse recruiter when you get home is unrealistic. A week or more may go by without any indication on the status of your application. You are one of possibly a hundred or so candidates applying for the many jobs that are posted on the healthcare facility's website. The nurse recruiter usually waits until all interviews are completed before arranging for the next round of interviews with prospective candidates.

Send a brief thank you email to the nurse recruiter listing three examples of how you meet the job requirements. At the end of the email, indicate that you look forward to meeting with the nurse recruiter again to discuss the position. Don't expect a reply. The nurse recruiter knows that you are anxiously pursuing the position, but let the nurse recruiter completely process all the applications – including yours.

You will be contacted if the nurse recruiter feels you are a viable candidate but there is no set time period for when this will happen. Much is happening behind the scenes (see Chapter 2 "The Dreaded Application Tracking System"). Your application, along with those of other qualified candidates, is sent for review to the hiring nurse manager. The nurse manager may get back to the nurse recruiter within a few hours or a few weeks.

Don't harass the nurse recruiter! Wait ten days after the interview to send the nurse recruiter an email asking a relevant follow-up question about the position – not "Am I still being considered?" Be sure to clearly identify the position by name since the nurse recruiter is likely interviewing many candidates for many different positions. The follow-up question might be about tuition reimbursement, the use of seniority for scheduling, or health insurance benefits. It is reasonable for you to clarify these issues. The nurse recruiter might provide the status of your application when answering your email.

Don't stop looking for a position! Although you may think you're the perfect candidate for this particular position, you have no facts to compare you with the other candidates. They, too, may be perfect candidates. The nurse recruiter and the hiring nurse manager typically select three or four candidates for the next round of interviews. You'll probably receive a rejection email quickly if you are not one of those selected. However, some nurse recruiters don't send rejection emails to viable candidates until a selected candidate accepts the job offer. This is one reason there might be a delay hearing from the nurse recruiter after your last interview. At some point you'll be invited to meet with the hiring nurse manager or be told that someone more qualified for the position accepted the job offer.

Meeting the Hiring Nurse Manager

Getting a call rather than an email from the nurse recruiter is a sign that you still are in the running for the position. The next step is meeting the hiring nurse manager. The nurse manager is looking for an experienced nurse who will fit well with the current healthcare team. Unfortunately, there is no checklist that helps decide if you are a fit. The nurse manager wants you to communicate well; listen carefully; demonstrate that you understand what is being said; and respond professionally. A nurse manager typically goes with her gut feeling when choosing a nurse to join her team.

Follow the same procedures you did for your interview with the nurse recruiter. Give yourself time to get lost and find your way. Arrive for the interview about fifteen minutes early. Greet the nurse manager with small talk, always making eye contact and speaking in complete sentences. The nurse manager may or may not ask similar questions posed by the nurse recruiter. Each manager has her own style of interviewing and has far less experience interviewing than the nurse recruiter.

Some nurse managers may describe their unit and the open position to you before asking you any questions. Don't take this as an indication that you are a good candidate for the position. Instead, the nurse manager may simply be managing your expectations describing the positives and negatives about the job before asking you to present yourself.

Feel free to ask the nurse manager specifics about the unit and the position before responding to questions. You can always tell the nurse manager that you want to frame your answers based on the needs of the unit. Prepare to give a two-minute synopsis of your story tailored to what you know of the unit and position. Focus on your recent nursing experience. Try to include something humorous but not negative. Describe how you are a team player in your current position. Give examples of how you use critical thinking when you care for your patients. Fill in information that the nurse manager probably needs to know about you but may have forgotten to ask. Your goal is to show the nurse manager that you are a skilled nurse who will be a valued asset to the nurse manager's team.

Summarize your understanding of the position and how your background complements the job requirements at the conclusion of the interview with the nurse manager. Tell the nurse manager whether or not you think this is a fit. Be honest. Raise any deal breakers for you before the end of the interview. The nurse manager may or may not be able to accommodate you. If no accommodations can be made then you are not a fit for the job ... but the nurse manager or the nurse recruiter may have other job openings in the future that are a fit. So leave on an upbeat note.

Follow up with an email to the nurse manager after the interview. Also email the nurse recruiter describing how well your interview went with the nurse manager. Give the nurse manager and nurse recruiter time to make a decision. This may take several weeks. You'll have to sit tight; however, emailing the nurse manager after ten days asking a relevant question is permissible. You might be given an inkling of information on the status of your application.

You have a lot to offer a healthcare facility as an experienced nurse. You've demonstrated your expertise throughout your nursing career. Now you must convince the hiring nurse manager that you are a good fit for her team. You can provide leadership while delivering primary nursing care to their patients.

Chapter 5
Choosing a Nursing Specialty

Developing a Career Path

Few nurses actually plan their nursing career aside from graduating nursing school and finding their first nursing job. A nursing career seems to evolve from circumstances and opportunities that just happen – not from deliberate planning. Downsizing may force you to explore a different type of nursing. Openings within your hospital may give you a chance to branch into a new specialty. However, you probably don't have a master plan – a career path.

A career path is a plan that states a goal and enumerates the tasks necessary to reach that goal. You had such a plan when you first thought about becoming a nurse. The goal was to become a licensed nurse. You selected a nursing school, identified and completed prerequisites, and then passed each course required for graduation. You prepped for the nursing boards, you passed, and you became a licensed nurse.

Nurse recruiters are noted for asking, "Where you do see yourself five years from now?" They want to determine if you have a career plan and whether or not the position you are interviewing for provides a stepping stone toward reaching your career goal. Some candidates simply fake a response to make it sound as though they have a well-thought-out master plan for their career, ensuring that the open position is the next step in their career plan.

Consider asking yourself, where do you want to be in five years? Your answer may surprise you. You might want to pursue emergency nursing, legal nursing, or nursing informatics. These are just a few of the many nursing opportunities that are available to you, which you'll learn more about later in this chapter. Each area of nursing has its own requirements – many of which are not standardized – but they usually follow a traditional career path from novice nurse to expert nurse.

Your initial career goal was to become a professional nurse. During the novice stage, you acquired the know-how to perform nursing tasks through learning from preceptors and from your own experience. You followed rules and had little responsibility for the outcomes of your task. As an advanced beginner, you learned more sophisticated rules and practices and you were able to prioritize tasks based on importance. You formed the foundation for making nursing decisions and accepted responsibility for those decisions. You problem-solved with little assistance from more experienced colleagues.

DOI 10.1515/9781501506109-005

Next, you became a proficient nurse, using the wealth of experience as the basis for your nursing intuition. You made calculated decisions that produced an effective result. You finally became an expert nurse able to perform all nursing duties fluidly with most actions performed unconsciously based on your broad library of experience. You respond to most clinical situations, including those with critical outcomes, as routine.

Novice nurse to expert nurse provides the framework for you career path. Suppose you set your goal on becoming a nurse practitioner. Explore the requirements – educational and experience -- to attain that goal, then develop and execute a career path. Once you've completed the basic educational and licensing requirements, focus changes to the novice-nurse-to-expert-nurse framework. Regardless of your nursing experience, you'll start off as a novice when you enter an area of nursing that is new to you and you need to work through each stage before becoming an expert nurse. You may move quickly through each stage if you are an expert nurse in a complementary field of nursing such as going from medical-surgical nursing to cardiac nursing. However, expect a slower transition if you are moving to a completely different type of nursing such as to legal nursing or nursing informatics where your skills are not directly transferable.

Consider developing an ultimate career path. Do you really want to continue providing bedside care when you are in your 50s or 60s? Bedside nursing takes a toll on your body as you grow older. There will likely be a time when you can no longer provide quality bedside care to patients. This doesn't mean you need to give up on nursing. Bedside nursing gives you a wealth of skills that can be transferred to many other areas of nursing as you'll see later in this chapter. Developing an ultimate career path helps you build the experience and educational requirements to move to areas of nursing aside from the bedside.

Obstacles to Change

Remember your first clinical experience in nursing school? You had butterflies in your stomach. There was a sense of excitement of the unknown challenges that lay before you. You probably were on your "A" game. The spark and excitement probably left you years ago as you became the expert nurse. You know what to expect each day and even the unknowns become routine. There is little excitement and no butterflies in your stomach. Changing to a new career path in nursing rekindles the spark that makes nursing exciting again – new challenges, new learning opportunities, and new ways to care for patients.

If there were no obstacles, what different area of nursing would you explore? Give an honest answer, then investigate obstacles that really stand between you and your dream – and determine how to eliminate those obstacles by going around them or breaking them down. Begin your investigation by reviewing a general description of the job. You'll find the more common ones in this chapter. Then look at actual job postings at healthcare facilities around your area. You'll notice what you think might be job requirements are listed as optional: nice to have but not a requirement. You'll find listed educational and professional certification requirements.

Assume you can meet all requirements with a little work on your part such as returning to school or sitting for the professional certification exam. Make a list of the requirements. Check off those requirements that you meet. Identify what you need to do to satisfy the remaining requirements and investigate how to go about it. Finally, develop a strategy for fulfilling the unmet requirements.

Assess Your Current Nursing Career

Nurse managers use SWOT (Strengths, Weaknesses, Opportunities, and Threats) analysis to assess the effectiveness of nursing operations such as a unit or division of the healthcare facility. You can use SWOT analysis to assess the current status of your nursing career. Begin by dividing a piece of paper into fourths – upper left, upper right, lower left, and lower right. Label the upper left as Strengths, upper right as weaknesses, lower left as opportunities, and lower right as threats.

List your strengths in the upper left portion of the paper. Be sure to consider your education, certifications, leadership roles (for example, serving on committees, functioning as a preceptor), nursing experience, and non-nursing experience (that is, your previous career).

List your weaknesses in the upper right portion of the paper. Be honest and list items that you see are or could be weaknesses. For example, you may have an associate's degree in nursing and healthcare facilities in your area prefer or require a BSN. You might hold an LPN (licensed practical nurse) license, which may limit your choice of employers. The distance between your home and local healthcare facilities may also be a weakness, especially if the nearest healthcare facility is a two-hour drive one way.

List what you see are opportunities in the lower left portion of the page. Opportunities might be to transfer positions within your current healthcare facility. Your healthcare facility may offer incentives to continue your nursing education.

Your family situation (for example, having an empty nest) may give you the chance to refocus on your nursing career. You may have developed a strong network of former colleagues and friends who can "open doors" to new employment opportunities.

List threats to your nursing career in the lower right portion of the page. For example, healthcare facilities in your area may be merging or closing down, placing you at risk for termination. Your healthcare facility may be phasing out LPN or associate's degree nurses and require you to obtain an RN license or BSN within a specific timeframe to maintain your employment. You have new family obligations (for example, caring for an elderly parent) that place limitations on work performance. You're getting older and working the floors is taking a toll on your body. You are the sole supporter of your family and changing jobs is too risky. You and your new boss are not hitting it off well.

Your goal is to take advantage of your strengths and opportunities while minimizing your weaknesses, as well as preparing a strategy for handling threats to your nursing career. For example, stay with your present employer while you go back to school for your RN or BSN, taking advantage of your employer's tuition reimbursement policy. Doing so strengthens your weakness and places you in a better position should your employer phase out LPN or associate's degree RNs. Likewise, if you find yourself in a nurse specialty that is in low demand, you can use your network of colleagues to move to a high-demand nursing specialty within your organization.

Changing Nursing Specialty

Time for a change? If so, then anxiety is likely holding you back from making the move because change means you'll face new challenges – and the risk that you may not be able to meet those challenges. The risk of failure is a strong roadblock to exploring new areas of nursing. A nurse executive once commented, you know when it is time for a new pair of shoes but you may not know if the new pair is a fit until you try them for a few weeks. The same is true about changing nursing specialties. Should you give up a job that you've mastered? What happens if you fail at your new specialty? These aren't easy questions to answer.

It is usually best to change specialties within your current healthcare facility for a number of reasons. First, you are a known quantity. You've proven yourself as an excellent reliable nurse who provides quality care for your patients. Even good candidates from outside the organization still must prove to management that they are reliable and provide quality patient care. Next, you can use your network of colleagues to explore the open position before you apply for a transfer.

You'll learn what it is really like to work on that unit for that manager. You won't find this information if you accept a position elsewhere until you're on the job.

And most important, you know from other employees who transferred how Human Resources and management handle situations when the "new shoe" isn't a fit. Technically, Human Resources will probably tell you that you are on probation for the first 90 days on your new job. You can be terminated at will at any time during that 90-day period. Practically, this may not occur unless you were a marginal employee in your current position or you made grave errors in your new position. If the organization terminated employees following a transfer, it would send the message "don't transfer from your current job." This simply doesn't help the organization. A better approach is to acknowledge that all "new shoes" don't fit. Sometimes you can go back to wearing your "old shoe" – that is, they purposely hold off replacing you until everyone believes that the "new shoe" is a fit. Other times, you might be offered a position that is comparable to your old position – "another pair of old shoes." That position, maybe on a different unit, different shift, or in the float pool – but a position that is practically identical to your old position. You are unlikely to find such consideration as a new employee in another healthcare facility.

You'll need to meet the job requirements for the new specialty even if you are transferring within your organization. One of the toughest requirements to meet is the "3 – 5 years of experience" requirement. You have to solve the chicken or the egg problem. How can you get experience if you don't have experience in the specialty? Here's a technique that might work for you. You likely have job skills that are transferable to the specialty – starting an I.V., administering I.V. medications, assessing patients, admissions, discharges. Ask the specialty unit manager in your current organization if you can float to the unit whenever they are short. That is, pick up a shift outside your current position. In this way, you can get a feel for what it is like to work on the specialty unit while helping out the manager. Show that you are willing to learn the specialty. The current staff is likely to help you get up to speed. If both you and the unit manager feel you are a fit, then you become the ideal candidate for the next opening – and the 3 – 5 years of experience may no longer be a requirement in your case because you've already been cross-trained.

Don't be cocky thinking that you are an expert nurse in the new specialty – you're not. You have a wealth of experience but that experience is in a different specialty. Some experience is transferable and other experiences are meaningless in the new specialty. You still must work your way through the novice, advanced beginner, and proficient nurse stages. Don't let your pride get in the way of learning your new specialty.

Realize that changing specialty is a major life change that may be stressful. You are moving from being an expert at one specialty to being a novice who has to learn the new specialty by going back to school, reading nursing books about the specialty and taking directions from nurses who could be your younger sibling or your child. You need to ask your colleagues for help – something you don't do often in your present job. This may not come naturally, but there is a high risk for failure if you don't ask for help.

Changing specialty is a family decision, in many cases for both your work family and your home family. Family members can be supportive by helping you objectively explore the pros and cons of the move. Also consult your bargaining unit representatives, if your current or future position is a bargaining unit position. The bargaining unit representative can speak to you about your rights based on the bargaining contract and past practices of your healthcare facility setting realistic expectations for the transfer. For example, you might be at the top of the clinical ladder. Changing specialty could place you back on the first rung of the clinical ladder and affect your pay.

Consider a nursing specialty change when your present nursing position is no longer challenging, when your new patient begins to look like the hundreds of patients that you've cared for over the years. There is a risk that the quality of your care may be unintentionally lowered. Don't change specialties to avoid conflicts in your current position. It is always better to the leave your position on a positive note because the "new shoe" may not fit and you need the support from your current management to go back your "old shoe."

Is Management for You?

Nurse management is challenging and is more than just being the boss. The nurse manager has total responsibility for the operations of a unit(s). This includes: estimating needs, planning to meet needs, and executing that plan. Each unit has a license for a specific number of beds within a specialty, such as medical-surgical beds. The flow of admissions and discharges dictate the number of patients on the unit at any specific time. The nurse manager must meet the needs of those patients based on standards of care defined by The Joint Commission and state and federal regulators. The nurse manager must determine resources (personnel and material) and policies and procedures to meet those needs.

Success is usually defined by staying within budget; passing audits by The Joint Commission and state and Federal regulators; having an excellent customer service rating; and providing a safe and stable working environment for staff. All of these must be accomplished without you – the nurse manager – performing patient care and support services yourself.

Some experienced nurses see nurse management as the next logical step in their nursing career because they've already handled the day-to-day challenges of bedside nursing and possibly managed a shift as a charge nurse. You know the problems of providing quality care on the unit – and you have a few possible solutions to rectify those problems that you can implement if you became the boss.

Other experienced nurses see nurse management as a lose-lose situation. Everything that goes wrong on the unit becomes your problem to solve. Upper management usually doesn't want to hear about your problems and your staff simply asks you, "What do you want me to do?" You have to deal with staffing issues: staff who don't show up for work; staff who don't want to follow work rules; staff who are just waiting to be terminated. Upper management orders you to keep within your overtime budget while some staff create situations where they get paid overtime. The nurse manager seems to always be the bad guy.

Consider the following before accepting a nurse manager's position:

- Healthcare facilities typically require nurse managers to hold an MSN degree although they may accept a nurse with a BSN degree who is working toward the MSN degree. Will you recoup the expense of an MSN degree?
- Nurse managers don't receive overtime pay.
- Staff nurses can forget about their job once they are off shift. Nurse managers have 24/7 responsibility for their unit(s).
- Experienced nurses who are at the highest salary scale may take a pay reduction by becoming a manager when considering the loss of overtime and pay differential.
- Some healthcare facilities may not permit you to return to a non-management role once you become a manager.
- Nurse managers usually lose their bedside nursing skills because they don't provide bedside care. This may limit career opportunities in the future.
- Nurse managers are usually not part of a bargaining unit. The nurse loses protection of the bargaining unit by becoming a nurse manager.
- Nurse managers are expected to fix all problems on their unit – even those that are nearly impossible to fix.
- Pay increases for nurse managers may not be as frequent as staff nurses who belong to a bargaining unit.

The nurse manager is no longer seen as a colleague – you're the boss. You hire new staff. Approve transfers. You write annual evaluations. You discipline staff. You're the person who says "You're fired!"

Nurse management is a good experience as long as you are a "take charge" person who is well-organized, likes dealing with people fairly, doesn't take failure of others personally, and feels a sense of accomplishment when your staff provides quality patient care. Understand there is little glory in being the nurse manager when compared with the overall responsibility for patient care and for your staff.

Successful nurse managers can rise to a director's level within the healthcare facility where they are responsible for managing a major function within the organization such as the acute division, infection control, emergency department, and staff development. A nurse manager may also become the chief nurse administrator responsible for all nursing in the healthcare facility. There seems to be a trend where directors and administrators jobs require a Doctor of Nursing Practice (DNP) degree.

Agency Nursing

An agency nurse is a nurse who works for an organization that supplies nurses to a healthcare facility to supplement the healthcare facility's own staffing needs. The agency nurse does not work directly for the healthcare facility but performs the same duties as the healthcare facility's own staff nurses.

An agency typically has a contract with the healthcare facility and may or may not have a contract with you. The contract with the healthcare facility specifies the hourly or daily rate that the agency is to receive from the healthcare facility, which is typically much higher than the healthcare facility pays its own staff nurses. However, as an agency nurse you receive a fraction of what the agency receives from the healthcare facility.

The agency is responsible for your performance and certifies that you are competent to perform the tasks assigned by the healthcare facility. The healthcare facility is responsible for educating you on the healthcare facility's policies and procedures and for orienting you to the facility and to each unit.

You will fill out the traditional employment forms for the agency and provide the healthcare facility with a copy of your nursing license and health record. It is likely that you'll go through the healthcare facility's orientation process including a probationary period. However, you are not terminated if you don't successfully complete orientation or the probation period because you work for the agency and not the healthcare facility. The healthcare facility simply tells your agency that they no longer require your services and the agency sends another nurse to fill that spot.

There are benefits for working for an agency:
- You have the opportunity to work for different healthcare facilities.
- You get exposed to different specialties and patient demographics.
- You don't get involved in the internal politics of the healthcare facility.
- You are an earner for the agency not an overhead expense. Agency nurses bring in revenue for the agency whereas staff nurses are seen as a necessary expense for the healthcare facility. You have leverage to negotiate your compensation with the agency because without you – and the other agency nurses – the agency won't make money.
- You may be able to create your own schedule.
- You may receive higher pay than if you were an employee at the healthcare facility. However, higher pay may reflect that the agency isn't providing you with benefits.

And there are drawbacks being an agency nurse:
- There are usually no paid sick days or holidays. If you don't work, then you don't get paid.
- Work may or may not be consistent depending on the agency's contract with the healthcare facility. There are contracts where the agency supplies full-time nurses for a period of time (for example, three to six months). Other contracts are on an as-needed basis. That is, you get called only if regular staff is unavailable. Agencies usually don't pay you to stand by.
- Agencies usually don't offer any benefits. Any benefits that are offered to you are likely at a higher amount then if you worked for a healthcare facility.
- You're considered an outsider in the healthcare facility. You don't get the same treatment by the healthcare facility as they treat their own employees (for example, no parking discount, training).
- You may be prohibited from being an employee of the healthcare facility for six months to a year after you leave the employ of the agency even if you don't have a contract with the agency. The healthcare facility's contract with the agency usually specifies terms under which the healthcare facility can convert an agency nurse to an employee. In some cases, the agency wants the healthcare facility to pay the agency an amount equal to one year's salary of the agency nurse. This makes it too expensive for the healthcare facility to hire you. And some agencies don't tell you about this clause in the contract until you apply for a position at the healthcare facility.
- You're always starting over unless your agency places you in the same healthcare facility for a long time period. You have to continually prove yourself to the staff and manager.

– You are unappreciated and seen as a hired hand. There are no rewards (that is, promotions, bonuses) even if you are a star performer.
– Some agencies may send you out on jobs that are outside your experience in an effort to bring in revenue for the agency.
– You will probably be required to provide your own malpractice insurance.

It is critical that you are totally honest with the agency about your experience and skills because the agency places you on assignments based on what you tell them. You never want to be placed in a position where there are surprises. An agency nurse is considered experienced and able to provide quality patient care with little orientation to the unit. You'll need to be told where things are, not how to perform the job.

Agency nursing isn't for new grads or nurses looking to change specialties. There is little opportunity for training and nurturing. Agency nurses are expected to hit the ground running, otherwise the healthcare facility may tell the agency that you are not right for their position. The agency may then place you in a more appropriate position in another healthcare facility or not call you for assignments.

Travel Nursing

A travel nurse is a type of agency nurse, except a travel nurse usually relocates to various parts of the country to work rather than working within the vicinity of their home. Some healthcare facilities bring in travel nurses when there is disruption in their current staffing such as having to rapidly train the current staff; staff-wide illness (flu); or when labor negotiations with nurses may lead to a labor strike.

A travel nurse should be an expert nurse with the confidence to handle any situation with minimum orientation to the unit. During a labor strike there may not be anyone at the healthcare facility to provide a good orientation to the unit. The agency nurse must be a self-starter able to find supplies and anything else needed to provide quality patient care.

There are advantages to being a travel nurse:
– You have the opportunity to live in different parts of the country.
– All travel expenses, room, and board are paid by the agency.
– Many agencies offer a bonus for completing a contract.
– Travel nurses receive premium compensation rates.
– You decide your schedule.

There are some disadvantages:

– You are in a state of constant change, living in different housing (the agency selects your housing), different communities, and working in different healthcare facilities. You may have a different charge every three months.
– Each contract has a different rate of pay.
– There is inconsistency of work to consider as you depend on the agency to find your next assignment. You may be out of work once your present contract is fulfilled.
– You are constantly away from family and friends living in unfamiliar surroundings. Packing and unpacking every three months.
– There is the challenge of meeting state licensing requirements for each state where you work. Typically, the agency assists you in meeting these licensing requirements.
– You may not have benefits – and benefits that are offered may be less than those offered to employees at a healthcare facility. No sick days. No holidays.
– You may be working in a hostile work environment especially if the current nursing staff is on strike.
– You are treated as an outsider.
– There is a higher than normal stress environment because you must constantly adapt to change (that is, new healthcare facilities, new policies and procedures). Change also brings with it a higher than normal chance of making errors.

Whether you are a travel nurse or a local agency nurse, it is crucial that you deal only with a well-established agency. The agency is representing you to healthcare facilities just as much as you are representing the agency. Smaller unestablished agencies are prone to two considerable problems. First, the agency may lack the depth of nursing experience to fulfill contracts, resulting in inexperienced nurses (inexperienced outside their specialty) being assigned to a healthcare facility. Cash flow is the other issue. There is usually a gap between when the agency receives payment from the healthcare facility and when the agency has to pay you. Well-established agencies have the financial resources to finance this gap. You get paid even if the agency hasn't received payment from the healthcare facility. Smaller agencies may not be able to finance payroll – you'll get paid when the agency gets paid.

Home Healthcare Nursing

There is an increasing trend to provide healthcare in the home to avoid extended stays in a healthcare facility. Some patients prefer the comforts and convenience of home by having the healthcare team come to them rather than by remaining extra days in a healthcare facility. Insurers find home healthcare less expensive than the most costly care given in a healthcare facility.

A home healthcare nurse plays a pivotal role in treating a patient at home. Typically the nurse is the first member of the healthcare team to visit the patient at home to make an assessment of the patient's needs. The assessment determines if home healthcare is the appropriate level of care for the patient and determines the support level that must be provided to maintain quality care at home. The goal of a home healthcare nurse is to identify health issues with the patient, diagnose problems, administer medication, and coordinate care with the practitioner who oversees the patient's medical care.

Usually the home healthcare nurse works for a home healthcare agency or a division of a healthcare facility that provides home healthcare services. Based on the nurse's assessment and the practitioner's orders, the home healthcare agency assigns other members of the home healthcare team to perform specific levels of care required by the patient. For example, the nurse may determine that the patient requires 24-hour 7-day a week care by a certified nursing assistant. The home healthcare agency then assigns CNAs to shifts at the patient's house. Specialty nurses such as a wound care nurse may be assigned to treat and monitor wounds.

You'll need bedside experience – not for new grads -- and be able to work independently to become a home healthcare nurse because you'll be caring for a patient in the patient's home with little or no support. For example, you'll be expected to draw blood, provide Foley catheter care, and provide tracheotomy care all within the home. You must bring all necessary supplies with you and perform all tasks without assistance. Although this can be challenging, home healthcare nursing provides a degree of satisfaction not found in bedside nurses since you develop a care plan, execute the care plan, and know that your effort was a key factor in restoring the patient's health.

There are advantages to being a home healthcare nurse:
- You make your own schedule. You determine when you visit your patients each day.
- You teach patients how to care for themselves.
- Improvement in the patient's health is primarily because of the care you give to the patient.
- You get to use nursing skills that you may not use in the healthcare facility.

- You bond with each of your patients and their families.
- You take control of the situation based on your critical thinking skills

There are disadvantages to being a home healthcare nurse:
- You are on your own. There is little or no support.
- There is a lot of driving in all weather. You'll visit four or five patients per day and they may not live near each other. You'll use your own car.
- Your day is not over after you leave the patient. You have to provide detailed documentation, usually using computer-based software, on each visit. In some situations, 50% of your job is paperwork.
- You are always going into a stranger's home and the home may not be in a safe neighborhood.
- Expect to be on-call several days a month.
- You may still have to work weekends and holidays.

Case Management

A case manager is employed by a healthcare facility to coordinate patient care among healthcare providers, insurers, other healthcare facilities, and resources that are available in the community. The goal is to ensure that the patient receives the most efficient and cost-effective level of care based on widely accepted medical protocols. Some case managers are also utilization managers whose goal it is to make sure all the assets of the healthcare facility are in use. For example, the case manager may refer the patient to the healthcare facility's home healthcare service rather than to an outside home healthcare agency. Still other case managers focus on discharge planning, ensuring that the patient has proper follow-up care that will prevent the patient from returning to the healthcare facility for the same diagnosis shortly after discharge.

Case management is a critical factor in providing quality, cost-effective care because the case manager bridges the gap among care providers. They have an in-depth knowledge of the healthcare system. Each care provider has a defined scope of practice. For example, the primary care practitioner diagnoses and treats common illnesses and may refer the patient to a surgeon if the patient's condition warrants it. Once surgery is completed and the surgeon determines that the patient has recovered, the surgeon discharges the patient from care and refers the patient back to the patient's primary practitioner. However, the patient may require additional services such as rehabilitation, home healthcare, or need to be seen by another specialist. The case manager steps in to ensure there is continuity of care – and that care is acceptable to third-party payers.

Case managers work very closely with the patient, the patient's family, the patient health insurer, and practitioners to make sure that quality patient care doesn't fall through the cracks in care providers. Case managers also identify care paths that are least costly to the patient yet provide quality care. For example, the case manager may arrange for a patient to receive step-down care in another healthcare facility which is more cost-effective than in the patient's primary healthcare facility. Likewise, the case manager may arrange rehabilitation services when the patient arrives home rather than sending the patient to a more costly rehabilitation facility.

There are advantages to being a nurse case manager:
- You ensure that patients receive quality care without duplication of tests and treatments.
- You reduce unnecessary medical expenses.
- You help patients and their families navigate the medical system.
- You learn the business rules surrounding medicine and health insurance.
- You are an advocate for your patients by discussing each patient's case with insurers, practitioners, and healthcare facilities, and by directly arranging for patient care.
- You can work for insurers and healthcare facilities or work privately.
- There are no evenings, nights, weekends, or holidays.
- You develop your own contacts to provide continued patient care.
- You work with all disciplines.
- You are well-paid since you help the healthcare facility bring in reimbursements. You know the ins-and-outs of third-party payers.
- You use a wide array of interpersonal skills.

There are disadvantages to being a nurse case manager:
- Some patients may feel that you are being intrusive and working for insurers to make sure that they pay the lowest cost in lieu of receiving quality patient care.
- Patients may also feel that you are working for the healthcare facility to make sure that they receive the highest reimbursement while performing the least amount of patient care.
- You may find yourself working for the betterment of the healthcare facility rather than the patient since you are employed by the healthcare facility.
- You may have 28 or more patients to manage.
- You are the bearer of bad news to the patient, the patient's family, and practitioners. You tell the patient and practitioner that the patient must be discharged to another healthcare facility or to home-based care due to the

healthcare facility's policy, and you relay reimbursement limitations of the patient's health insurance. They may feel you are throwing the patient out of the healthcare facility.

- You are focused on costs vs. benefits. You have to prove that the extra expense is beneficial to the patient.
- You work at a desk focused on the phone and emails to get your job done.
- There are a lot of politics, business, and law involved in case management. These can get you in trouble if you do not adhere to them.

Nurse Practitioner

A nurse practitioner is a nurse who has completed advanced studies and passed licensing boards that permit the nurse practitioner to make medical diagnoses, order medical tests, and prescribe treatments and medications to patients. The nurse practitioner may or may not be able to work without a collaborative relationship with a physician depending on state regulations. The nurse practitioner's practice is restricted to a specialized area of medicine such as family medicine. Additional training and licenses are required for the nurse practitioner to practice in another specialty.

A nurse practitioner can function as a nurse. However, it is important that the scope of the nurse's practice is well-defined when hired by the healthcare facility. The nurse is hired as either a nurse or a nurse practitioner — not both. In a nurse's role, the nurse works within the scope of a nurse and follow orders written by a practitioner. As a nurse practitioner, the nurse works within the scope of a practitioner — not a nurse.

The nurse practitioner takes on the same responsibilities as a physician. You diagnose the patient and order treatment. You are solely to blame if you're incorrect. You may face malpractice claims and civil lawsuits if you incorrectly order the wrong medication or the wrong dose or overlook a serious medical condition. You can't say, "I followed the doctor's order" because you are the practitioner.

There are many advantages to becoming a nurse practitioner:

- You have autonomy because you take on the role of a physician in many settings.
- There is no bedside nursing. The nurse practitioner assesses the patient and writes orders that are carried out by the medical team.
- The nurse practitioner has full responsibility to identify and treat the patient.
- You may have a flexible schedule depending on your practice setting.
- Your work is less physically demanding.

There are also drawbacks to becoming a nurse practitioner:

- There are typically more opportunities for nurses than nurse practitioners, since one nurse practitioner can care for many more patients than a bedside nurse.
- There is increased competition for nurse practitioners since many nursing schools offer nurse practitioner programs.
- There can be bias against a nurse practitioner by the practitioners and by patients. Some practitioners see nurse practitioners as competitors who have less medical training than physicians yet are expected to perform the same tasks as physicians — reducing the need for physicians. Some patients refuse to be seen by a nurse practitioner and would rather be seen by a physician because they feel the nurse practitioner is unqualified to provide care.
- There is no residency program. Physicians must complete a three- or four-year residency program working under the mentorship of an experienced physician before they can work independently. Nurse practitioners have no such programs and therefore may lack that mentorship.
- The nurse practitioner may be assigned tasks that the physician doesn't want to perform such as being on-call 24/7, hospital rounding, and follow-up assessment of patients.
- You may not recoup the expense associated with becoming a nurse practitioner when you consider tuition, nurse practitioner compensation, and the increased professional insurance coverage that you need.

Flight Transport Nurse

A flight transport nurse is an exciting career choice because you mix the fast pace of the emergency department with the thrill of airlifting critical care patients from the scene of an accident or natural disaster to the nearest trauma center. You are responsible for the care of the patient during the flight under the direction of a practitioner. Flight transport nurses are also involved in transporting more stable patients by air between facilities.

Flight transport nurses usually have years of experience in a trauma center, have worked as critical care nurses, and may have worked as paramedics in the field. You must be in very good physical condition and be able to quickly board and off-board the aircraft in less than ideal locations such as car accidents. You'll be expected to carry emergency equipment and operate hoists used to lift the patient aboard the aircraft. Advanced Cardiac Life Support (ACLS) Certification, Pediatric Advanced Life Support (PALS) Certification, and Neonatal Resuscitation

Program (NRP) Certification are necessary, along with the completion of nationally recognized trauma programs. These include: Transport Nurse Advanced Trauma Course (TPATC), Basic Trauma Life Support, and Pre-Hospital Trauma Life Support (PHTLS).

There are advantages to being a flight transport nurse:

- You are a first responder where your skills save the lives of critically injured patients.
- You work independently and are able to apply critical thinking to save lives.
- You learn to intubate, insert chest tubes, read x-rays, insert central lines, and learn to identify and treat life threatening problems.
- You are trained to handle any emergency condition in the field.

There are disadvantages to being a flight transport nurse:

- There are few jobs. Level I trauma centers usually have flight transportation services although in some states the state police provide such services due to the cost of aircraft maintenance.
- You work under dangerous conditions. There is always the risk of an air crash since the aircraft typically lands in areas other than airports (for example, highways or fields).
- You have minimal backup. You are the primary care giver and you must work within the confined space of the aircraft.
- There is limited growth potential other than returning to bedside trauma care. It is also difficult to change employers since few hospitals require a flight transport nurse.

Nursing Informatics

In nursing informatics, nurses take an active role in maintaining a healthcare facility's electronic medical records (EMR) system. The nursing informatics nurse documents clinical workflows; modifies the EMR system to conform to existing workflows; writes training materials; trains staff; and oversees the implementation of the EMR system with the clinical staff. In doing so, the nurse directly interacts with all levels of administration and the clinical team in addition to the management information systems (MIS) department and vendors who supply the EMR system.

Nursing informatics requires formal computer training that focuses on systems analysis, database analysis, project management, and other aspects of computer science. Although the informatics nurse won't be programming the EMR system, the nurse will be applying the EMR system to meet the needs of the healthcare facility. In some cases, this means adjusting the clinical workflows to meet requirements of the EMR system. In other cases, the nurse will use computer programs supplied by the vendor to modify the EMR system to conform to the healthcare facility's clinical workflows.

You'll probably require a BSN degree or an MSN degree focused on nursing informatics and several years as a staff nurse. Although the informatics nurse performs many of the same functions as an MIS systems analyst (non-nursing), healthcare facilities tend to prefer nurses in such a role because nurses have a broad knowledge of clinical operations and can easily identify the needs of the clinical staff.

There are advantages to being an informatics nurse:
- Every healthcare facility requires informatics nurses because Federal regulations require healthcare facilities to use computerized medical records.
- You use analytical skills to incorporate clinical workflows into the electronic medical records system workflows.
- You use your critical thinking skills to problem-solve with an EMR system.
- You can implement your own ideas to streamline clinical workflows throughout the healthcare facility.
- You become directly involved with all levels of administration and staff in the healthcare facility.
- You make the EMR system work for the healthcare facility and the clinical team.
- You train the clinical team on the use of the EMR system.
- You may be able to work from home.
- You may have a flexible schedule; however, expect to work long hours when you are on deadline for releasing an update to the EMR system.

There are disadvantages to being an informatics nurse:
- You must translate tedious regulatory requirements into clinical workflows that are incorporated into the electronic medical records system.
- You tend to get blamed by administration and the clinical team when the EMR system doesn't work as they expect it to work.
- You are expected to fix all EMR system problems – problems that only the vendor can fix. The vendor can take months and years to make fixes.
- You have no contact with patients or with the clinical units.
- You will perform hours and days of tedious testing at your desk prior to releasing updates of the EMR system to the clinical team.
- You are blamed for delays in implementation that are beyond your control.

- You are likely to have difficulty explaining what causes problems with the EMR system because few members of administration and the clinical team understand the technical aspects of the system.
- You can lose your clinical skills.

Hospice Nurse

A hospice nurse cares for a patient who is in the final days of their life. Your goal is to make sure the patient and family members are comfortable and that all needs are met. You provide a blend of patient care and education explaining to the patient and the patient's family what is happening. Not all nurses are cut out to work hospice, primarily because all your patients are terminal. Nothing you do will save their life.

You'll work either in a healthcare facility that provides inpatient hospice care or provide at-home hospice care through a hospice agency. Many hospice patients are not geriatric patients. Many patients are middle-age and some hospice patients are children.

There are benefits to being a hospice nurse:
- You make a difference in the lives of your patients and their families.
- You advocate for your patients and families.
- You help the patient and family understand the end-of-life process.
- You help to bring a painless (as possible) death to a patient.
- You develop sensitive communication skills.
- You stay abreast of clinical skills such as pain management.

There are disadvantages to being a hospice nurse:
- All your patients are terminal. You build a bond with your patients – and then they pass away.
- The constant stress of facing death daily is difficult to balance with your personal life.
- On-call for home hospice patients requires you to travel distances to patients' homes at any time.
- There is too much to do when multiple patients require your services at the same time.
- Providing care in the last stages of life in the home environment with little or no support can be unpredictable. You don't have immediate access to supplies and the clinical team as you would in an inpatient hospice setting.
- There is a high risk for burnout.

- Conflict of roles may occur when the employer has you performing roles other than that of a hospice nurse, such as that of a case manager.

Infection Control Nurse

An infection control nurse is responsible for preventing the spread of infections in a healthcare facility by monitoring admissions, lab results, and daily assessments of patients to identify potential risks for infection. The infection control nurse is usually on-call to answer inquiries from staff nurses and practitioners about situations related to infection such as the proper handling of suspected infected samples.

Healthcare facilities are required to report results of this monitoring to regulatory authorities. This is also performed by the infection control nurse. If there appears to be an outbreak of infection, the infection control nurse implements measures to identify the source of the infection and contain, treat, and monitor the affected area of the healthcare facility. On an ongoing basis, the infection control nurse makes rounds on units, educating staff on infection control prevention methods and observing if those preventive measures are being properly implemented. The infection control nurse also coordinates with vendors on the proper procedures for sanitizing vendor equipment.

There are advantages to being an infection control nurse:
- You are the first responder to identify and contain infections within the healthcare facility.
- You play a critical role in keeping patients and staff safe from hospital-acquired infections.
- You gain a vast knowledge of infectious agents and how to prevent the spread of infections.

There are disadvantages to being an infection control nurse:
- Most of your time is spent in your office gathering and reporting statistics about infection.
- At times you are more of a coordinator between regulators and the healthcare facility rather than actively preventing infections.
- Staff may see you more as an "inspector" looking to catch their errors rather than as a colleague in a mutual effort to prevent infection.
- You will lose your bedside nursing skills.

Military Nursing

Military service offers the opportunity for nurses to gain a unique experience that can be transferred to civilian nursing. Military nurses work in military hospitals and may be deployed to the field in times of conflict to care for soldiers who are ill or wounded. Nurses provide the full breadth of nursing care in the military – trauma care, urgent care, acute care, primary care, and rehabilitation. Care is provided in military installations both abroad and in the United States.

You'll need to pass a background check that results in security clearance so you can be deployed around the world. You also must have no felony convictions, pass a physical, and meet age requirements. You'll need at least a BSN to be a commissioned officer with some experience as a nurse. You need to be a United States citizen; although nurses who are legal residents of the United States may also be eligible. You also have to agree to be a military nurse for at least three years.

You may choose to be an active-duty nurse or a reserve-status nurse. An active-duty nurse is full-time and can be deployed anywhere at any time. A reserve-status nurse is a part-time nurse (after the initial active-duty period) and usually participants in military functions on one weekend per month and for two full weeks per year. However, the reserve-status nurse can be called up for active duty at any time during an international conflict.

The U.S. Navy Nurse Corps services both the Navy and the Marines. At times you may be deployed at sea on a ship. The Air Force offers the opportunity to become a flight nurse. Expect a vast cultural change once you join. The military is highly structured and follows a very formal process. You are a soldier first, then a nurse.

Expect a long work week especially in MEDCEN (the United States Army Medical Center), which are large military hospitals.

You may qualify for an educational loan repayment program. Read the fine print and don't assume full loan repayment. You may be responsible for interest payments and any taxes associated with the educational loan repayment.

There are advantages to becoming a military nurse:
- You are a commissioned officer.
- You may be able to continue your nursing education at the expense of the military.
- The military usually employs cutting-edge medical technology that you'll be trained to use.
- You get to travel, although not as a tourist.
- Usually you have a 30-day paid vacation annually.
- Nurses may command an entire military healthcare facility.

There are disadvantages to becoming a military nurse:

- Military nursing may be unpredictable because the military assigns you to a job and decides where you are going to live during a deployment period. You may be away from your family for 12 months or more.
- You may be called into harm's way treating soldiers who are involved in armed conflicts around the world.
- Avoid joining under enlisted (non-officer) status. Enlisted nurses are usually assigned as hospital corpsmen with a civilian nursing license – not as a nurse. There is usually little free time to continue your nursing education and the pay is low.
- Don't believe everything the recruiter tells you. The recruiter cannot guarantee you anything once you join the military.
- Commissioned officers pay for their own food, uniforms, and have other out-of-pocket expenses not incurred by enlisted personnel.
- You'll need to join as enlisted personnel if your academic credentials are no higher than an associate's degree and the same is true if you have less than an RN license, and you won't work as an RN. Officers must be an RN with at least a BSN.

Nurse Educator

A nurse educator is an experienced nurse who is responsible for developing curriculum and educating nurses on nursing-related subjects. Education takes place online, in the classroom, using computer-based simulations, and in the clinical setting. Schools of nursing employ nurse educators as faculty members in pre-licensing and post-licensing programs. Healthcare facilities employ nurse educators to develop and implement nursing orientation programs, annual competencies, in-service training, continuing education, and provide remediation as part of disciplinary action.

You'll be updating curriculum based on current regulatory requirements and translating the curriculum into training material, online courses, classroom presentations, and clinical training — and you'll be teaching in the classroom and clinical setting. You'll implement testing procedures that identify if nurses are able to understand and implement curriculum. You'll also develop remediation for nurses who fail.

Schools of nursing and healthcare facilities typically require a nurse educator to have completed an MSN (master of nursing) degree, hold board certification in their specialty, and have several years of experience in their specialty. Healthcare facilities may accept a nurse who is working toward an MSN. You must be a leader and be comfortable speaking before groups of strangers. Good presentation skills are critical to the success of a nurse educator. You should be well-versed in the use of presentation software since you are expected to create your own presentations.

In a healthcare facility, you may be responsible for clinical education for a division of the healthcare facility or for a number of clinical units. You'll be expected to make sure that the clinical staff has completed all necessary training, and you must provide documentation to support your findings should regulatory authorities audit those units.

Schools of nursing usually offer part-time teaching positions, referred to as 'adjunct.' This is worth exploring as a way to see if you like teaching. You'll be responsible to teach either a lecture or clinical course for an academic term. Pay is minimal. There are usually no benefits. If you like teaching, then you may want to consider working as an adjunct and keep your full-time nursing job.

There are advantages to being a nurse educator:
– You mentor new and current nurses.
– You keep your nursing skills current and provide training that keeps other nurses current with their skills.
– You help correct clinical problems.
– You have no work on weekends or holidays.
– Usually you work a day shift except when in-service training is scheduled for off shift (healthcare facilities).
– Schools of nursing require a minimum number of classes to teach (for example, 24 credit hours), specific office hours, and committee assignments. You work during the academic year (that is, 10 months).
– Nurse educators in healthcare facilities typically have broad responsibilities to create and maintain training for all clinical staff, including managers, and advise on facility-wide policies and procedures.
– Nurse educators in healthcare facilities may also serve as mock auditors surveying clinical units prior to regulatory audits.
– You have autonomy in both schools of nursing and in a healthcare facility as a nurse educator.
– You have minimal patient care. You directly supervise nurses during in-service training (healthcare facility) and clinical rotation (schools of nursing).

There are disadvantages to being a nurse educator:
– Schools of nursing may offer lower salaries compared with a clinical nurse who holds an MSN.

- Schools of nursing may require faculty members to perform research and publish frequently to maintain employment. Expect to work during school breaks and vacations without additional compensation.
- Your assessment may determine if a nursing student becomes a nurse or a current nurse continues employment due to possible incompetence.
- You'll be expected to manage multiple assessments (for example, orienting multiple nurses, teaching classes, performing in-service training, and preparing curriculum) simultaneously.
- Minimal patient care can lead to you to lose your nursing skills.
- The job requires a lot of prep work.
- You are fully responsible for patient care during clinical rotations in pre-license programs (schools of nursing).

Legal Nursing

A legal nurse assists the legal system in interpreting medical records; helps attorneys interview clients related to medical issues; and collaborates with the legal staff on strategies for legal actions related to a client's medical condition. No advanced degree is required although you should hold a Legal Nurse Consulting certificate and have several years of staff nurse experience. Experience in nurse management is a plus.

A legal nurse consultant typically participants in personal injury cases where the nurse reviews medical records, treatments, and other technical aspects of the case and compares it to standards of practices. The nurse then advises attorneys whether or not actions of the medical team conformed to standards of care. The nurse's assessment provides a foundation for building a case, formulating deposition questions, and determining if cases should be settled or go to trial.

There are part-time and full-time opportunities for a legal nurse consultant. The nurse participates in interviews with clients, conducts medical literature searches, identifies a timeline of care, educates the legal staff on medical issues, and may serve as an expert witness during a case.

There are advantages to being a legal nurse consultant:
- If you work as an independent legal nurse consultant:
  o You set your own work schedule.
  o You can keep your clinical nurse position.
- If you work on an in-house staff:
  o You receive a regular salary and benefits.
  o You have regular working hours — no weekends, plus holidays off.
  o It's possible you receive a bonus

There are disadvantages to being a legal nurse consultant:
- If you work as an independent legal nurse consultant:
  - o   You must constantly market yourself to attorneys.
  - o   Your clinical nursing employer may frown upon your legal nurse consulting activities.
  - o   You must always be available to be deposed by your attorneys and the opposing party's attorneys.
  - o   You will likely have to testify in court and be held responsible for your testimony.
  - o   You must meet with potential clients (that is, attorneys) without pay to sell your services.
  - o   You may wait to be paid after providing services. You don't get a regular pay check.
- If you work on the in-house staff:
  - o   You receive no overtime pay.
  - o   You have no flex time. You are expected to work normal business hours.
  - o   There are few full-time in-house staff positions available.

Forensic Nurse

Forensic nurses work with patients who are involved with the court system either as a victim or as a detainee. Some forensic nurses respond to emergency situations providing care to crime victims, such as victims of rape, abuse, domestic violence and neglect. These nurses collect evidence that can be used in investigations and criminal trials. Another type of forensic nurse works in jails and prisons providing first-line medical care to detainees. There are situations when the forensic nurse also collects evidence when providing first-line medical care, should the detainee become a victim within jail or prison.

You'll need the emotional stability to work with victims immediately after they have been traumatized and be able to work within the jail and prison systems if you provide care to detainees. You must have good nursing skills as a staff nurse and be trained and certified to collect evidence. The legal case against a perpetrator depends on correctly gathering evidence from the victim.

There are advantages to being a forensic nurse:
- You directly comfort crime victims in their time of need.
- You collect evidence that is key to building a case against the perpetrator.

- You typically work for a government agency such as the Sheriff's department, although some forensic nurses work for hospitals that are designated trauma centers.

There are disadvantages to being a forensic nurse:
- You are on-call and respond to either the scene of the crime or at the trauma center.
- Your patients are either crime victims or detainees who are incarcerated.
- You may work within the jail or prison system daily where your safety is a concern if you care for detainees.

Utilization Review Nurse

A utilization review nurse ensures that care provided to patients is covered by third-party payers and results in the cost-effective treatment of patients. The utilization review nurse is assigned several patient care units in a healthcare facility. The utilization review nurse monitors and works closely with the patient's case manager, treatment team, and third-party payers to be sure treatment conforms to third-party payer's guidelines and that treatment is supported by pre-certification where required and documentation of need and results.

The utilization review nurse also follows up with third-party payers to address any denial of payment. The goal is for the utilization review nurse to take action that ensures payment from third-party payers is received in a timely manner both as care is being provided and for care that has previously been provided by the healthcare facility.

You'll need several years of bedside nursing and need to master the business of reimbursements. In addition, you'll need excellent verbal and written communications skills, be comfortable using electronic charting software, and be detailed oriented. You'll need to interact with the case manager, treatment team, healthcare facility administrators, and insurers.

There are advantages to being a utilization review nurse:
- You are on the first-line to prevent financial losses to the healthcare facility by making sure that requirements of third-party payers are met prior to treatment.
- You recommend changes in procedures within the healthcare facility to ensure every opportunity is taken for reimbursement.
- You are the person who provides additional information to convince insurers to reconsider denial of payment.
- Your skills are transferable to other healthcare facilities and health insurers.

– You don't work weekends or holidays.
– There is potential to work from home.
– You get to work independently.

There are disadvantages to being a utilization review nurse:
– You may feel like the person in the healthcare facility who denies care to the patient because you transmit requirements for reimbursements to the case manager, treatment team, and the healthcare facility's administration.
– You work in an office and review charts all day. There is no patient contact.
– You lose your bedside nursing skills since you provide no patient care.
– You must learn the details of reimbursement requirements for many third-party payers.
– You will potentially have a heavy workload.

Telehealth Nursing

A telehealth nurse is hired by a health insurer to assist patients over the phone by answering health-related questions, assessing the patient's needs, and directing the patient to the proper level of care. Telehealth nursing is also used to help chronically ill patients manage their diseases. The telehealth nurse is a triage nurse and not a replacement for a practitioner. The goal is for the patient to efficiently receive medical help.

The telehealth nurse should have several years of bedside patient care experience and experience in the emergency department as a triage nurse. You'll need to be comfortable communicating with patients over the phone, asking pertinent medical questions that help to direct the patient to the proper level of care or providing home or over-the-counter remedies that will address the patient's immediate needs.

There are advantages to being a telehealth nurse:
– You work independently.
– You don't work weekends or holidays until you agree to be on-call during those shifts.
– You have the possibility of working from home.
– You assist patients and address their immediate medical needs.

There are disadvantages to being a telehealth nurse:
– You make recommendations without seeing the patient.
– You lose your bedside nursing skills.
– You are unable to perform a complete assessment (for example, vital signs).

- The patient may feel your recommendations are in the best interests of the insurer and not those of the patient since you work for the insurer.

School Nursing

Public and private schools, including colleges, are required to have a nurse on staff to respond to general health issues and accidents. The school nurse typically maintains medical records of students and staff; administers or oversees administration (actually performed by the student) treatments ordered by the practitioner, such as inhalation treatment for acute asthma or insulin injections; and performs triage. In some instances, the school nurse also teaches health related classes.

School nurses may require a special state certification. You must like working with children of all ages, including high school students. Each age group has their own unique needs and challenges. And you must like working with parents. You're the person who notifies a parent when their child has taken ill in school and must care for the child until the parent arrives at the school.

There are advantages to being a school nurse:
- You work during the school day and school year and are usually off during the summer months and during inclement weather.
- There are no weekends, holidays, or evenings.
- You may receive tenure after three years of work, depending on the school district.
- You may have the same schedule as your school-age children which eliminates the need for after school childcare.
- You work relatively independently.
- You directly help children and their parents.

There are disadvantages to being a school nurse:
- You are limited in the care that you can give to students. Some states limit you to performing first aid.
- You lose your bedside nursing skills.
- You have no support since you are usually the only school nurse on duty in the building.
- Dealing with some parents can be challenging.

Cruise Ship Nursing

If you like cruising, then you may want to explore becoming a nurse aboard a cruise ship. Cruise ship lines frequently require onboard nurses to have emergency department experience to assist the ship's practitioner in managing onboard emergencies. The small cruise ship medical team provides first-line medical care to passengers and crew once at sea. Typically, cruise ship nurses sign a contract for several months (for example, 6 months). The contract is likely renewable by either the nurse or the cruise ship line at the end of the contract period. Staff may take off a couple of months between contracts.

You are expected to have at least three years nursing experience in emergency medicine or acute care since you are expected to handle all first-line medical care, along with the medical team. You'll be expected to work the clinic from 8 a.m. to 11 a.m. and from 3 p.m. to 6 p.m. and be on-call outside clinic hours. Depending on the cruise line, you may have a private cabin and will have free food and uniforms. You are paid twice a month (usually) in U.S. dollars. Federal taxes are automatically deducted for U.S. citizens and residents. You will have out-of-pocket expenses purchasing items from the crew shop.

There are advantages to being a cruise ship nurse:
- You'll have time to visit ports-of-call when the ship is at dockside.
- You can take shore excursions at discount prices when space is available.
- There are crew activities onboard (for example, parties, tournaments).
- There is usually a crew gym and crew bar.
- You can use the onboard spa and hair salon at discount prices.
- You and your family may take advantage of discount cruises, if available.
- You are one of the ship's officers.

There are disadvantages to being a cruise ship nurse:
- You are not on a cruise and have limited or no access to passenger accommodations.
- You may not choose your assignment. Assignments to specific cruise ships are made based on business needs.
- You may have to pay a per-minute fee for Internet access even if you bring your own computer.
- Cell phone service is usually available onboard but international roaming rates apply.
- You can make long distance calls at your expense.
- There is no guarantee that you'll be offered another contract.

Medical Sales Representative

Medical device and pharmaceutical manufacturers employ nurses to represent their products to the medical community. The medical sales representatives visit practitioners in private offices and in healthcare facilities to explain the technical advancement of products that can improve the quality of patient care. The goal is to make direct or indirect sales. Direct sales are when the medical sales representative places an order. Indirect sales occur when the medical sales representative influences the decision to use the product, such as a when a practitioner prescribes medication that was presented by the medical sales representative.

Nurses usually make good medical sales representatives because the nurse has the clinical background to relate how the product actually helps the provider take better care of the patient. Nurses are particularly successful when describing products that are used by nurses such as wound care products, syringes, and IV catheter products.

You must have excellent communication skills and have a confident outgoing personality to walk up to a stranger (perhaps a practitioner) and tell her how your product will improve her practice – and she may have little or no time to listen to you. You'll also require a good sense of business, which is not normally found in bedside nursing. Your job is to sell your products.

There are advantages to being a medical sales representative:
- You create your own work hours as long as you meet your sales goals.
- Your compensation is based on performance. Generally, the harder you work the more money you earn.
- You develop professional relationships with healthcare providers.
- You have autonomy to run your own territory and "your own" business within the organization.
- You have the feeling of accomplishment by selling products that can change a patient's life

There are disadvantages to being a medical sales representative:
- There are risks of layoffs due to the volatility of the industry.
- Unrealistic performance expectations may lead to termination if you fail to meet your sales goal.
- There is a trend by firms to decrease financial incentives for meeting or exceeding sales goals.
- You limit growth within your territory because your focus is on price rather than quality that requires a higher startup cost.
- Consolidation and mergers of competitors limits your employment opportunities.

—   There can be too much company politics focused on the bottom-line and not on patient care.

Nursing is a unique profession. There are many different opportunities available to a nurse. If you find yourself pigeon-holed into one nursing specialty, you can always move into a more interesting specialty by taking a few courses then honing your new nursing skills into a fully competent nurse in your new specialty. The challenge is to move outside your comfort zone and test the waters in a new specialty.

Chapter 6
Preparing for the Interview

Whether you are a new grad looking for your first job or a seasoned professional seeking to move on to a different healthcare facility, you'll need to prepare for the pre-employment interviews, which can be challenging since you have no idea what you'll be asked during the interviews. It is safe to say that the nurse recruiter will try to discover if you fit the healthcare facility's culture, if you meet all requirements for the position, and if there is anything in your work history that might imply you are not a good worker.

Ask your colleagues and friends if they know what it is like to work for your prospective employer. You might see a trend in their replies that gives you a hint about the culture within the healthcare facility. Sometimes you'll hear that the pay is above average but the workload is also above average. Take comments with a grain of salt since opinions are based on perceptions – and misperceptions. Aside from asking around, there is little you can do to prepare for questions that explore whether you fit the healthcare facility's culture, primarily because you don't know much about it.

Questions about job requirements are something you can prepare to answer. Get a piece of paper and make two columns: one containing job requirements and the other evidence that proves you meet each requirement. The goal is to help the nurse recruiter match your background to the position. Don't be concerned if you are unable to match every job requirement as few candidates meet all requirements (see Chapters 3 and 4). Take time before the interview to match as many requirements as you can and come up with a way that you might be able to meet missing requirements in the near future. Keep in mind that the nurse recruiter believes you meet enough of the requirements to invite you in for an interview.

Your resume presents your work history (see Chapter 2). The ideal candidate will have stayed five or six years with each employer and shows progress in increasing responsibilities, such as membership on committees. There are few ideal candidates. The reality is that sometimes jobs don't work out the way you and the nurse manager anticipated. It's like walking around in a new pair of shoes and you've discovered they don't fit so you change shoes. The nurse recruiter understands that work histories may not be pristine. Prepare a reasonable response to potential questions related to any employment gaps or short-term employment (see Chapter 4). Be honest and consider bringing up these situations even before the nurse recruiter asks the question. This shows that you're not hiding any information.

DOI 10.1515/9781501506109-006

Preparing Your "Script"

Become a good sales representative for yourself by anticipating probable and possible questions that might be asked during your interviews. Later on we'll focus on technical questions, but before any technique questions come your way, the nurse recruiter and the nurse manager need to get to know you by asking some probing questions. No one knows the questions that will be asked – sometimes the interviewer comes up with the question on the spot. However, you can anticipate typical questions asked in interviews and anticipate questions that your background might generate, such as gaps in employment or short periods of employment.

Prepare a response to each anticipated question similar to how politicians prepare for questions posed by the media or are asked at public events. Prepared responses (talking points) are commonly referred to as a script. The script is carefully written with words and phrases that convey a response that will satisfy the audience's curiosity. Politicians memorize the script and "stay on script" (recite the script) and avoid "going off script" (ad-libbing) when answering questions. You should do the same so you won't be flustered and appear confused at the time of the interview. Instead you'll come off appearing confident and honest. The script should be a few short sentences that clearly answer the question. The goal is to deliver a succinct response.

Here are some likely questions that you'll be asked. Write a script for each one.
- So tell me about yourself.
- What do you know about our facility?
- Why do you want to work here?
- What makes you feel you are qualified for this position?
- Why did you become a nurse?
- Where do you see yourself in five years?
- What are your likes and dislikes about nursing?
- What are your strengths and weaknesses?
- Why should we hire you?
- What is your most important accomplishment?
- What failures have your encountered and what would you have done differently?
- Describe your ideal position.
- What motivates you?
- How would you resolve a conflict with your nurse manager?
- What is your strategy for multi-tasking?
- Why are you leaving your present position?

- What do you like and dislike about your present position?
- How do you keep your nursing skills current?

Make a list of questions based on the job requirements listed in the job posting. The nurse recruiter will probably walk you through each job requirement to determine which requirements you meet. You should have a script prepared for each requirement that clearly links your background to the requirement. Be forthright if you don't meet the requirement. Your script should acknowledge that you're lacking the requirement, however, show how something in your background is similar to the requirement or how you plan to meet it in the near future. For example, "I'm not ACLS certified; however, I'm scheduled to take the ACLS course in four weeks." But if you don't meet a particular requirement – and will not in the future – say so. The nurse recruiter will decide if that's a deal breaker or not.

Here are some basic considerations that you should be prepared to address (see Bring a List of Questions to Ask, later in this Chapter):
- Shifts: eight-hour shifts, 12-hour shifts, day/evening/night shifts, start/end times, breaks
- Work schedule: three-day week, five-day week, every-other-weekend, days off during the week, holidays, day mandated to work (emergencies, weather related, short staffing)
- Assignments: assignment to a unit, floating, populations, staffing ratios, support staff availability, management expectations
- Commuting: travel distance from home, travel time during rush hour, public transportation availability and schedules, parking (employee parking, parking fees, location)
- Employment: pay period, probation period, transfer to another position, education benefits, pay increases, union positions, time off (vacation, personal days, and sick days), non-compensated time (required online training on your own time)

Create an opening "script" for the initial meeting with the nurse recruiter that includes the greeting and small talk such as "this was an easy place to find" or about the current weather – something to set the stage for the interview. Keep everything upbeat. Speak with confidence. Be yourself. The worst that can happen is you're not invited back to the next interview, but you might be surprised.

Scripts have stage direction that tell you what you should be doing. Some nurses include stage direction in their interview "script." Active listening is the stage direction found in many "scripts." You stop, listen, and process what the interviewer is saying to you. This is the most important action you can take during an interview. You learn by listening, a nursing instructor once said.

Remember that the nurse recruiter leads the interview – not you. The nurse recruiter can take any number of directions once the small talk is over. Some nurse recruiters begin with an open-ended question such as "tell me about yourself." Others may step through your resume quizzing your experience such as, "I see you are a med-surg nurse at ABC Medical Center. Tell me about what you do."

Be prepared to follow the nurse recruiter in any direction that he or she takes during the interview. Anticipate questions similar to those mentioned in this chapter and then prepare a "script" to respond to each question. "Scripts" help you speak with confidence on anything about your background and nursing. You'll come across as a professional especially when the nurse recruiter compares you to other candidates who apply for the same position.

The Game Plan

You know that you can do the job successfully but you still must make it through the pre-employment gauntlet before you'll get a chance to prove your clinical skills to the nurse manager. This can be a frustrating period but you must put aside those frustrations and perform every task requested of you as if each task is an exciting new challenge. Leave the "attitude" at the doorstep especially if you feel that your experience and training should exempt you from some pre-employment activities (for example, testing). You are being carefully observed during all phases of pre-employment (as well as during the probation period if you are offered the job). Typically, the nurse recruiter and the nurse manager will stop the pre-employment process if the candidate appears to have an "attitude." They would rather cut their losses sooner than be saddled with a problem employee for the long haul.

There can exist situations that you prefer the nurse recruiter to gloss over rather than explore in detail. For example, you might have had a position that didn't work as well as you had hoped and it clearly appears on your resume. Expect that the nurse recruiter will bring this up during the interview; however, your response determines how much time is spent exploring the situation. Here's a strategy that may help you deal with uncomfortable situations in your background.

– Don't try to hide the situation. It is best to bring this out during the interview rather than have the nurse recruiter learn about it as a result of a background check.

- Be consistent on your resume and in your responses to the nurse recruiter's questions. If a position didn't work out, still list the employer, position, dates of employment, and a brief description of your duties on your resume in the same format as used to describe your other positions.
- Limit details both on your resume and in your response about the potentially negative situation. Be specific but light on details. Try to satisfy the most obvious concerns without dwelling on the problem. Be prepared to give a brief reason why a position didn't work out such as the position required a more experienced nurse.
- Don't blame others for the situation. That is, the position didn't work out because you lacked the required experience. It wasn't that "they" didn't train you or didn't give you time to prove yourself. This demonstrates that you objectively assessed the problem and accept responsibility. It isn't that you are a bad nurse, the shoe simply didn't fit.
- Keep your response short and to the point. The nurse recruiter wants the headline, not the full story. If the headline conveys sufficient information, then the nurse recruiter is not interested in the whole story.
- Acknowledge the negative situation, then try to refocus the interview on positive situations. After explaining that the position didn't work out because you lacked experience, mention that you found a more appropriate position at ABC Medical Center where you were successful, and now have the needed experience.
- Use a three-part structure to respond to questions. Describe the situation succinctly, then describe the action you took to deal with the situation. Follow this with the outcome of your action. Don't elaborate! The nurse recruiter will ask for more information about the situation, if necessary.
- Speak about you – not the team. The nurse recruiter wants to know what you can do and how you do it, not how your team operates.
- Time is on your side – not on that of the nurse recruiter. You have about an hour to convince the nurse recruiter that you are a viable candidate. The nurse recruiter has the same amount of time to decide if you are a viable candidate. Don't spend time explaining negative situations; focus on your positive attributes. Briefly explain negative situations then refocus the conversation on positive ones.

It's a Wrap

Plan your conclusion as the interview winds down by preparing a "script" for your closing act. Leave on a positive note and imply that you want to remain a candidate for the position, even if you don't want that position. You don't want to bring closure to your candidacy during the interviewing process. Wait until they offer you the position before telling the nurse recruiter that you are no longer interested in the position.

Rarely will you be offered the position on the spot, although that might happen if the hiring nurse manager conducts the interview. Be cautious if you get such an offer. Have a "script" prepared that politely probes why the offer is being made on the spot ("I wasn't expecting such a quick decision"). This opens the door for the nurse manager to explain the situation. You might have been the last candidate interviewed and you surpassed the qualifications of the other candidates. On the other hand, it might also be that not many other candidates applied for the position – you're the first one who wanted the position since the job was posted months ago and they're desperate to hire someone. This may not be a good sign for you. Why didn't others apply for the position? Did they know something you didn't about the nurse manager, the unit, or the healthcare facility that would make the position undesirable?

Even if you're "hired on the spot," it is not official. The nurse manager needs to process the hiring decision with the nurse recruiter. Typically, the nurse recruiter formally reviews the job requirements and compensation with you. You must verbally agree before the nurse recruiter sends you the official offer letter in writing. The offer letter states the terms of employment and supersedes all verbal and written communication about the job. Any arrangements you made with the nurse manager that are not contained in the terms of employment might not be enforceable. For example, if the nurse manager agreed to give you every Wednesday off and this is not stated in the offer letter, then you may not be getting every Wednesday off and should address this before formal acceptance of the offer.

Interviews tend to end either because you're not a fit for the position, or you are no longer a viable candidate compared with other candidates. The nurse recruiter is usually straightforward and will tell you if you are no longer a viable candidate. Don't take the rejection personally. The nurse recruiter knows the culture and personalities on the unit plus performance expectations and feels that you won't be successful in the position. Prepare a "script" on how you are going to respond to the rejection ("I appreciate that you're being upfront. Are there other open positions that might be a better fit?").

You might be asked to meet with the hiring nurse manager if you're still in the running for the position. Be accommodating. Try to meet with the nurse manager immediately following your interview with the nurse recruiter if offered. You're already warmed up for the interview with the nurse manager – and you don't have to come back. You finish the interviews in one day. If the nurse manager is unavailable, then schedule an interview as soon as possible.

Don't become overly optimistic. A good nurse recruiter always gives candidates the feeling that everything is on track for a job offer, though it might not be necessarily true. The nurse recruiter usually hedge bets if the top candidate turns down the job. Prepare a "script" that you can use if you're still a viable candidate ("Thank you for the opportunity to explore the position. I'd like to continue our discussions. Do you have any timeframe when I might hear from you?").

Some Thorny Questions

There are questions that in the United States are illegal to ask during a pre-employment interview, and some questions that might be asked are simply inappropriate. The nurse recruiter probably knows what questions cannot be asked during the interview; however, some nurse managers may be inexperienced at interviewing potential employees and may deviate into illegal or inappropriate questions during the interview.

Areas off limits to pre-employment questions are:
– Age
– Birthplace
– Disability
– Marital and family status – including if you are pregnant
– National origin
– Race
– Religion
– Gender

Be aware that the interviewer may intentionally or inadvertently touch upon these areas indirectly during the conversation. Rarely will you be asked questions directly. For example, "We live in the same town. My daughter is a junior at the high school." This may lead you to continue the conversation that reveals "do not ask" information such as "My daughter is in the first grade." This reveals your family status. Although your response may seem inconsequential, the interviewer may extrapolate situations that may interfere with your employment – a young child at home raises childcare issues during working hours.

The nurse recruiter and experienced nurse managers may use carefully worded questions to explore "do not ask" information but are perfectly legal because the question focuses on whether or not you are able to perform the job function. For example, you might be asked if you can lift 50 pounds or stand for six hours per shift rather than "Do you have any disabilities that prevent you from working?" You can be asked if you can work overtime or if you are willing to travel, but you can't be asked questions about family status that may interfere with your job.

The interviewer can't ask you your age or cunningly asking the year you graduated from high school to estimate you age. You can be asked if you are over the age of 18, which is the legal age to work in most states. Likewise, you can't be asked if you are a U.S. citizen but you can be asked if you are authorized to work in the United States.

If you are asked directly or indirectly a "do not ask" question, then politely ask for clarification ("I'm a little puzzled by your question. Can you clarify it for me?"). Hopefully the interviewer picks up your hint that the "do not ask" line is about to be crossed. If not, then you can restate the question in a way that focuses on whether or not you can perform the job ("I'm not sure I understand the question, but if you're asking if I'm available to work overtime, I am as long as it is not every day.")

Some questions may probe how you would respond to a realistic situation where there is no easy answer. Simply think through the question and respond reasonably. Don't try to give an answer that you think the interviewer wants to hear. Here are a few of those questions.

The practitioner gave you a direct verbal order to obtain a written pre-procedure consent from the patient. Hospital policy requires the practitioner to obtain the signed consent directly from the patient. What would you do?

Two of your most difficult patients ring the call bell at the same time. You are the only staff member available on the floor. What would you do?

You and your colleague are at the nurse's station. A family member approaches your colleague stating that it is time to give her daughter pain medication. Your colleague is the daughter's primary nurse and tells the family member, "I'll be with you in a few minutes." The family member turns to you and tells you that it is time to give her daughter pain medication. What would you do?

Bring a List of Questions to Ask

You need to decide if the job is a fit for you and the best way to make your assessment is by gathering information that might influence your decision. Listing factors that you are looking for in a job is a good way to begin your assessment. Focus on the obvious — and the not so obvious – ways that they will affect your quality of life both at work and during off-hours.

Write a "script" using wording that doesn't imply the importance of the question to you accepting the position. For example, instead of asking "Is there adequate parking on campus for employees during all shifts?" you may want to rephrase the question as "How is the parking situation for employees?"

The nurse recruiter is likely to be forthright in responding to the question. Always respond positively even if the nurse recruiter's response is a possible deal breaker for you. Perhaps the nurse recruiter tells you that employees park in remote parking areas off-campus and are bussed to the campus and that employees are responsible for clocking-in on time. This could end up being a quality of life issue for you since your arrival time must consider the extra time to go to the remote parking area and the shuttle bus schedule during change of shift. The same consideration must be given at the end of shift. You may not want this hassle, but don't give the nurse recruiter any hint that this is a problem at this time. Make a list of pros and cons about the job if you are invited back for another round of interviews or are offered the position and then decide if any showstoppers are truly showstoppers. You'll be in a better mindset to make this decision than during the interview when the potential showstopper appears.

Here are a few questions that you may want to consider:

- What are the staffing ratios for your shift and on your unit(s)?
- How are work schedules decided (at the discretion of the nurse manager, collaboration with the employee, or by seniority)?
- Can I be floated to other units (assuming you are hired for a specific unit)?
- In what conditions would I be mandated to stay at work?
- How are vacations and holiday requests approved (at the discretion of the nurse manager, by seniority)?
- Will you be assigned to a unit without orientation to the unit?
- What are the benefits (health insurance, educational benefits, 401(k), others)?
- How are weather-related emergencies handled (will you be mandated to stay, provided sleeping accommodations, given extra pay, or be allowed to call out)?
- How are workplace injuries handled (disability leave, mandated medical provider, time off, light duty)?
- What is the annual review process?
- What opportunities are there to increase compensation (annual increases, extra pay for meeting/exceeding goals, bonuses, longevity increases, shift differential, board certification increases, advanced nursing degree increases)?
- What is the parking situation (remote parking areas, parking fees, designated parking for employees, and adequate parking for all shifts)?

- Is there any non-compensated time (online training at home)?
- How are sick days handled (doctor's note, length of time before required to go on disability, disability pay)?
- What is orientation like (length, time in classroom, time on units, extension if necessary, online classes, simulation lab, when transferring to a different unit)?
- What are the nurse manager's expectations and what should your expectations be during the first six months on the job?
- Is this a new position? If so, why was the new position created?
- Why did the previous person leave the position?
- How long was the previous person in the position before they left?
- How long has this position been available?
- Can you tell me about performance reviews (annually, goal setting, basis for evaluation)?
- Why should I work here?
- What is the compensation?
- Are there special incentives for accepting the position (for example, signing bonus, pay for bilingual nurses)?

If the Interview Doesn't Go Well

Be prepared if something does not go well during the interview. Something you said might be taken the wrong way, or there may be a misunderstanding about what the nurse recruiter is saying. Whatever the case, the temperature of the interview changes from warm and cozy to chilly. You'll notice this right away when the upbeat tone switches to uncertainty — focusing on mismatches to job requirements rather than matches.

You may not experience this; however, prepare for this possibility. A good strategy is to acknowledge the concern immediately when you detect the change in direction ("It seems that you have some concerns"). The nurse recruiter will likely appreciate your observation because there is an issue that the nurse recruiter needs to resolve and you'll be able to get the interview back on course.

Plan to ask the nurse recruiter to tell you about her concerns. Listen carefully to the response. The nurse recruiter's response may indicate that your original choice of words might have been misleading or words used by the nurse recruiter may have misled you. Clarify the issue using different words. Better yet, plan to describe a scenario that illustrates the situation in conflict and how you would handle that situation.

There might be deal breakers for you or the nurse recruiter that make it impossible to continue the pre-employment process. You'll probably know where your qualifications are weak when you compare your background to the job requirements. These weaknesses might have been noticed for the first time by the nurse recruiter during the interview, which dampens the upbeat tone of the interview. Write "scripts" to address each potential issue. Don't hide the mismatch. Explain your plan to meet those requirements shortly after being hired, or why your other qualifications weigh more than your deficient. Write another "script" that you can use if this truly turns into a showstopper. Thank the nurse recruiter for taking the time to chat with you about the position and ask if you would be considered for future positions in the healthcare facility.

Be Prepared to Walk Away

Prepare to negotiate. The initial interview with the nurse recruiter is probably not the time to enter into negotiations unless you are offered the position on-the-spot. However, you should do your homework to prepare to negotiate if and when that time comes. Senior management negotiates a contract that has a start and end date and contains specific expectations of both the healthcare facility and the senior manager. Employment terminates at the end of the contract period. Both sides need to sign a new contract to continue employment.

Most employees are not senior level and will not be offered a contract. In place of a contract, you receive an offer of employment letter that states terms of employment. The letter contains your title, where you are going to work (for example, float pool, unit), shift, wages, and when to report to work. Terms of employment generally reflect the healthcare facility's contract with the bargaining unit, if your position is covered by the bargaining unit. You still abide by the bargaining unit contract even if you decide not to join the union (if permitted by law) as long as your position is a bargaining unit position.

You and the nurse recruiter may have some discretion to modify the standard terms of employment. Depending on your position and the healthcare facility's policies, this discretion may not exist or is very narrow. Assume that it exists and prepare to negotiate terms of employment at the appropriate time during the pre-employment process. You might be surprised that a barrier to employment for you isn't one for the nurse recruiter who can remove that barrier.

Decide the minimum terms of employment that you will accept and list them before meeting with the nurse recruiter. Also create a list of ideal terms of employment: the perfect job. For example, you have off every weekend in the perfect world; however you are willing to work every Sunday if you have off every Saturday because you have another job on Saturday that you need to keep. No weekends would be an ideal term. No Saturdays is a minimum term.

Minimum terms of employment are the "line in the sand" that you won't cross. This is your "walking away" point. The nurse recruiter also has minimum terms of employment or a "line in the sand" that won't be crossed — their "walking away" point. Don't waver on your minimum terms of employment and feel that you'll figure out something when the conflict occurs. The pre-employment period is where you identify and resolve conflicts, not after you begin work.

Ask the nurse recruiter toward the end of the initial interview to walk you through details of the pre-employment period, orientation, probation period, and remaining of the work year. Take good notes and refer to your notes when developing your minimum terms of employment and ideal terms of employment. For example, you might be expected to work the day shift during your orientation then change to the nightshift, which is your regular shift. This might conflict if you already have a day job and want this new job to be your second job.

Be assertive if your minimum terms of employment cannot be met. The job may not be a fit for your current situation. Your situation may change in the future and a similar position in the healthcare facility might be a fit, so you don't want to burn bridges. Plan to point out the conflict to the nurse recruiter at the appropriate time during the pre-employment process. Bring up the conflict sooner rather than later because the nurse recruiter doesn't want to spend time and money continuing with your pre-employment process if you already know there is a conflict that prevents you from accepting a job offer.

Prepare for the Online Pre-Employment Tests

Online medication administration tests that some healthcare facilities use during the pre-employment process follow the NCLEX style of questions. There are three parts to the question: the stem, the case, and the distractor. The stem is the portion that asks the question. The case describes the situation. The distractor is either a wrong answer or not the best answer. It is critical to identify these parts of the question before selecting a response.

Identify keywords or phrases in the stem of the question. There may be many words in the question but only one or two words that are important for answering the question. This helps to focus on the aspect of the problem that you need to address. Key words or phrases in the stem or a synonym may appear in the correct answer too.

Here are a few hints that may help narrow your focus on the likely answer to the question:
- Two answers that are opposite may imply that one of them is the correct answer.
- Absolute answers that use words such as all, always and never are typically incorrect.
- Answers that have the same concepts are likely incorrect. An answer that is different from other answers *may* be the correct answer.
- If at least two of the answers seem to be correct, then the "all of the above" choice is probably the correct answer.
- Calling the practitioner is usually the incorrect answer unless your nursing interventions have failed and there is nothing more you can do as a nurse.
- Remember that you need to assess the patient and collect data (that is, vital signs) before calling the practitioner.
- Know the difference between signs and symptoms of potential complications and signs and symptoms that are expected of the disease process. For example, a patient who is beginning antibiotic therapy will likely have a fever. This is not a complication.
- There are no patterns of correct answers. Question "A" might be the answer to the next five questions.
- When in doubt, choose the answer that focuses on patient safety.
- Choose your answers based on the perfect world and not the real world.

There will likely be questions requiring you to prioritize your response. These usually have words such as "first" or "initial." However, the question doesn't usually give you any clues on how to prioritize your response. You should be able to prioritize by using the ABCs, the nursing process, or Maslow's Hierarchy of Needs:
- The ABCs are airway, breathing, and circulation. If the patient's airway is obstructed and he or she is not breathing, or if the patient's heart or circulatory system is not functioning, then all other issues related to the patient are secondary. Focus on answers that don't involve the ABCs only if the patient is breathing and the patient's heart is working fine.
- The nursing process is assessment, diagnosis, planning, intervention, and evaluation (ADPIE). Remember that you must identify the problem and decide your response (assessment, diagnosis, planning) before you respond (intervention), and you need to determine if your response was appropriate (evaluation) before doing something else. The question may focus on one

part of the nursing process. Incorrect answers may focus on different parts of the nursing process.

— Maslow's Hierarchy of Needs is another suitable tool to use to help prioritize your actions. Physiological need (breathing, food, water, excretion) is top priority followed by safety. Next is the sense of belonging (friends, family) and then self-esteem (confidence, achievement, respect from others). The lowest priority is self-actualization (acceptance of facts, creativity, morality, problem solving).

Don't look for cookie-cutter accuracy when trying to apply ABCs, the nursing process, and/or Maslow's Hierarchy of Needs in answering a question that involves prioritizing. These are general guidelines that help to prioritize your actions. You are expected to apply your knowledge and not simply repeat facts. You are to find the *best* answer not the *right* answer.

Also remember the *rights* of medication administration if the question is on this topic. There are seven rights: right medication, right patient, right dose, right time, right route, right reason, and right documentation.

Remember to use the five "Ps" of assessing fractures if the stem involves a fracture. These are pain, pallor (poor circulation), pulselessness (poor circulation), paresthesia (burning or prickling sensation indicating a neurological problem), and paralysis.

Let's say a patient returns from surgery to her bed in the medical-surgical unit and you are her nurse. Before reading the stem, focus on what you know about surgery – any surgery. You want to assess the patient – check breathing, check level of consciousness, monitor vital signs, make sure there is no bleeding at the surgery site or internally, make sure that the patient is not in pain, take precautions to prevent blood clots (that is, apply the leg massaging pump), elevate the head of the bed (if appropriate), check for normal capillary refill and relatively normal color, note the presence of a pedal pulse. Next read the stem and the case. The answer may involve following the standard nursing process following surgery.

Understand what is normal for the patient at that time by determining the timeline before answering the question. An answer may be irrelevant depending on the time. For example, you would expect your patient to be in pain 24-hours following surgery but probably not five days after surgery. Pain days after surgery may indicate that the patient is experiencing complications.

Eliminate two answers that don't seem to involve post-surgery care, then focus on the remaining two answers. Think of each question as a true or false statement. If the statement is true, related to the surgery, and seems to answer the stem, then you've found the correct answer. If the statement is false, then the remaining question is the correct answer. Any exception to the stem indicates that the answer is likely incorrect.

Don't overanalyze the question. Don't assume facts not stated in the question. Usually the most comprehensive, therapeutic, age appropriate, reasonable and patient-centered answer that is within the nurse's role is correct. Strange answers that are exceptions to common nursing practice are likely incorrect answers. The obvious answer or the answer that will cause the least harm to the patient is likely the correct answer.

Pre-employment tests usually don't ask multiple-choice type questions where you are expected to select possible answers to the question from a list of items. However, you should be prepared to answer such a question should one appear on the test. Keep in mind that selecting one incorrect item or failing to select one correct item will make your answer incorrect regardless of whether you correctly select others on the list. A good approach is to focus on each item individually, asking if the statement is true or false based on the stem.

Prep for the Technical Interview

In addition to being prepared for pre-employment tests on your nursing knowledge, you'll need to prepare for technical interviews by the hiring nurse managers and other staff who want to learn the level of your nursing knowledge. Technical interviews are informal. Questions may not be formally vetted for clarity and accuracy. You can be asked anything about nursing. And your response to questions may be subjectively evaluated. You don't know what is a passing score, the interviewer may not have defined a passing grade either. Passing might be the overall impression that you leave with the interviewer.

Challenging as a technical interview may seem, you still have to prepare to answer questions to the best of your abilities — and your best may not be adequate to pass the technical interview, especially if you are an inexperienced nurse. You are probably an excellent nurse, but it might have been a while since you've been quizzed on details (by the book) of nursing. You likely take shortcuts that pose no harm to the patient but you wouldn't pass muster if your nursing supervisor, or nurse professor, was watching you.

Furthermore, you have no clue as to what you might be asked. The remaining chapters of this book will help you prepare for both technical pre-employment tests and technical interviews. Questions tend to focus on critical thinking skills and patient safety rather than fine details of nursing procedures or medications.

You probably know the answers, you might simply need something to jog your memory. You'll find those memory-joggers in the next few chapters.

Chapter 7 focuses on medication and medication administration. Four types of medication commonly administered on practically all types of units are reviewed. These are antihypertension medication, diabetic medication, antibiotics, and pain medication. In addition, you'll review the basics of safe medication administration. Chapter 8 concentrates on nursing skills.

Part Two: **Key Facts Every Candidate Should Know**

Part Two is an overview—a big cheat sheet or memory jogger—of what you may be expected to know in the interviews. It is a simple review of over 2,500 topics and facts that you are expected to know as a nurse. For ease of use, Part 2 is broken into chapters on medication types and body systems.

Chapter 7
Preparing for Medication Questions

There is a saying that only the two elderly nurses who make up NCLEX questions know what you'll be asked on the nursing boards – not your instructor or authors of NCLEX prep books. There aren't two elderly nurses who make up NCLEX questions; however, NCLEX questions, of course, aren't shared with your instructor or an author of NCLEX prep books. Likewise, only the interviewer and the test preparers know the medication questions that you'll be asked during the pre-employment process.

Throughout this chapter, you will review the kinds of questions (and answers) that cover topics that you might be asked by a nurse manager or find on a pre-employment medication administration test. This chapter reviews medication topics helping you to brush up on some basics that may have slipped your mind. This is a good way to prepare for your pre-employment medication questioning.

You Don't Need to Be a Genius

You will need to be prepared to be asked questions about medications during interviews with the nurse manager. Some healthcare facilities require that you pass an online medication administration test even before you meet with the nurse manager. One thing is for certain: there are no standards when it comes to quizzing you about medication. In fact, you may be lucky and have no one challenge your knowledge about medication until you begin your job orientation.

There may be general questions about medication and medication administration and then there may be questions that focus on medications that you administer in a specialty area, if this is a requirement for your job. The format of the questions may range from a simple one formulated by the nurse manager or more complex (NCLEX) online questions supplied by a vendor.

Don't panic! You probably know the answer. Nurse managers tend to ask questions related to patient safety rather than those that require knowledge of obscure facts about medications. For example, the nurse manager may ask you how you administered Lopressor. The nurse manager is looking for more than making sure you have the right patient, the right medication, the right time, the right dose, and the right route. That's a given, especially since many healthcare facilities use an electronic medication administration record (eMAR) system that checks this for you. Think safety. The nurse manager is hoping you say that you'll

DOI 10.1515/9781501506109-007

take the patient's blood pressure before administering Lopressor. Lopressor is a medication that lowers blood pressure. You want to be sure that the patient's blood pressure isn't low already. Giving Lopressor in that case may cause the patient to fall.

Listen carefully to each question asked by the nurse manager. The question may not be as precisely worded as an NCLEX question. Ask the nurse manager if she can restate the question if you don't understand it. You, too, can restate the question before answering to ensure that you understood it.

Rather than give a brief textbook answer, walk through a clinical situation that you experienced, highlighting the problem mentioned in the question, and then explain how you handled the situation. For example, you might say that you once had a patient who had relatively unstable blood pressure. You made sure to take the patient's blood pressure before each administration of Lopressor because sometimes the medication had to be held since the patient's blood pressure was low. You might also say that you make these standing procedures before administering any medication that affects blood pressure. Walking through a clinical situation when answering a question gives you an opportunity to share your critical thinking abilities with the nurse manager.

Walking through a clinical scenario is also a good approach to take when you are unsure of what the nurse manager is looking for in the answer. The walkthrough may satisfy the nurse manager because somewhere during the walkthrough you answered the nurse manager's question. Even if you don't specifically answer the question, the walkthrough may provide the nurse manager with sufficient insight into your nursing skills.

Each nurse manager establishes her own criteria when selecting the ideal candidate for the position. You don't know what medication questions – if any – will be asked. You don't know how the nurse manager will evaluate your problem-solving ability. You don't know the passing grade except on a medication online test.

The nurse manager is likely evaluating how you approach solving the question and is less concerned that you use the perfect language or recite policy and procedures. Can you think on your feet? Are you focused on patient safety? How do you compare with other candidates who might have been asked the same questions?

Expect that some questions can be vague or difficult to answer. As a result, you might give the wrong answer. Typically, the nurse manager may give you additional information (hints) that get your thoughts back on track. Don't take this as a negative. Other candidates may have needed help answering the question. What is important is how you handle incorrect questions. That is, how many hints do you need before you answer correctly?

Also expect that you'll sometimes answer questions incorrectly. That's okay too. Rarely does anyone answer all questions correctly. Be honest and tell the nurse manager that you are unsure of the answer, however, also state how you would find the answer if you were on the unit. This shows how you would solve problems in real life. Doing so changes an incorrect response – not knowing the answer – to a correct response – how you would find the answer.

Online Medication Tests

You may have to take an online medication administration test prior to employment as a way for the healthcare facility to remove unqualified candidates from the mix before time and money is spent on the interview process. Online medication administration tests are more structured and more predictable than medication questions asked during interviews because typically online tests are provided by a vendor.

Some healthcare facilities use vendors that supply nursing schools with exit exams. In fact, the pre-employment online medication administration test is likely to have elements of the exit exam used by nursing schools. This is a good thing if you are a recent graduate because you have recent testing skills and the content is fresh in your mind. The test might be a challenge for experienced nurses who haven't prepped for a medication administration test in years.

Don't assume that you can whiz through the online medication administration test because you administer hundreds of medications per month to your patients. Some healthcare facilities report that more nurses fail than pass their online medication administration test. It is not that they are asked about strange medications – nearly all medications on the test are the basic meds that you find in a typical medical-surgical unit. The problem is that experienced nurses don't prepare for the test.

Vendors tend to use NCLEX-type multiple-choice questions where two answers are wrong and two answers are correct – one more correct than the other. You may also find medication calculation questions, which can frustrate experienced nurses, since many healthcare facilities use single-dose medication. Nurses rarely calculate the medication dose and some healthcare facilities have policies that prohibit nurses from calculating doses, leaving the calculation to the pharmacist.

The margin of safety is identified by the Therapeutic Index (TI) and determines the safe range of dose levels. The TI is a ratio that compares the blood concentration at which a drug becomes toxic and the concentration at which the drug is effective. A TI closer to 1 indicates danger of toxicity. The level of medication in the bloodstream is measured with a trough level. A sample of blood is drawn right before the next dose is to be administered to the patient. The trough level indicates if the medication is near the toxic level and also indicates the rate at which the medication is excreted from the body.

A medication contains active and inactive ingredients. The active ingredient provides the therapeutic effect and the inactive ingredient is commonly referred to as a filler and has no therapeutic effect. For example, inactive ingredients include the enteric coating around a time-release capsule that delays the onset of therapeutic effect.

Medication directly enters the bloodstream through intravenous injection. Other routes require that medication be absorbed before the medication enters the bloodstream. Medication attaches to a target receptor sites in the body where the medication provides a therapeutic benefit (*primary effect*). Some medications attach to non-targeted receptor sites resulting in a side effect (*secondary effect*) or an adverse side effect. For example, the primary effect of Benadryl is to reduce allergy symptoms. A side effect of Benadryl is drowsiness. A rare adverse side effect of Benadryl is blurred vision.

Once in the bloodstream, medications typically bind to proteins (albumin or globulins) in plasma that carry the medication throughout the body. Most, but not all, medications are delivered to the liver where the medication is metabolized (called the *first pass*). The active ingredient is returned to the bloodstream where it is carried to receptor sites in areas of the body that require therapeutic treatment. The inactive ingredients (metabolites) are returned to the bloodstream where they are carried to the kidneys for excretion. Some inactive ingredients are also excreted in bile.

Here are elements of absorption that you should keep in mind during your interview:

- Absorption usually occurs in the small intestine when the medication is given orally
- Tissue absorbs medication when medication is given sublingually (under the tongue) or buccally (between the gum and the cheek.) Sublingual and buccal administration bypass the first pass
- The skin absorbs medication when administered transdermally (the patch)
- Subcutaneous injection has a slow absorption rate
- Intramuscular injection has fast absorption and bypasses the first pass

- Inhalation medications are absorbed by lung tissue
- Intravenous injection has instant absorption in the bloodstream and by-passes the first pass

Facts to Remember

- Up to 40% of medications administered orally are bioavailable (enter the bloodstream). The remaining medication is impaired through the absorption process. In contrast, 100% of intravenous medication is bioavailable.
- Oral medications have typically four times the dose of intravenous medication to compensate for the relatively low bioavailability.
- Absorption rate and metabolism can be impaired by:
    o Poorly functioning intestine
    o Liver disease
    o Kidney disease
    o Impaired blood flow may decrease circulation of medication and circulation to organs
    o Food can slow or block absorption of some medication
- The deltoid muscle has more blood vessels and absorbs medication faster than the gluteal muscle.
- Subcutaneous tissues have fewer blood vessels than muscle and absorb medication more slowly than muscle.
- Free medication that is absorbed but not bound to a receptor site may result in toxicity.
- Low levels of plasma protein (malnourishment) may increase free medication in the bloodstream.
- Low levels of fat tissue may increase free medication for medications that attach to receptors in fat tissue for storage.
- Two or more medications (Inderal and Warfarin) may compete for the same receptor site in the body leading to increased free medication in the bloodstream.
- Dialysis can be used to increase excretion of medication in an emergency.
- Children have an immature liver that may affect metabolism of medication.
- Geriatric patients may have diminished liver, kidney, and circulation function that may affect metabolism of medication.
- The patient's metabolism (fast/slow) may affect the therapeutic effect of medication. A fast metabolism may fail to give the medication time to work before the medication is excreted. A slow metabolism may cause a backup of

         o   Fentanyl: chest, flank or upper arm
- Date, time, and initial the patch.

Topical Medication

- Topical medication has a local effect.
- Apply using a glove, cotton-tipped applicator, or tongue blade.
- Stroke topical medication firmly on the skin.
- If skin is broken or burned, use a clean or sterile technique when applying medication.
- Make the patient comfortable when medication is applied to painful areas.

Eye Drop Medication

- Have the patient look toward the ceiling.
- Pull down the skin below the eye exposing the conjunctival sac.
- Administer the appropriate number of drops in the center of the conjunctival sac.
- Don't touch the dropper to the eyelids or eyelashes.
- Release the skin. Pressure the inner corner of the eye (lacrimal duct) with a sterile cotton ball or tissues for two minutes. This prevents medication from being absorbed through the lacrimal canal.

Eye Ointment Medication

- Have the patient look towards the ceiling.
- Pull down the skin below the eye exposing the conjunctival sac.
- Squeeze a half-inch of ointment into the conjunctival sac. Don't place medication on the cornea. This may damage the cornea and cause discomfort to the patient.
- The patient may experience temporary blurred visions.
- Keep eyes closed for two minutes.

Ear Drop Medication

- Tilt head slightly toward the unaffected side.
- Pull auricle (earlobe) up and back for patients three years and older and down for patients under three years to straighten the external ear canal.
- Drop medication into the ear.
- Don't touch the ear with the dropper to avoid contamination.
- The head should be tilted for three minutes.

Nose Drop Medication

- Ask the patient to blow his nose.
- If the infection is in the frontal sinus, then tilt the patient's head back.
- If the infection is in the ethmoid sinus, then place the patient's head to the affected side.
- Administer the drops.
- Place the patient's head backwards for five minutes after administering the medication.

Nose Spray Medication

- Ask the patient to close the unaffected nostril.
- Tilt the patient head to the side of the closed nostril.
- Spray the medication.
- The patient should open the closed nostril or briefly hold his breath depending on manufacturer's instructions.

Inhalation Medication

- Hand-held nebulizer inhalers change liquid medication to a fine spray, while a push-button-activated hand-held metered dose inhaler sprays the medication into the patient's mouth.
- Inhalers deliver 9% of the medication to the lungs. A spacer is used with an inhaler to deliver 21% of medications to the lungs. The spacer is a funnel-like device that attaches to the mouthpiece of a metered dose inhaler.

- Patients should inhale slowly and deeply so the medication fully enters the patient's lungs.
- Place the patient in a semi- or high-Fowler's position (sitting up).
- Wait two minutes between puffs if a hand-held metered dose inhaler is used.
- Rinse the patient's mouth with water to prevent oral fungal infections if a steroid inhalant is administered to the patient.

Nasogastric and Gastrostomy Tube Medication

- Used for patients who are unable to swallow or ingest orally.
- Nasogastric tubes pass through the nose into the stomach allowing medication and food to be placed into the stomach and to remove the stomach contents using suction.
- Gastrostomy tubes are inserted directly through the skin into the stomach to form a permanent feeding tube.
- Before administering medications, make sure that the tube is patent.
- Open the clamp on the tube.
- Inject 20 mL of air into the tube as you listen for the air entering the stomach.
- Aspirate the contents of the stomach and test the pH level of the contents. A pH ≤5.5 indicates that the tube is in the proper position.
- Remove the plunger from the syringe.
- Pour the medication into the syringe.
- Flush the tube with 30 mL of water.
- Close the clamp and remove the syringe.

Suppository Medication

- Used when the upper GI tract is not functioning or when digestive enzymes change the medication.
- The rectum contains a vast network of blood vessels.
- Provide privacy for the patient.
- Place the patient in the Sims' position (lying on the left side).
- Wash hands, apply gloves, and lubricate the suppository as necessary.
- Ask the patient to break wind to relax the anal sphincter.
- Insert the suppository.
- The patient should remain in the Sims position for 20 minutes.

Intradermal Injection

- Intradermal injection is commonly used for the Mantoux tuberculin test.
- Injection sites are inner forearm, scapular area of the back, Medial thigh or the upper chest.
- Use a 26- or 27-gauge needle with a 1 mL syringe that is calibrated in increments of 0.01 mL.
- Clean the injection site with alcohol or betadine.
- Hold skin taut.
- Position the bevel of the needle up.
- Insert the needle at a 10 to 15-degree angle so you can see the needle through the skin. Medication does not enter the bloodstream.
- Slowly form a wheal and remove the needle.
- Don't massage the injection site.
- Assess the site 48 to 72 hours after the injection.

Subcutaneous Injection

- Used for medications that need to be absorbed slowly, such as insulin and heparin.
- Injection sites are: abdomen, upper hips, upper back, lateral upper arms, and lateral thighs.
- Use a 25- to 27-gauge needle 1/2 or 5/8 inches in length and a 1 to 3 mL syringe. The syringe should be calibrated 0.5 to 1.5 mL. Syringes used for insulin are calibrated in *units*.
- Clean the injection site with alcohol.
- Pinch the skin.
- Insert the needle at a 45 to 90-degree angle – the smaller degree is best for a patient with a small amount of subcutaneous tissue.
- Release the skin.
- Inject the medication slowly
- Remove the needle quickly.
- Massage the injection site unless the medication heparin is injected.

Intramuscular Injection

- Medication is rapidly absorbed.
- There should be no more than 3 mL of medication delivered in the same injection.
- Select the injection site based on the size of the muscle and minimum of nerves and blood vessels at the site.
- Injection sites: Ventrogluteal (hip), Dorsogluteal (buttocks), Deltoid (upper arm), or Vastus lateralis (front of thigh).
- Use a 20- to 23-gauge needle 1 to 1.5 inches in length. The syringe should be 1 to 3 mL and calibrated with 0.5 to 1.5 mL.
- Clean the injection site with alcohol
- Flatten the skin with your thumb and index finger.
- Insert the needle at a 90-degree angle into the muscle.
- Release the skin.
- Slowly inject the medication.
- Quickly remove the needle.
- Massage the area unless not recommended by the medication manufacturer.

Z-Track Injection

- Used to prevent medication (for example, dextran iron) from leaking back into the subcutaneous tissue of where the medication is injected that might result in permanent skin discoloration.
- Clean the injection site with alcohol.
- Pull and hold the skin to one side.
- Insert the needle at a 90-degree angle.
- Inject the medication.
- Withdraw the needle.
- Release the skin.

Intravenous Injections

- Provides rapid onset of the medication.
- Insert the intravenous catheter (butterfly needle, angiocatheter) in the cephalic vein in the arm or the dorsal vein in the hand. Start with the hand, then work towards the cubital vein.

- Avoid the cubital vein except in emergencies since the cubital vein is used for drawing blood specimens.
- Use a 14-gauge intravenous catheter for whole blood and 23-gauge for rapid infusion.
- Medication may be directly injected into a vein using a 21- to 23-gauge needle 1 to 1.5 inches in length. Use the larger needle for more viscous medications.
- Clean the insertion site based on hospital protocol.
- Apply a tourniquet above the site.
- Insert the intravenous catheter until there is a blood return.
- Remove the tourniquet.
- Dress the intravenous catheter per hospital protocol.
- Monitor the site:
  - Skin color (redness)
  - Infiltration (swelling)
  - Distal pulse
  - Skin temperature
- Flush the intravenous catheter before and after administering an IV push medication.

Before Administering Medications

You know how to give medication to a patient but over the years some nurses – not you – may deviate from the proper way to administer them. Let's say that the way some nurses gave medication in front of your nursing instructor during clinicals is not exactly the way some nurses give medication today. It is not that the medication is administered incorrectly but some factors are assumed to be correct and, therefore, not verified unless something goes amiss. It is probably best to describe how you gave medication during your clinicals if asked during your pre-employment interviews with the nurse manager. Let's review the basics.

Make sure the medication order is valid. Each order must have:
- Date and time
- Name of the medication
- Dose
- Route of administration
- Frequency of administration
- Duration that the patient is to receive the medication
- Signature of the prescriber
- When administering the medication make sure you:
- Have the right patient

- Are administering the medication at the right time
- Have the right medication
- Know why the medication is prescribed
- Know the symptoms the patient exhibits
- Know the expected outcome of taking the medication
- Know how the medication is absorbed, distributed, metabolized, and eliminated. Current status of the patient may have changed since the order was written, making the medication contraindicated.
- Know onset and peak times of the medication
- Know side effects and adverse side effects of the medication (know what signs and symptoms must be monitored)
- Is the medication available?
- Has the medication expired?
- Is it the right dose?
- Is it the right route? (The patient's current status may indicate that a route different from the order is necessary.)
- Know and assess for contraindications for administering the medication.

Things to Remember

- Reference recent vital signs and labs before administering medication to assess the patient's current status
- Identify patient allergies
- Wash hands before administering medication
- *Never* administer medication prepared by someone else
- Tell the patient the name of the medication and why the patient is receiving the medication before administering it
- Show the medication to the patient. Stop immediately if the patient doesn't recognize the medication. You may have the wrong medication or the pharmacy switched vendors and the medication looks different but is still the medication ordered by the practitioner.
- Explain the possible side effects to the patient.
- The patient has the right to refuse the medication. Notify the practitioner if the patient refuses to take the medication.
- Stay with the patient until the medication is swallowed.
- Monitor the patient for the therapeutic effect, side effects, and adverse side effects.
- Wash hands after administering the medication.

- Chart that the medication was administered.
- Reassess the patient within an hour of administering the medication if this was the initial dose of the medication or if it was a PRN medication. Document your reassessment, especially whether or not symptoms subsided in the case of a PRN medication.
- Don't recap needles.
- Place needles and syringes in a sharpie container.
- Dispose of wasted medication according to hospital policy. Have another nurse witness and document waste of a controlled substance.

Experienced nurses implement tricks of the trade that make administering medication efficient. Here are some of the ones you may want to bring up during your interview with the nurse manager.

- Give ice chips before administering bad tasting medication since ice chips numb the taste buds. Also give bad tasting medication first and then pleasant tasting medication to shorten the duration of the bad taste.
- Administer medication last to patients who require extra help with the medication.
- Replace the needle after withdrawing medication from a vial with a new needle. Withdrawing medication may damage the needle.
- Ask the patient to relax before inserting the needle to reduce pain when giving an injection.
- Avoid injecting into hardened tissue or sensitive tissues.

Remember that the nurse manager is likely to focus on safety during the interview. Try to interject into the conversation procedures that you use to avoid medication errors. Here are common ways to prevent medication errors:

- Avoid distraction when preparing medication
- Pour medications from clearly marked containers
- Open single-dose packages in front of the patient after telling the patient about the medication
- *Never* guess at the name of the medication or dose if you cannot understand the medication order
- Avoid administering medications that appear different than normal (that is, discolored, cloudy)
- Don't leave medication by the patient's bedside
- *You* administer the medication – not the patient, visitors, or unlicensed staff
- Hold the medication if the patient states the he is allergic to the medication
- Identify the patient by name and date of birth – and electronically if available

– Notify the charge nurse and practitioner immediately upon recognizing that a medication error has occurred and document appropriately

Common Medications That Are Helpful to Know

It's not feasible to memorize facts on all medications that might be asked about in your pre-employment interview. There are simply too many medications, most of which would never come up in the interview or on the pre-employment medication test. You should, however, review medications that are commonly prescribed in your specialty if you are applying for a similar position at another healthcare facility. For example, brushing up on facts about cardiac-related medications is probably a good move if you are applying to work on a cardiac unit.

There are four types of medications – antihypertensive medication, diabetic medication, antibiotics, and pain medication – that are commonly administered on virtually all units, which is why we'll take a few moments to review these medications. This review focuses on patient safety, safe medication administration, and patient education.

Hypertension Medication

Medication prescribed for hypertension lowers blood pressure. Make sure that you assess the patient's blood pressure before you administer any medication that may affect blood pressure – including medications that are prescribed for purposes other than hypertension – that may lower blood pressure.

Diuretics

Diuretics are often the first choice to lower blood pressure because diuretics cause the kidneys to increase elimination of sodium and water, resulting in decreased blood volume and the relaxing of blood pressure walls.
– Thiazide diuretics (HCT, Maxzide) are usually prescribed with another hypertensive medication
– Quinazoline diuretics (Metolazone, Zaroxolyn) are used for patients who have kidney problems or when other diuretics have not worked
– Loop diuretics (Lasix, furosemide, bumetanide, Demadex) are used for patients who have kidney problems, heart failure, or for swollen legs as a result of heart failure

- Potassium-sparing diuretics (Aldactazide, Aldactone) are used for patients who have low potassium levels
- Safety issues to consider:
- Difficulty breathing and swelling may indicate that the medication needs adjustment. Hold the medication and notify the practitioner immediately.
- Confusion, muscle cramps, or an irregular heartbeat may indicate a change in potassium level. Diuretics, except for potassium-sparing diuretics, may cause a decrease in potassium. The practitioner may order that the patient take a potassium supplement.
- Dry mouth or increased thirst may indicate dehydration as a result of loss of fluids and require a medication adjustment and rehydration.
- Make sure that the patient is able to safely go to the toilet since the patient will experience increased urination especially when the patient begins taking the medication.

Consider asking the practitioner to modify the schedule for taking hypertension medication if increased urination interferes with the patient's lifestyle, especially for patients who tend to skip a dose when it is inconvenient to urinate.

Non-diuretic medication is also use for hypertension and is sometimes administered along with a diuretic medication. Commonly prescribed non-diuretic medications are:

- Beta blockers (Lopressor, Corgard, Inderal, Sectral, Tenormin) relax blood vessels, decreasing the workload of the heart. This results in decreased heart rhythm and decreased force of blood flow. Beta blockers are more effective when combined with other antihypertensive medications.
- Angiotensin-converting enzyme (ACE) inhibitors (Zestril, Capoten, Accupril, Monopril) block angiotensin-converting enzyme which forms chemicals that narrow blood vessels, as a result blood vessels relax.
- Angiotensin II receptor blockers (ARBs) (Cozaar, Micardis, Diovan, Benicar, Avapro) prevents the action of chemicals that narrow blood vessels.
- Calcium channel blockers (Norvasc, Cardizem, Calan, Felodipine) prevent calcium from entering the cells of blood vessel walls, causing muscles in arterial walls to relax and resulting in the widening of blood vessels.
- Renin inhibitors (Tekturna, Aliskiren) decrease production of renin. Renin is an enzyme produced in the kidneys that causes increased blood pressure.
- Alpha blockers (Minipress, Cardura) reduce nerve impulses to blood vessels, resulting in the widening of blood vessels.
- Alpha-beta blockers (Coreg, Trandate) combine the effects of alpha and beta blockers by reducing nerve impulses to narrow blood vessels and reduce the

heartbeat, this decreases the amount of blood pumped through blood vessels.
- Central-acting agents (Catapres, Intuniv, Methyldopa) inhibit the nervous system from increasing the heart rate and narrowing blood vessels.
- Vasodilators (Hydralazine, Minoxidil) relax muscles in arterial walls, preventing the narrowing of arteries.

Medications That Interfere with Hypertensive Medications

- Pain medication (indomethacin, Indocin, and anti-inflammatory (Naproxen, Aleve, Ibuprofen, Advil, Motrin) medications) may cause the patient to retain water resulting in increased blood pressure.
- Antidepressants (Prozac, Sarafem, fluoxetine, Effector) may increase blood pressure.
- Birth control pills and hormonal birth control devices may increase blood pressure.
- Caffeine may increase blood pressure temporarily.
- Decongestants (Sudafed, Neo-Synephrine) narrows blood vessels, resulting in increased blood pressure.
- Herbal supplements (Ginkgo, Ginseng, St. John's Wort, Senna) can increase blood pressure.

Always be prepared to answer questions relative to what a nurse can do to care for a patient diagnosed with hypertension. A good response is to educate the patient on non-medication methods of lowering blood pressure. These include:
- The *Dietary Approaches to Stop Hypertension* (DASH) diet is a lifestyle change that emphasizes eating fruits, vegetables, whole grains, poultry, fish, low-fat dairy products, and potassium-containing foods.
- Decrease salt intake to no more than 1,500 milligrams per day. Don't use the salt shaker. Be aware of salt contained in processed foods.
- Decrease intake of saturated fat and trans fats.
- Lose weight, if the patient is overweight.
- Don't smoke.
- Exercise regularly. At least three hours of moderate aerobic activity weekly.
- Decrease stress.
- Limit alcohol use.

Some Facts to Remember

– Normal blood pressure is 120/80 (systolic over diastolic).
– Hypertensive crisis is systolic pressure equal to or greater than 180 millimeters of mercury or a diastolic pressure equal to or greater than 120 millimeters of mercury. This may also include headache, confusion, blurred vision, nausea/vomiting, shortness of breath, and severe anxiety.
– Low blood pressure is systolic pressure lower than 90 millimeters of mercury or diastolic pressure lower than 60 millimeters of mercury. This may result in dizziness or fainting. Severe low blood pressure may result in poor perfusion of organs.
– Take the patient's blood pressure before administering any medication that will lower blood pressure. Hold the medication if blood pressure is less than 90 mm systolic or less than 60 mm diastolic. Also hold the medication if the heartrate is less than 60.
– Always consult with the practitioner if you held a patient's medication that would lower the patient's blood pressure (medication other than antihypertensive medications lower blood pressure). For example, Librium lowers blood pressure and can be prescribed to prevent seizures. The practitioner may want the patient who had moderately low blood pressure to receive the scheduled dose of Librium to prevent seizures. The practitioner may have the patient lie in bed for several hours after taking Librium to prevent the patient from falling related to moderately low blood pressure.
– If blood pressure is marginally low, ask the patient to drink water and walk around (assuming the patient isn't dizzy). This will increase blood pressure.

Diabetic Medications

Medications for diabetes is another area where you might be asked questions during the pre-employment process because diabetic medication is commonly prescribed and may lead to patient safety issues if improperly administered to the patient. There are two types of diabetic medications. These are for Type I diabetes, an autoimmune disease where the body is unable to produce insulin, and Type II, where the body is making insufficient insulin or is unable to use the insulin that is made by the body.

Blood glucose levels vary throughout the day. A patient who does not have diabetes will have a blood glucose level under 100 mg/dl when they awaken. Before meals the patient should experience blood glucose level of 70 – 99 mg/dl (3.9 – 5.5 mmol/L). Two hours after meals, blood glucose should be less than

140 mg/dl (7.8 mmol/L). In contrast, a patient who has diabetes will have a blood glucose level between 80 – 130 mg/dl (4.5 – 72 mmol/L) when they awaken and less than 180 mg/dl (10 mmol/L) two hours after their meal.

Insulin

Insulin is injected as replacement for the patient's own insulin when they have Type 1 diabetes because the patient is unable to make insulin. There are a number of insulin types. The choice depends on the severity of the insulin depletion. Some patients are prescribed a combination of insulins that are identified by percentages such as Humulin 70/30, which is a mixture of human insulin intermediate-acting (NPH) and human insulin regular.

Amylinomimetic medication (pramlintide, SymlinPen) is sometimes prescribed for patients diagnosed with Type I diabetes. Amylinomimetic medication delays emptying of the stomach, resulting in decreased glucagon secretion after meals, leading to lower blood glucose levels. Glucagon is a hormone produced by the pancreas that raises blood glucose levels.

- Short-acting (regular insulin, Humulin, Novolin) has on onset of 30 to 45 minutes and peaks between 2 hours and 3.5 hours.
- Rapid-Acting (aspart, NovoLog, FlexPen, glulisine, Apidra, lispro, Humalog) has an onset of 1 hour to 3 hours and peaks between 4 hours and 9 hours.
- Intermediate-acting (NPH) insulin (isophane, Humulin N, Novolin N) has on onset of 1 to 20 minutes and peaks between 1.5 and 2.5 hours.
- Long-acting insulin (degludec, Tresiba, insulin detemir, Levemir, glargine, Lantus, Toujeo) has on onset of 1 hour to 3 hours and peaks between 6 hours and 10 hours.

Type 2 Diabetic Medication

The purpose of Type 2 diabetic medication is to decrease blood glucose levels by making better use of existing insulin. Typically, Type 2 diabetic medication is taken orally and not injected. Some patients are prescribed a combination of Type 2 diabetic medications.

- Alpha-glucosidase Inhibitors (acarbose, Precose, miglitol, Glyst) assist the body in metabolizing table sugar and starchy foods.
- Biguanides (Fortamet, Metformin, Glucophage, Glumetza, Riomet) decrease glucose absorption by the intestine, decrease glucose production by the liver,

and increase glucose absorption by muscles. Biguanides also makes cells more sensitive to insulin.

– Dopamine agonist (bromocriptine, Parlodel) reduces the resistance to insulin by cells.

– DPP-4 inhibitors (sitaglipin, Januvia, alogliptin-metformin, Kazano) increase insulin production by the pancreas and lowers blood glucose without causing hypoglycemia.

– Glucagon-like peptides (Bydureon, Tanzeum, Byetta) are metabolic hormones called incretin that stimulate insulin secretion whenever food is ingested leading to an increased production of insulin by the pancreas.

– Meglitinides (Prandin, Prandimet, Starlix) increases the release of insulin by the pancreas; however, there may be a tendency for over-production of insulin resulting in hypoglycemia.

– Sodium Glucose Co-Transporter-2 inhibitors (SGLT2) (Farxiga, Jardiance, Invokana) increase glucose excretion by the kidneys.

– Sulfonylureas (Glucotrol, DiaBeta, Diabinese, Metaglip) stimulates the pancreas to increase insulin production.

– Thiazolidinediones (Actos, Duetact, Amaryl M, Avandia) decrease glucose in the liver and increase the use of insulin by adipose cells. There is an increased risk of heart disease with these medications.

Some Facts to Remember

– Blood glucose levels are raised shortly after meals and gradually return to normal levels if the patient is not diabetic.

– Patients who have Type I diabetes typically require insulin injections to help the body return to normal blood glucose levels.

– Always draw "clear" regular insulin first before "cloudy" insulin when mixing insulin in the same syringe to prevent the "cloudy" intermediate-acting (NPH) insulin from entering the "clear" insulin vial.

– Rotate the insulin injection sites to prevent development of hard lumps or fat deposits at the site.

– Rapid-acting and regular insulin are used to cover meals and lower periods of high levels of blood glucose that may occur.

– Intermediate-acting insulin and long-acting insulin are used to maintain blood glucose levels throughout the day.

- Rapid-acting or short-acting insulin should be administered 15 minutes before the patient eats. The patient may experience hypoglycemia if insulin is administered earlier.
- If insulin is taken 15 minutes before eating high-fat foods such as pizza, blood glucose levels may drop immediately then rapidly increase hours later once the body absorbs and metabolizes the food.
- Exercise lowers blood glucose levels.
- Patients who have Type II diabetes usually use oral diabetic medications to maintain a relatively normal blood glucose level.
- Hyperglycemia:
   - Normal blood glucose level range is 90 – 160 mg/dl
   - Blood glucose level range of 240 – 300 mg/dl may indicate diabetes is out of control.
   - Diabetic ketoacidosis (DKA) is when the body breaks down stored fat because there is insufficient blood glucose to supply muscles and ketones build up in the body and appear in urine. Diabetic ketoacidosis can lead to diabetic coma. This may be the first sign of Type I diabetes. The patient may have thirst that lasts for days resulting in frequent urination. The patient may also have a fruity smell to their breath. Treat with insulin injection.
   - Diabetic hyperosmolar syndrome (HSS) occurs when the blood glucose level is 600 mg/dl (3.33 mmol/L) or higher, resulting in the blood becoming syrupy. The patient may become dehydrated as fluid is brought into blood vessels from other areas of the body and can lead to diabetic coma. Treat with insulin injection.
- Hypoglycemia:
   - A blood glucose level below 70 mg/dl indicates hypoglycemia.
   - The patient may feel hungry, shaky, sweating, and have tachycardia symptoms.
   - Give the patient glucose tablets, orange juice with two packs of sugar added, two sugar lumps, two teaspoons of granulated sugar, or hard candy if the patient is conscious.
   - Give the patient I.V. 75 – 90 ml 20% glucose. If I.V. access cannot be established, then give glucagon 1 mg IM or SC.
   - Mental confusion, antagonistic behaviors, unconsciousness, or seizures are signs of life-threatening hypoglycemia.

o Hypoglycemia may be from too much diabetic medication being administered to the patient or from vigorous exercise or drinking too much alcohol.

o Hypoglycemia is more serious than hyperglycemia because the body has insufficient glucose to maintain bodily functions.

- Brittle diabetes is usually Type I diabetes that is difficult to control, leading to blood glucose levels rapidly spiking and then dropping unpredictably leading to dramatic symptoms. Patients typically receive insulin by a subcutaneous insulin pump.
- Some patients with brittle diabetes may experience severe hypoglycemia when they are sleeping. As a result, the patient may be unable to awaken. Checking blood glucose on a schedule during sleeping hours – even if the patient has to be awakened – may be necessary.

Antibiotics

Antibiotics are another area of medication that you might be questioned about during your pre-employment interview and testing. Don't expect questions about prescribing antibiotics unless you are applying for a nurse practitioner's position. Questions will likely focus on patient safety, managing side effects of the medication, and patient education.

Typically, a practitioner will order a broad-spectrum antibiotic when the practitioner suspects that the patient has a relatively common bacterial infection. A culture and sensitivity test will also be ordered as a precaution if the broad-spectrum antibiotic doesn't work. The culture and sensitivity test identifies the bacteria and identifies antibiotics that kill the particular bacteria. It is critical that the specimen for the culture be taken before the patient receives the antibiotic otherwise the antibiotic may kill the bacteria before the bacteria is cultured. Also make sure that you follow hospital policies for taking samples (that is, use the clean catch method for sampling urine). A contaminated sample invalidates the culture and sensitivity test.

Facts to Remember

- The patient may experience common side effects of soft stool, diarrhea, or mild stomach upset. Administering probiotics or yogurt may reduce diarrhea.
- Some antibiotics should be taken on an empty stomach and others with food. Be sure to follow the manufacturer's instructions.

- Hold the antibiotic and contact the practitioner if the patient experiences more severe side effects such as vomiting, severe diarrhea, abdominal cramps, rash, itching, white patching on the tongue, or an allergic reaction.
- Antibiotics assist the immune system in combatting a bacterial infection. The antibiotic reduces the level of bacteria that is causing the infection to a level where the immune system can finish the job.
- Antibiotics don't work for the flu or cold. These are viral, as you probably know, but this is an important fact to share with your patients who demand an antibiotic.
- The color of mucus or phlegm is not always an indication of a bacterial infection.
- If the patient's symptoms don't improve after taking an antibiotic, then either the wrong antibiotic was prescribed or the patient doesn't have a bacterial infection.

There are many antibiotics available to the practitioner and new antibiotics continue to reach the market as bacteria become resistant to older antibiotics. Here are twelve of the common classes of antibiotics. You may not be quizzed on specific classes during the pre-employment process, but it might be worth a review just in case an antibiotic or a class of antibiotics slips into a question.

- **Penicillins** include amoxicillin, Augmentin, and penicillin G and penicillin V
- **Penicillinase-Resistant** antibiotics include nafcillin and oxacillin
- **Tetracyclines** are broad spectrum antibiotics that are prescribed for urinary tract infections, intestinal tract infections, and sexually transmitted diseases. These include demeclocyline, doxycycline, and tetracycline
- **Cephalosporins** have evolved into five generations, each of which treats additional types of bacteria. Cephalosporins are prescribed for strep throat, urinary tract infections, meningitis, skin infections, and ear infections. The fifth generation is prescribed for methicillin-resistant *Staphylococcus aureus* (MRSA).
  - o First generation includes Keflex, and cefadroxil
  - o Second generation includes Cefoxtin, cefprozil and cefuroxime
  - o Third generation includes Rocephin, Ceptaz, and Tazicef
  - o Fourth generation includes Cefepime and Maxipime
  - o Fifth generation includes ceftaroline (Teflao)
- **Fluoroquinolones** also known as quinolones are a broad-spectrum type of antibiotics that are prescribed for difficult to treat bacterial infections such as urinary tract infections, hospital acquired pneumonia, anthrax, and the plague. Fluoroquinolones includes Levaquin, Avelox, and Cipro.

- **Lincomycins** are prescribed for serious infections such as joint and bone infections, lower respiratory tract infections, and pelvic inflammatory infections because they are effective against gram-positive aerobes and anaerobes. Lincomycins include lincomycin and clindamycin.
- **Macrolides** are antibiotics prescribed for pertussis, community-acquired pneumonia, and for simple skin infections. In recent years, some bacteria have become resistant to Macrolides and practitioners have begun to use the Ketolides class of antibiotics in place of Macrolides. Macrolides include Zithromax, erythromycin, and Biaxin.
- **Sulfonamides** are prescribed for ear infections, urinary tract infections, and pneumocystis pneumonia. Sulfonamides include Bactrim, Septra, Azulfidine, and sulfisoxazole.
- **Glycopeptides** are prescribed for methicillin-resistant *Staphylococcus aureus* (MRSA), C.difficile-related diarrhea, endocarditis that is resistance to other antibiotics, and complicated skin infections. Glycopeptides include vancomycin, telavancin, and dalbavancin.
- **Aminoglycosides** are fast-acting antibiotics that are typically administered intravenously. Aminoglycosides include amikacin, gentamicin, and tobramycin.
- **Carbapenems** are a wide spectrum antibiotic commonly prescribed for life-threatening bacterial infections in the stomach, kidney, and lungs include multi-antibiotic resistant hospital acquired infections. Carbapenems include meropenem, ertapenem, Doribax, Invanz, and Primaxin.

Pain Medications

Managing a patient's pain is bound to come up in the pre-employment interview with the nurse manager or may appear on a pre-employment test because the nurse manager wants to be sure that you appropriately respond to a patient's report of pain. Remember that pain is defined by the patient. Don't second guess the patient based on your observations of the patient or your own pain tolerance. Some patients don't display outward signs of pain yet they are still experiencing pain – and you may have higher pain threshold than the patient.

Pain is commonly measured using the numeric rating scale by asking the patient to rate his pain on a scale from zero to 10 where zero is no pain and 10 is the worst pain. The Wong-Baker FACES Pain Rating scale uses a series six of simple faces to indicate the level of pain. Each face is assigned a numeric value and a two or three word description. A smiley face indicates no hurt and has a value of zero. A sad face showing tears has a value of 10 and states that the pain hurts worst. This is a good scale to use for patients who have difficulty expressing themselves in English.

Patients who are unable to convey the feeling of pain usually give you clues that they are in pain. Look for:
— Facial grimacing
— Frowning
— Rapid blinking
— Shifting in bed
— Groaning
— Agitation
— Restlessness
— Inactivity
— Acting withdrawn
— Increased heart rate, blood pressure, breathing
— Guarding the area of pain
— Resisting care
— Irritability
— Increased confusion
— Changes in sleep and appetite
— Diaphoresis (sweating)
— Dilated pupils

Be sure to explain how you assess pain. The numeric pain scale (older children and adults), the Wong-Baker FACES Pain Rating Scale (non-verbal patients and children three years and older), and clinical signs of pain (patients unable to speak) are used to describe the severity of pain. You also want to assess the acceptable level of pain, location of pain, does the pain move or stay in one place, when did the pain begin, what predicated the pain, and what makes the pain better or worse. You may also suggest that the patient use a pain log to track incidents of pain to better determine the pattern of pain.

Think about discussing non-medication approaches to pain management during your pre-employment interview with the nurse manager. This shows that you are using critical thinking skills to help the patient. Some commonly used non-medication techniques for managing pain are:
— *Distraction* helps to refocus the mind and is a good technique for relatively minor pain and for periods between pain medication administrations.
— *Relaxation techniques* such as guided imagery, breathing techniques, and the gentle movements of tai chi.
— *Pet therapy* refocuses the patient away from the pain and onto a pet.

- *Warm or cold gel packs* can treat localized pain.

Non-medication techniques have their limitations when reducing pain. Pain medication (analgesics) is sometimes the only treatment for pain. Pain medication either blocks the pain signal from reaching the brain or modifies how the brain interprets the pain signal. Keep in mind that pain medication does not fix the cause of the pain. The pain persists unless the underlying cause of the pain is addressed.

For example, pain for a soft tissue injury may be caused by swelling as the inflammation process repairs the injured site. Applying a cold then warm compress to the site may reduce the swelling and reduce the pain. Anti-inflammatory medication decreases the inflammation process, reducing the swelling and pain.

There are two primary types of pain medications. These are non-narcotic and narcotic. Non-narcotic medication is not controlled and narcotics are controlled. Non-narcotic medications include analgesics for mild to moderate pain such as acetaminophen. Nonsteroidal anti-inflammatory drugs (NSAIDs) (ibuprofen, naproxen) are also non-narcotic medications that are used to treat pain that is associated with inflammation such as muscle strains and osteoarthritis.

Facts to Remember

- The practitioner must specify in the order the reason for prescribing a non-narcotic medication (acetaminophen) that can be prescribed for pain and for fever especially if the medication is a PRN medication.
- Non-narcotic pain medication is available without prescription; however, a prescription may be written for a non-narcotic pain medication at a higher therapeutic dose (ibuprofen 200 mg per tablet OTC and 600 mg per tablet prescribed).
- Alert the patient about the dangers associated with taking more than the recommended OTC dose. For example, 800 mg is the maximum dose for ibuprofen with a four dose maximum per day. Patients in pain may increase the dose rather than consulting a practitioner for a more appropriate medication.
- NSAIDs
    o Increase the risk of stomach bleeding for patients with stomach disorders.
    o May cause an upset stomach, heartburn, and nausea
    o Long-term use may lead to stomach ulcers, cardiovascular event, kidney disorders, and liver disorders

        o   Non-traditional NSAIDs medication (celecoxib, Celebrex) do not cause stomach problems

Narcotic medications are opioid-based drugs that attach to opioid receptors, changing the way the patient experiences pain. These are prescribed for severe injury. Narcotics are a controlled substance classified in five schedules.

Schedule I medications have no currently accepted medical use in the United States and have a high potential for abuse. These medications include heroin, lysergic acid diethylamide (LSD), cannabis, peyote, methaqualone, and 3, 4-methylenedioxymethamphetamine (Ecstasy).

Schedule II medications have a high potential for abuse that can lead to physical and psychological dependency. These medications include Dilaudid, Demerol, Oxycodone, Percocet, fentanyl and methadone.

Schedule IIN medications are stimulants rather than pain medication. These include amphetamine (Dexedrine, Adderall), methamphetamine (Desoxyn), and methylphenidate (Ritalin).

Schedule III medications may lead to moderate or low physical dependence or high psychological dependency but have a lower potential for abuse than medications in Schedules I and II. These medications include Vicodin, Suboxone, and Tylenol with codeine.

Schedule IIIN medications are non-narcotics that may have the same risk for physical and psychological dependency as Schedule III. These include Didrex (stimulant), anabolic steroids, phendimetrazine (stimulant), and ketamine (anesthetic).

Schedule IV medications have a low potential for abuse. These include Xanax, Klonopin, Valium, Ativan, Versed, Restoril, and Halcion.

Schedule V medications have the lowest potential for abuse. These medications include Robitussin AC, Phenergan with codeine, and ezogabine (anticonvulsant).

Facts to Remember

- A patient is unlikely to become addicted to narcotic medication if the medication is administered as prescribed and the practitioner closely supervises the patient.
- Administer pain medication an hour before any painful treatment to allow time for the pain medication to work.

- Narcotic medications may lead to constipation. The practitioner should anticipate this problem and order a stool softener or other therapeutic treatment to reduce constipation.
- High doses of narcotic medication can lead to respiratory depression and depress the cough reflex.
- Patients administered pain medication may be at risk for falls.
- Chronic pain may lead to depression. Antidepressant medication may relieve pain and depression associated with pain. These medications include Celexa, Prozac, Zoloft, Cymbalta, and Wellbutrin.

You don't have to be a whiz at pharmacology to pass a pre-employment pharmacology test or to answer medication questions asked by the hiring nurse manager. However, you do need to have a good knowledge of basic medications that are common in most practices. This chapter no doubt brought back memories of the pharmacology course in nurse school. Keep in mind that no one except the nurse manager knows the medication questions that you'll be asked on your interview, but this chapter gives you an edge when answering her medication questions.

Chapter 8
Preparing for Nursing Questions

You don't know what you don't know until you are interviewed by a nurse manager or sit for a pre-employment online nursing test – and by then it's too late. No one knows what you'll be asked on a job interview or pre-employment test except the nurse manager and the people who created the pre-employment test. However, it is likely that you'll be asked questions that involve nursing judgment and patient safety.

Like many nurses, you have good skills within your area of nursing. You can whiz through any nursing quiz in your specialty but how would you fare with questions outside your current nursing job? Can you provide the textbook approach to procedures that you perform daily? These can be challenging and trip you up during the pre-employment process. It's not that you don't know the answer, but you don't remember it. Somewhere in your brain it sits. How far back depends on how long ago you graduated from nursing school.

Don't fret. This chapter provides a review of nursing basics — a good foundation for answering critical thinking and patient safety questions. Consider this review as a tune-up – maybe a long overdue tune-up depending on how long ago you interviewed for a nursing job.

Physiological Compensation

When the patient encounters a stressful situation – a disorder — the patient's body automatically changes from normal operations to modified operations in order to compensate for the stressful situation. Respiration increases to raise the oxygen level in the blood. Some blood vessels contract while others dilate to increase blood volume to vital organs and away from less vital organs. The heart rate escalates pumping the increased oxygenated blood throughout the body. Normal function returns once the stressful situation subsides.

This is referred to as *physiological compensation*. The capability of the patient's body to compensate for abnormal situations (such as infection) is called the body's *physiological reserves*. The patient requires medical intervention when the physiological reserves are low or unable to compensate for the changes. For example, the patient's immune system destroys and removes bacteria that enter the body by increasing the white blood cell (WBC) count. The WBC count returns to normal once the bacterial infection is resolved. However, the severity of the bacterial infection may eventually deplete the patient's physiological reserves –

DOI 10.1515/9781501506109-008

the immune system can't keep up fighting the bacteria – and the patient requires antibiotic medication to help fight the bacterial infection. Without the additional help (antibiotics), the bacteria will "win" because the patient's physiological reserves are exhausted — the patient becomes septic and dies.

The lower the physiological reserves, the more medical intervention is required to help the patient compensate for the abnormal situation. The combination of medical intervention and the patient's physiological reserves enables the patient's body to compensate for the disorder. The objective is to intervene before the physiological reserves are depleted and the patient develops multiple organ dysfunction syndrome (MODS) where failure of one organ to compensate has a cascading effect of taxing the physiological reserves of other organs. For example, depletion of respiratory reserves increase CO_2 in arterial blood leading to an increased heart rate as the heart pumps more blood to compensate for low oxygen levels in the blood. At some point, cardiac reserves are depleted and no blood is supplied to organs. The kidneys fail. The liver fails. The heart fails. And the brain fails.

Physiological reserves decrease with:

– Aging. Parts of the body are old and don't work like they use to work. For example, an aging liver may be unable to properly metabolize some medications leading to ineffective therapeutic effect of the medication and the risk of an overdose of medication.

– Disorders. Parts of the body are not functioning properly. For example, bone marrow and other blood forming organs produce an increasing number of immature WBC (leukemia) leading to an impaired immune system.

Estimating the Physiological Reserves

The patient's physiological reserve can be estimated by measuring some systems of the body – but not all systems. Sometimes attempting to measure the physiological reserve of a system may produce misleading results.

– *Cardiac reserve*. Cardiac reserve is measured as the difference between the resting heart rate and the heart rate when ischemia and angina occurs during a stress test. A narrow range indicates a low reserve. Cardiac reserve is also measured by the mean arterial pressure (MAP), which is the average arterial pressure during a cardiac cycle. A value less than 50 mmHg indicates a low reserve.

- *Pulmonary reserve.* Pulmonary reserve is measured as partial pressure of the end-tidal CO_2 ($PaCO_2$) in arterial blood gas. Increased CO_2 indicates a low reserve. Lower arterial oxygen levels indicate low reserve. An arterial oxygen level lower than 200 mmHg may require that the patient be placed on mechanical ventilation.
- *Renal reserve.* Renal reserve is measured by serum creatinine. A value greater than 5 mg/dl indicates a low renal reserve. Creatinine is a byproduct of muscle metabolism and is filtered by the kidneys and excreted in urine.
- *Blood production reserve.* Blood production (hematopoietic) reserve is measured by serum hemoglobin and the platelet count. Hemoglobin 7g/L indicates a low reserve. A platelet count below 50,000 indicates a low reserve.
- *Liver reserve.* Liver reserve is measured by total bilirubin in serum. Total bilirubin greater than 12 mg/dl indicate a low reserve.
- *Coagulation reserve.* Coagulation reserve is measured by the serum platelet count. A serum platelet count of less than150,000 platelets indicates a low reserve.
- *Neurological system reserve.* The neurological system reserve is measured by the *Glasgow Coma Scale*. A Glasgow Coma Scale value of less than 9 indicates a low reserve.
- *Immune system reserves.* The immune system reserves are measured by testing the amount of immunoglobulins (antibodies) in the patient's blood. The white blood cell (WBC) count (B-cells and T-cells) is also an indicator of the immune system reserves. A low WBC indicates a low reserve indicating that the patient is at risk for infection.

The Call for Help

The average patient visits a practitioner when all else has failed to address the problem. The body compensates for many disorders without the patient noticing a change. For example, the immune system attacks microorganisms routinely. It is only when the immune system reserves are being overtaxed that the patient notices symptoms (for example, fever). At this point, the average patient tries to "tough it out" and let the body's compensation take over. The patient may rest more than normal but as the symptoms become more uncomfortable the patient may use home remedies and over-the-counter (OTC) medications most of which treat the symptoms and not the underlying cause. For example, an OTC pain medication may help a headache but does nothing for the bacterial infection that triggered the inflammation response that lead to the headache. Sometimes home remedies and OTC medications are sufficient to give the body time to resolve the problem. However, when home remedies and OTC medications fail, the patient goes to the practitioner for help.

The practitioner is faced with a puzzle — diagnose the problem and develop a treatment plan that either fixes the problem (acute condition) or minimizes the symptoms (chronic condition). However, in the real world there may be more that the practitioner considers other than identifying and treating the problem.

The patient is thinking, "I hope the practitioner can fix my problem."

The practitioner is thinking, "I hope you have a problem that I can fix."

The practitioner creates a database of information about the patient especially focusing on the current episode. Questions are asked; a physical assessment is performed; and medical tests are likely ordered, if necessary. The direction taken by the practitioner depends on the symptoms (subjective) reported by the patients and the signs (objective) identified by the physical assessment.

The practitioner then decides if she can fix the problem. If so, a medication is likely ordered to supplement the patient's physiological reserves. Sometimes treatment can only be performed in a hospital if the patient's physiological reserves are low and more involved treatment is needed to supplement the physiological reserves. The practitioner may also decide to refer the patient to another practitioner if the practitioner is unable to reach a diagnosis or is unable to treat the patient.

There are times when the practitioner is capable of treating the patient but doesn't want to treat the patient. In the real world, practitioners have the following concerns when deciding to treat a patient:

- Avoid being sued.
- Keep the professional license.
- Make money.
- Treat the patient.

Practitioners tend to build a practice (outpatient/inpatient) focused on a specific group of disorders that the practitioner finds relatively safe to treat and that is profitable. Some focus on family practice while others become experts in a specialty. This expertise is not only for diagnosing and treating patients but also navigating third party payer rules to ensure maximum profit.

The goal of the practitioner — regardless of motivation — is to fix the problem. But if this is not feasible, the goal is to return the patient to activities of daily living (ADL), to reduce the symptoms so that the patient is more comfortable than when the patient presented to the practitioner.

The Cascading Effect

A symptom may be caused by a complex array of events take place in a patient's body. Think of each symptom as a dot. The task is to identify and connect all the dots to "see" what is really happening with the patient. This is similar to the "connect-the-dots" books that children use to "draw" pictures.

Let's look at a patient who is a heavy smoker.

- Tobacco causes increased growth in cells in the lung that produce mucus. This leads to an overproduction of mucus (thick mucus).
- Cilia (hair-like cells) "clean the lungs." Tobacco consumption decreases the number of functioning cilia. Mucus cannot be removed.
- The buildup of mucus clogs the airway and the patient develops a chronic cough as the body attempts to remove the mucus.
- Airway narrows reducing air flow resulting in increased CO_2 levels and decreased oxygen levels in the blood.
- Wheezing is heard as air moves through mucus.
- Mucus retained in the lungs make a perfect medium for the growth of microorganism leading to chronic lung infection (chronic bronchitis and COPD).
- Over time the alveoli (the site of gas exchange in the lungs) collapse, trapping air in the alveolar sac (emphysema) thus reducing the area of the lung that can be used for gas exchange.
- Decreased gas exchange leads to decreased oxygen in the blood resulting in bluish tint seen in nail bed, nose, and earlobe (cyanosis).
- Increased levels of CO_2 in blood signals the brain to compensate by increasing the heart rate (tachycardia) to pump more blood through the body to perfuse organs and increase respiration (tachypnea, shortness of breath) to increase gas exchange.
- Increased respiratory workload leads to the patient using accessory muscles to breath (raised shoulders). Accessory muscles are used to compensate for low respiratory reserve.
- The increased cardiac workload to compensate for increase CO_2 levels in blood leads to right-side heart failure as cardiac reserves are depleted. The heart is unable to effectively pump blood through the cardiovascular system leading to accumulation of fluid in the legs, ankles, and eventually the lungs (edema).
- Eventually low oxygen levels affect the brain and the patient dies.

Resolving the underlying problem (that is, smoking tobacco), may reverse the cascading effect or begin to reduce dependency on the physiological reserves. Effective treatment may also reduce dependency on physiological reserves, if the underlying problem is not resolved. For example, respiratory treatment reduces some of the accumulated mucus resulting in a decreased risk of infection and possibly an increase in effective gas exchange in the lungs.

Assessments

The patient assessment is where you learn why the patient is seeking help. There are times when the patient reports *classic symptoms* that lead to a diagnosis. You'll find classic symptoms for various body systems disorders later in this chapter. Classic symptoms help to define the patient's current problem (episode); however, always consider the whole patient when making the assessment. Some symptoms may not be related to the current problem but may indicate other problems that haven't fully materialized.

Also consider than signs that seem abnormal may be perfectly normal for the patient under the circumstances. For example, an 80-year-old male complained about random pain and drove himself to the emergency department. Blood tests were taken and his blood glucose level was near 300 mg/dL. This is considered an abnormal sign unless it was learned that the patient ate a large breakfast a little over an hour ago. This was normal.

The initial assessment is to identify systems that are being stressed by the underlying problem as indicated by signs and symptoms — and systems that are normal. The results direct the focus of the assessment to the current problem and then possible treatment options.

Quick Assessment

Remember your first bedside clinical assessment in nursing school that took nearly an hour to complete — and the five-minute assessment that you probably perform daily at bedside today?

"Mr. Jones, I'm Jim. I'll be your nurse today. How are you feeling?"

"I'm feeling much better."

This brief conversation tells you that the patient is breathing (no signs of any respiratory distress); heart is working (no signs of cardiac distress); alert and oriented (no signs of cognitive impairment); skin color is normal (no signs of cyanosis); he moved his head and followed you (no signs of hearing or loss of sight); he was reading, and holding a magazine when you walked in (arms and hands are functional, no tremors).

"Mr. Jones, were you able to go to the bathroom this morning?"

"No problem in that category. I went a few minutes ago."

There is no bowel obstruction; no reported problems urinating; no incontinence; and the patient is ambulatory.

Although a quick assessment is no replacement for a thorough head-to-toe assessment, quick assessments are commonly used to identify likely causes of the patient's complaints based on probabilities rather than possibilities. Here are three commonly used approaches to a quick patient assessment.

SAMPLE
- **S**igns and Symptoms (What bothers you?)
- **A**llergies (Is the patient having an allergic reaction to something?)
- **M**edication (Has the patient taken any new medications that may be causing an adverse side effect?)
- **P**ertinent past medical history (Has a previous problem reoccurred or lead to the present problem?)
- **L**ast oral intake (What did you ingest recently?)
- **E**vents leading up to the problem (Have you been doing anything different recently?)

OPQRST
- **O**nset: When did the problem start?
- **P**rovocation: What makes the problem worse?
- **Q**uality: How do you feel?
- **R**adiation: Does the pain or discomfort move?
- **S**everity: How bad is the problem?
- **T**ime: How long have you had this problem?

PQRST
A relatively efficient way of assessing pain is to use the PQRST method.
- P = Provocation
  - o Where did the pain start?
  - o What caused the pain?
  - o What aggravates the pain?
  - o What relieves the pain?
  - o Was the pain sudden or gradual?

- Q = Quality
  - o Describe the pain as sharp, dull, stabbing, burning, crushing, throbbing, shooting, and/or nauseating
- R = Region and Radiation
  - o Where is the pain located?
  - o Is the pain located in one place?
  - o Is it radiating pain? If so, where does the pain travel?
- S = Severity
  - o On a scale of 0 to 10 with zero being no pain and 10 being the worst pain, what is your pain?
- T = Timing
  - o What time did the pain begin?
  - o How long did the pain last?
  - o What time of day did you experience the pain?
  - o Did you ever have this pain before now?

Five P's of musculoskeletal injury (head to toe)
- Pain
- Paralysis
- Paresthesia
- Pulse
- Pallor

Risk of Mortality

In critical situations, it is important to assess the risk of mortality resulting from multi-organ failure to determine if treatment is beneficial or futile. Remember that treatment is designed to supplement the patient's body's capability to compensate for the physiological imbalance. There are times when the patient's body is no longer capable of compensating and, therefore, treatment is futile. There are four assessment models that are commonly used to assess the probability of mortality. These are:

Multiple Organ Failure (MOF)
- Multiple Organ Failure (MOF) predicts the patient's mortality based on the number of the patient's organs that have depleted their physiological reserves.

Mortality Probability Model (MPM)
- The Mortality Probability Model is used in the intensive care unit to predict the probability of the patient's mortality in 24 hours, 48 hours, and 72 hours of admission. Here are the factors that are evaluated in this assessment:
    - Age
    - Type of admission
    - Hours admitted
    - Metastatic Cancer
    - Cirrhosis
    - Diuresis < 150 mL/8h
    - Creatinine > 2 mg/dL
    - Coma (Glasgow Coma Scale 3-5)
    - Intracranial Mass Effect
    - Vasoactive drug (increases/decreases blood pressure) >= 1h
    - Mechanical Ventilation
    - PaO2 < 60 mmHg
    - Proven Infection
    - Pt > standard + 3 sec

Simplified Acute Physiology Score (SAPS)
- The Simplified Acute Physiology Score is used after the first 24 hours of admission to a critical care unit using 12 physiological measurements. These are:
    - Age
    - Heart Rate
    - Systolic Blood Pressure
    - Temperature
    - Glasgow coma score
    - Mechanical ventilation in use
    - PaO_2
    - FiO_2 (A fraction of the amount of oxygen inhaled using an oxygen device)
    - Urine output per hour
    - BUN
    - Sodium
    - Potassium
    - Bicarbonate
    - Bilirubin
    - WBC

- o   Metastatic cancer
- o   Hematologic malignancy
- o   AIDS
- o   Type of admission

Sequential Organ Failure Assessment (SOFA) Score

- The Sequential Organ Failure Assessment Score uses six factors to evaluate the risk of sequential organ failure. The higher the score the lower the physiological reserves. These are:
  - o   Respiratory
  - o   Cardiovascular
  - o   Hepatic
  - o   Coagulation
  - o   Renal
  - o   Neurological

Acute Physiology and Chronic Health Evaluation (APACHE)

- The Acute Physiology and Chronic Health Evaluation measures physiological factors during the first 24 hours of admission to measure the severity of disease for adults. The higher the APACHE score, the higher risk that the patient will die. Factors measured are:
  - o   Age
  - o PaO_2 or $AaDO_2$ (which to select to assess is based on FiO_2 value)
  - o   Rectal Temperature
  - o   Mean arterial pressure (MAP)
  - o   Arterial pH
  - o   Heart rate
  - o   Respiratory rate
  - o   Serum sodium
  - o   Serum potassium
  - o   Creatinine
  - o   Hematocrit
  - o   White blood cell count
  - o   Glasgow Coma Scale

Baseline Assessment

The baseline assessment provides a database of information about the patient that helps you identify what is normal and potentially abnormal physiologically with the patient. Trust what the patient reports; however, be sure to verify the information with the patient's other healthcare providers and the patient's family. Some patients are poor historians. Develop a potential problem list reported by the patient. The practitioner will also develop a problem list containing targets for treatment.

- Age, occupation, psychosocial information
- Presenting problem that caused the patient to seek treatment
- Current/past medical problems and chronic medical conditions
- Timeline of events leading the patient to seek treatment
- Head:
  - o Eyes open. Pupils equal and reacting to light.
  - o Mouth free from trauma
  - o Patent airway
  - o All tubes are patent
- Chest:
  - o Heart
    - Heart sounds
    - Heart rate
    - Blood pressure
    - Mean arterial pressure to measure end-organ perfusion
    - Urinary output to measure end-organ perfusion
  - o Respiration
    - Respiratory rate
    - Partial pressure of arterial O_2 (PaO_2)
    - Partial pressure of end-tidal CO_2 ($PaCO_2$)
  - o Chest expansion
  - o Lungs
  - o Drainage tubes are patent
- Arms and hands:
  - o Skin
  - o Range of motion (ROM)
  - o Patent I.V. lines
- Abdomen:
  - o Bowel sounds present
  - o Bowel movement

- o Passing flatus
- o Urinary output
- o Drainage tubes are patent
- o Femoral line patent
– Legs and feet:
  - o Skin
  - o Range of motion (ROM)
– Blood Labs (abnormal)
  - o HCT low
  - o Hgb low
  - o TICB low
  - o Iron low
  - o Ferritin low
  - o RBC low
– Risk for bleeding
  - o Platelet < 37,000
  - o PTT high
  - o PT high
  - o INR high
– Nutrition (abnormal)
  - o Malnutrition
    - ▪ Prealbumin decreased
    - ▪ Albumin decreased
– Fluid balance (abnormal)
  - o Dehydration
    - ▪ HCT high.
    - ▪ Hgb high
    - ▪ RBC high
    - ▪ Albumin high
    - ▪ Urine specific gravity high
  - o Overhydration
    - ▪ HCT low
    - ▪ Hgb low
    - ▪ RBC low
    - ▪ Albumin low
    - ▪ Urine specific gravity low

- Immune system (abnormal)
    - ○ CD4 low
    - ○ WBC < 2,000
    - ○ ESR high
    - ○ Neutrophils high
    - ○ Eosinophils high
    - ○ Lymphocytes high
- Pancreas (abnormal)
    - ○ Amylase high
    - ○ Lipase high
- Liver function (abnormal)
    - ○ Albumin low
    - ○ ALT high
    - ○ AST high
    - ○ Total bilirubin high
    - ○ Direct bilirubin high
- Renal function (abnormal)
    - ○ Urine output less than 1 ml/kg/hr
    - ○ Creatinine high
    - ○ BUN high

Remember the methods used to physically examine the patient:
- All parts of the body except the abdomen
    - ○ Inspection: Look for abnormal signs.
    - ○ Palpation: Assess for location, size, texture, and consistency.
    - ○ Auscultation: Listen with a stethoscope.
    - ○ Percussion: Tap areas and listen for repercussion sounds.
- Examine the abdomen
    - ○ Inspection: Look for abnormal signs.
    - ○ Auscultation: Listen with a stethoscope.
    - ○ Palpation: Assess for location, size, texture, and consistency.
    - ○ Percussion: Tap areas and listen for repercussion sounds.

Level of Consciousness

The Glasgow Coma Scale (Table 8.1) is used to objectively measure the patient's level of consciousness based on the patient's eye response, verbal response, and motor response. A score of less than 13 is associated with decreased level of consciousness. The National Institutes of Health Stroke Scale (Table 8.2) is an objective way the measure impairment caused by a stroke by assessing consciousness, vision, sensory, motor responses, and speech and language function. An initial score greater than 4 indicates that the patient may benefit from thrombolytic medication to dissolve the blood clot.

Table 8.1: Glasgow Coma Scale

	1	2	3	4	5	6
Eyes	Does not open eyes	Opens eyes in response to painful stimuli	Opens eyes in response to voice	Opens eyes spontaneously	N/A	N/A
Verbal	Makes no sounds	Incomprehensible sounds	Utters inappropriate words	Confused, disoriented	Oriented, converses normally	N/A
Motor	Makes no movements	Extension to painful stimuli (decerebrate response)	Abnormal flexion to painful stimuli (decorticate response)	Flexion/withdrawal to painful stimuli	Localizes painful stimuli	Obeys commands

Table 8.2: The National Institutes of Health Stroke Scale

1a. Level of Consciousness	0= Alert; keenly responsive	1= Not alert; but arousable by minor stimulation to obey, answer, or respond	2 = Not alert; requires repeated stimulation to attend, or is obtunded and requires strong or painful stimulation to make movements (not stereotyped)	3 = Responds only with reflex motor or autonomic effects, or totally unresponsive, flaccid, and areflexic
1b. LOC Questions The patient is asked the month and his/her age.	0 = Answers both questions correctly	1 = Answers one question correctly or unable to speak because of endotracheal intubation, orotracheal trauma, severe dysarthria from any cause, language barrier, or any other problem not secondary to aphasia	2 = Answers neither question correctly or Aphasic and stuporous patients who do not comprehend the questions	
1c. LOC Questions The patient is asked to open and close the eyes and then to grip and release the non-paretic hand.	0= Performs both tasks correctly	1 = Performs one task correctly	3 = Performs neither task correctly	

Table 8.2: The National Institutes of Health Stroke Scale (continued)

2 horizontal eye movements by having patient 's eye follow a finger moving horizontally in front of the patient	0= Normal	1 = Partial gaze palsy; gaze is abnormal in one or both eyes, but forced deviation or total gaze paresis is not present	2 = Forced deviation, or total gaze paresis is not overcome by the oculocephalic maneuver	
3 Visual using finger counting	0 = No visual loss	1= Partial hemianopia	2= Complete hemianopia	3= Bilateral hemianopia (blind including cortical blindness)
4 Facial Palsy the patient shows teeth or raise eyebrows and close eyes	0 = Normal symmetrical movements	1= Minor paralysis (flattened nasolabial fold, asymmetry on smiling)	2= Partial paralysis (total or near-total paralysis of lower face)	3 = Complete paralysis of one or both sides (absence of facial movement in the upper and lower face)
5 Motor Arm extend the arms (palms down) 90 degrees (if sitting) or 45 degrees (if supine). Drift is scored if the arm falls before 10 seconds	0 = No drift; limb holds 90 (or 45) degrees for full 10 seconds	1 = Drift; limb holds 90 (or 45) degrees, but drifts down before full 10 seconds; does not hit bed or other support.	2= Some effort against gravity; limb cannot get to or maintain (if cued) 90 (or 45) degrees, drifts down to bed, but has some effort against gravity	3= No effort against gravity; limb falls 4 = No movement
6 Motor leg The limb is placed in the appropriate position: hold the leg at 30 degrees (always tested supine). Drift is scored if the leg falls before 5 seconds	0= No drift; leg holds 30-degree position for full 5 seconds	1 = Drift; leg falls by the end of the 5- second period but does not hit the bed	2 = Some effort against gravity; leg falls to bed by 5 seconds but has some effort against gravity	3 = No effort against gravity; leg falls to bed immediately 4 = No movement
7 **Limb Ataxia** (loss of full control of bodily movements) The fingernose- finger and heel-shin tests are performed on both sides with eyes open	0= Absent	1= Present in one limb	2 = Present in two limbs	
8 Sensory Sensation or grimace to pinprick when tested, or withdrawal from noxious stimulus in the obtunded or aphasic patient.	0= Normal; no sensory loss	1 = Mild-to-moderate sensory loss; patient feels pinprick is less sharp or is dull on the affected side; or there is a loss of superficial pain with pinprick, but patient is aware of being touched	2 = Severe or total sensory loss; patient is not aware of being touched in the face, arm, and leg	

Table 8.2: The National Institutes of Health Stroke Scale (continued)

9 Best Language ability to under- stand or express speech	0= No aphasia; normal	1=Mild-to-moderate aphasia; some obvi- ous loss of fluency or facility of compre- hension, without sig- nificant limitation on ideas expressed or form of expression. Reduction of speech and/or comprehen- sion, however, makes conversation about provided materials difficult or impossi- ble. For example, in conversation about provided materials, examiner can identify picture or naming card content from pa- tient's response	2=Severe aphasia; all communication is through fragmentary expression; great need for inference, questioning, and guessing by the lis- tener. Range of infor- mation that can be exchanged is limited; listener carries bur- den of communica- tion. Examiner cannot identify materials provided from patient response	3= Mute, global aphasia; no usable speech or auditory comprehension
10 Dysarthria Ask patient to read or repeat word	0= Normal	1= Mild-to-moderate dysarthria; patient slurs at least some words and, at worst, can be understood with some difficulty	2 = Severe dysar- thria; patient's speech is so slurred as to be unintelligible in the absence of or out of proportion to any dysphasia, or is mute/anarthric	
11 Extinction and Inattention Assessed from pre- vious testing	0= No abnormal- ity	1= Visual, tactile, au- ditory, spatial, or per- sonal inattention, or extinction to bilateral simultaneous stimu- lation in one of the sensory modalities	2 = Profound hemi- inattention or extinc- tion to more than one modality; does not recognize own hand or orients to only one side of space	

Ramsay Sedation Scale (RSS)
RSS is used to assess the rousability of a patient based on six levels.
1. anxious/agitated or restless, or both
2. cooperative, oriented, and tranquil
3. respond to commands only
4. exhibits brisk response to light tap or loud auditory stimulus
5. sluggish response to light tap or loud auditory stimulus
6. no response

Riker Sedation-Agitation Scale (SAS)
SAS provides a clear definition of sedation and agitation that can be used to measure the patient's sedation-agitation level throughout the course of treatment.

1. Unarousable. No response.
2. Very Sedated. Awakens to physical stimuli but doesn't follow commands.
3. Sedated. Difficult to arouse but awakens to gentle shaking and verbal stimuli and can follow simple commands before drifting back to the sedated state.
4. Calm and Cooperative.
5. Agitated. Mildly agitated or anxious but can be calm down with verbal intervention.
6. Very Agitated. Unable to calm down with verbal intervention and must by physically restrained.
7. Dangerous Agitation. Thrashing and is assaultive to staff.

Triage Revised Trauma Score (TRTS)

TRTS is an assessment tool (Table 8.3) that uses systolic blood pressure, respiration, and the Glasgow Coma Scale to prioritize treatment of patients in an emergency. The TRTS score ranges from 0 to 12 that corresponds to the status of the patient. Table 8.3 contains the TRTS assessment tool.

- Delayed: Walking Wounded. TRST Score 12
- Urgent: The patient can wait for a short time before being further assessed. TRST Score 11
- Immediate: The patient requires immediate attention. TRST Score 4 to 10
- Morgue: The patient is unlikely to survive TRST Score: < 4

Table 8.3: TRTS Scoring Table

Glasgow Coma Value	TRTS Score	Systolic Blood Pressure	TRTS Score	Respiration Rate	TRTS Score
3	0	0	0	0	0
4 to 5	1	1 to 49	1	1 to 5	1
6 to 8	2	50 to 75	2	6 to 9	2
9 to 12	3	76 to 89	3	> 29	3
13 to 15	4	> 89	4	10 to 29	4

Reverse Triage

Reverse triage is a technique used to manage scarce medical resources when assessing and treating patients. The goal is to stabilize the patient and return the medical staff to work. The initial step is to acquire information from the patient, those who accompanied the patient, and first responders (if involved in the care of the patient). Determine:

- What occurred
- When it occurred
- How it occurred
- Why it occurred
- What led up to the situation

Identify medical information gather from assessment and any treatment that was provided to the patient by first responders:

- Blood Pressure
- Pulse
- Oxygen saturation
- Respiration
- Temperature

Next, look for medical alert information on the patient (bracelets or medical alert cards in the patient's pocket or wallet). Use your critical thinking skills to verify all information you've gathered from the patient and other sources. Question each source of information then compare responses. Ask yourself, "does this make sense?" How did the person arrive at this information?

The final step is to use medical resources to treat more stable patients before less stable patients except in life threatening situations. There will likely be more stable patients that require minimum time to assess and treat compared with less stable patients, therefore, more patients can be treated by limited medical resources in the shortest amount of time by using reverse triage.

Dealing with Common Stressors

Always keep in mind that the presence of the medical team and the environment may create stress that also leads to symptoms. This is commonly referred to as "white coat syndrome." For example, a patient who presents with relatively high blood pressure each time she visits her practitioner may not have hypertension. Instead, the patient's body is compensating for anxiety by increasing blood pressure which becomes apparent when the patient is asked to measure her own blood pressure at home twice a day for two weeks.

Patients undergo stressful experiences when seeking medical treatment that exacerbates the patient's medical condition. An effort should be made to ease stressors by reducing the patient's anxiety at each stage of the episode. Here are common stressors that patients experience. Some have no basis in reality but appear real to the patient.

- Fear of death
- Fear of permanent disability
- Discomfort
- Loss of autonomy
- Lack of privacy
- Separation from loved ones and friends
- Frustration by the lack of immediate resolution of the patient's problem

Here are steps that you can take to reduce the stress level for your patients:
- Acknowledging the patient's concerns validates the patient's feelings.
- Educating the patient helps the patient learn about the unknowns of the patient's care and sets realistic expectations based on facts rather than speculation.
- Establishing milestones in the patient's experience. Explain what will happen and when it will happen.
- Making the patient comfortable at every stage of the encounter.
- Keeping the patient informed, continuing through every stage of the encounter. Don't let the patient sit for more than 15 minutes without a brief update of the patient's status.
- Minimizing disruptions by having fewer and longer interventions rather than frequent and short interventions.

Prepping for the "Quiz"

You may luck out and not be asked any technical questions during your interview with the nurse manager or have to take a pre-employment test that challenges your nursing knowledge. Realistically, however, expect that you'll be asked questions about nursing, some of which focuses on specific types of assessments, disorders, and nursing interventions. The nurse manager probably wants to know if you can recognize classic signs and symptoms and respond appropriately.

The rest of this chapter helps to prepare for your pre-employment nurse manager interview and pre-employment tests. Each section focuses on assessments, disorders, and nursing interventions for systems of the body. No doubt you learned about this information in nursing school. Some information you use daily in your practice and the rest is a good review before you go for your interview.

Pre- and Post-Operative Care

Special care must be given to patients who are to undergo an operative procedure and who return from an operative procedure. These are areas that should be your focus:

Pre-Operative Care

- Assess patients for contraindication for the procedures (for example, a bleeding disorder).
- Educate the patient and family on the procedures and what to expect pre- and post-procedure.
- Identify the patient's allergies.
- Determine if the patient signed informed consent for the procedure.
- Ensure that the patient has fasted before the procedure per practitioner's orders (usually, eight hours for heavy meal, two hours for clear liquid).
- Make sure the patient's vital signs are within acceptable range before the patient is transported to the procedure area.
- Address the patient's anxiety and fear, if necessary.
- Administer pre-procedure medication per practitioner's orders.
- Encourage the patient to void bladder and defecate before surgery.
- Ensure that baseline vital signs and laboratory tests have been completed.
- Remove all jewelry.
- Remove contact lenses.
- Remove dentures.
- Remove hair pieces.
- Remove hearing aids. Note on chart that the patient has a hearing deficiency.
- Remove makeup and dark nail polish
- Ensure that the patient has an ID band for allergies.
- Ensure that the patient's chart goes with the patient to the procedure area.
- Ensure that the pre-op checklist is completed.

Post-Operative Care

- Vital Signs. Identify changes in the patient's status.
- Pain Control. Ensure that the patient is free from pain.
- Monitor input and output. Ensure there is no buildup of fluids and the GI tract is working.

- Assess the wound site. Identify complications and proper drainage, if necessary.
- Apply compression stockings. Decreases the risk for deep vein thrombosis.
- Apply intermittent pneumatic compression (IPC) devices. Decreases the risk for deep vein thrombosis.
- Encourage early mobilization. Decreases the risk for deep vein thrombosis.
- Provide walking aids. Removes obstacles from early mobilization.
- Encourage deep breathing and coughing exercises. Increases lung capacity.
- Perform range of motion exercises. Regain mobility and muscle strength.
- Ensure adequate nutrition. Nutrition is required for healing.
- Turn patient every two hours. Prevents pressure sores and skin breakdown.
- Keep skin clean from urine and feces. Prevents skin breakdown.

Cardiovascular Assessment, Disorders, Interventions

Assessment
- Focus on the problem area.
- Stop the assessment if you need to intervene to stabilize the patient.

Interview
- Ask questions, short and to the point. Questions should be structured so they can be answered with a yes or no if the patient is in distress.
- Initial Questions:
    - What makes you feeling that something is wrong?
    - What happened prior to your noticing this problem?
    - Have you recently undergone any medical procedure?
- Follow up questions:
    - When did this problem start?
    - How long have you had this problem?
    - Can you describe the problem?
    - On a scale of 0 to 10 where 0 is no pain and 10 is the worst pain, what number is your pain?
    - Where is the pain?
    - When did the pain begin?
    - What makes the pain worse?
    - What makes the pain better?
    - Is the pain squeezing, burning, or tightening?
    - Does the pain move or remain in one place?

  o Are you nauseous?
  o Do you feel anything unusual with your heart, such as palpitation or your heart skipping a beat?
  o Do you feel short of breath?
  o You do have difficulty breathing when you wake up?
  o Do you feel dizzy?
  o Do you awaken to urinate?

Common Classic Signs
- Difficulty awakening: Related to decreased oxygenated blood (hypoxia) and possibly decreased circulation
- Bilateral swelling in ankles or feet related to right-side heart failure.
- Skipping heart beats related to irregular heart rhythm
- Heart pounding related to hypoxia
- Heart fluttering related to irregular heart rhythm
- Shortness of breath related to decreased oxygenation or decreased circulation
- Frequent night urination is a possible sign of right-side heart failure
- Dizziness is a sign of decreased oxygenation related to decreased circulation
- Pain might be a sign of decreased circulation to the heart muscle
- Cyanosis in nail beds, tip of the nose and ear lobes related to deoxygenating blood or poor circulation
- Clubbing of fingers related to chronic deoxygenating of blood
- Pale mucus membranes in dark skinned patients related to inadequate circulation
- Loss of hair on arms and legs related to decrease arterial circulation to the area
- Bilateral swelling is a possible sign of right-side heart failure, venous insufficiency, varicosities, or thrombophlebitis.
- Flushed skin related to increased circulation due to fever
- Capillary refill more than three seconds related to decrease circulation
- Cool skin temperature related to decreased circulation
- Warm skin temperature related to increased circulation
- Sound of turbulent blood flow related to aneurysm or heart valve malfunction
- Strong long pulse indicates increased cardiac output
- Diffuse pulse related to left ventricular hypertrophy
- Weak pulse indicates decreased cardiac output or increased peripheral vascular resistance
- Bounding pulse indicates hypertension or high cardiac output

- Dull sound from percussion over lung indicates pleural effusion related to biventricular failure allowing fluid to build up between the lung and the chest wall
- Bruits over the abdominal aorta indicates abdominal aortic aneurysm
- Pulmonary congestion (lungs) indicates left-side heart failure
- Sudden, sharp, continuous pain located below the sternum and radiating to the neck or left arm that gets worse lying on back or breathing deeply might be related to pericarditis
- Sudden, stabbing pain over the back that worsens on inspiration may be related to pulmonary emboli
- Sudden, severe, pain located at the side of the chest with difficulty breathing, and deviated trachea that worsens with normal breathing is related to pneumothorax
- Sudden, severe, tearing pain located in the upper abdomen or behind the sternum is related to a dissecting aortic aneurysm
- Squeezing, aching, burning pain below the sternum radiating to the arms, neck, back, and jaw that worsens on exertion, stress, eating, and lying down is related to angina pectoris (stable angina pectoris if resting resolves pain; unstable angina pectoris if pain continues upon resting).
- Pressure, aching, burning pain across the chest and radiating to the arms, neck, back, and jaw that worsens on exertion and increased anxiety is related to acute myocardial infarction.

Angina Pectoris

Narrowing of the coronary artery (arteriosclerosis) reduces blood flow to the heart.
- Stable Angina. Chest pain follows exercise or stress and is relieved by rest.
- Unstable Angina. Chest pain can occur at rest.
- Prinzmetal's angina (vasospastic angina). Chest pain occurs at night and at rest.

Classic Signs
- Chest pain, pressure, heaviness, squeezing, tightness for up to five minutes radiates to the jaw, back, or arms. Related to stress that increases oxygen demands on the heart
- Shortness of breath (dyspnea). Related to decrease oxygen in the blood.
- Tachycardia. The body attempting to increase oxygen flow to the heart.

- Increased anxiety. Related to decreased oxygen to cardiac muscles.
- Sweating (diaphoresis). Related to anxiety and increased cardiac workload.

Interventions
- Tell the patient to rest. Decreases cardiac workload.
- Place patient in a semi-Fowler's position. Decreases stress.
- Monitor vital signs.
- Measure fluid intake and output. Assess for renal output and renal perfusion. Normal is 1 ml per kg per hour. Critical is < 0.5 ml per kg per hour
- Perform 12-lead ECG during episodes of chest pain per orders.
- Place patient on a low cholesterol, low sodium, and low fat diet.
- Administer as ordered:
  - o 2 to 4 liters 100% oxygen. Use a non-rebreather face mask to increase oxygen supply to the patient
  - o Analgesic (Morphine). Decreases cardiac workload and pain.
  - o Nitrates (Nitroglycerin). Dilates blood vessels leading to increased blood flow to cardiac muscles.
    - ▪ Hold nitrate if systolic blood pressure < 90 mm Hg. Risk of reducing blood to the brain.
  - o Beta-adrenergic blocker. Decreases cardiac workload.
    - ▪ Hold Beta-adrenergic blocker if heart rate is less than 60 beats per minute. Risk of low cardiac output.
  - o Aspirin. Decreases formation of platelets.

Myocardial Infarction (MI)

Coronary artery blockage by atherosclerosis starves cardiac muscle of oxygen causing necrosis of cardiac muscle (infarction).

Classic Signs
- Feeling of impending doom. Related to decreased oxygen to the brain.
- Chest pain radiating to arms, jaw, back, and/or neck that is unrelieved by rest or nitroglycerin. Related to necrosis of cardiac muscle.
- Cool, clammy, pale skin. Related to decreased circulation.
- Diaphoresis (sweating). Related to increased anxiety from decreased oxygen to cardiac muscle.
- Tachycardia. The body attempting to increase oxygen flow to the heart.

- Nausea/vomiting. Related to decreased cardiac output.
- Variable blood pressure. Related to decreased cardiac output.
- Shortness of breath (dyspnea). Related to decreased oxygen in the blood.
- Asymptomatic. Symptoms varies in degree and a patient may have no symptoms of a MI.
- Urine output decreases (< 25 ml/hr). Related to lack of renal blood flow. Normal is 1 ml per kg per hour. Critical is < 0.5 ml per kg per hour
- Decreased pulse pressure (difference in systolic and diastolic). Related to decreased cardiac output.

Interventions
- Bed rest without bathroom privileges. Decreases cardiac workload.
- Place patient in a semi-Fowler's position. Decreases stress.
- Monitor vital signs.
- 12-lead ECG during episodes of chest pain per orders.
- Place patient on a low cholesterol, low sodium, and low fat diet
- Administer as ordered:
    o 2 to 4 liters 100% oxygen. Use a non-rebreather face mask to increase oxygen supply to the patient.
    o Analgesic. Decreases cardiac workload and pain.
    o Nitrates. Dilates blood vessels leading to increased blood flow to cardiac muscle.
        ▪ Hold nitrate if systolic blood pressure < 90 mm Hg. Risk of reduced blood to the brain.
    o Beta-adrenergic blocker. Decreases cardiac workload.
        ▪ Hold Beta-adrenergic blocker if heart rate is less than 60 beats per minute. Risk of low cardiac output.
    o Aspirin. Decreases formation of platelets.
    o Antiarrhythmics. Controls cardiac arrhythmias.
    o Antihypertensive. Decreases blood pressure.
    o Thrombolytic therapy (within 3 to 12 hours of an attack). Dissolves blockage.
    o Heparin. Prevents formation of blood clots following thrombolytic therapy.
    o Calcium channel blockers. Prevents re-infarction in a non-Q-wave infarction.

Cardiac Tamponade

The pericardium fills with fluid, blood, or pus increasing pressure in the pericardium and resulting in decreased filling of ventricles leading to decreased cardiac output.

Classic Signs
- Muffled cardiac sounds. Related to fluid, blood, or pus in the pericardium.
- Sweating (diaphoresis). Related to increased anxiety from decreased oxygen to cardiac muscle.
- Tachycardia. The body's attempts to increase oxygen flow to the heart.
- Shortness of breath (dyspnea). Related to decreased oxygen in the blood.
- Restlessness. Related to decreased oxygen to the brain.
- Paradoxical pulse (decrease of 15 mmHg or more in systolic blood pressure on inspiration). Related to pressure change within the chest on inspiration.
- Fatigue. Related to increase cardiac workload.
- Jugular vein distention. Related to fluid overload.

Interventions
- Monitor vital signs.
- Administer as ordered:
    o 2 to 4 liters 100% oxygen. Use a non-rebreather face mask to increase oxygen supply to the patient
    o Beta-adrenergic blocker. Decreases cardiac workload.
        ▪ Hold Beta-adrenergic blocker if heart rate is less than 60 beats per minute. Risk of low cardiac output.
- Pericardiocentesis: Aspirate fluid from the pericardium.

Cardiogenic Shock

Decreased blood pressure as a result of decreased cardiac output related to cardiomyopathies.

Classic Signs
- Distended jugular veins. Related to fluid overload.
- Hypotension. Related decreased cardiac output.
- Clammy, pale skin. Related to decreased circulation.

- Confusion. Related to decreased oxygen to the brain.
- Crackles. Related to build-up of fluids in the lungs.
- Decreased skin temperature. Related to decreased circulation.
- Cyanosis. Related to poor perfusion.
- Arrhythmias. Related to irritability of cardiac muscle from decreased oxygenation.
- Oliguria (urine output < 30 ml per hour) due to decreased kidney perfusion.
- Tachycardia. The body's attempts to increase oxygen flow to the heart.

Interventions
- Place patient on bed rest. Decreases cardiac workload.
- Monitor vital signs.
- Measure fluid intake and output. Assess for renal output and renal perfusion. Normal is 1 ml per kg per hour. Critical is < 0.5 ml per kg per hour.
- Measure weight daily. Weight increase indicates fluid retention.
- Place patient on a low sodium and low fat diet.
- Administer as ordered:
    o 2 to 4 liters 100% oxygen. Use a non-rebreather face mask to increase oxygen supply to the patient.
    o Vasodilator. Dilates blood vessels and decreases cardiac workload.
    o Adrenergic medication. Increases blood pressure and heart rate to perfuse organs.
    o Inotropes. Strengthens cardiac contractions.
    o Vasopressor. Increases blood flow.

Endocarditis

An infection of the inner lining of the heart (endocardium) and heart valves as a result of invasive medical procedures or secondary to rheumatic heart disease or degenerative heart disease.

Classic Signs
- Janeway lesions. Non-tender, small red areas on the soles and palms, or solid, elevated areas of tissue or fluid inside or under the skin of the soles or palms.
- Petechiae. Small, purple spots on fingernails and palate.

- Osler nodes. Painful, red, raised lesions found on the hands and feet.
- Fatigue. Related to increased cardiac workload.
- Murmurs. Related to turbulent blood flow caused by infected heart valves.
- Fever. Related to infection.

Interventions
- Bed rest. Decreases cardiac workload.
- Monitor for renal failure:
    o Decreased urine output. Related to decreased perfusion of the kidneys.
    o Increased BUN. Related to decreased perfusion of the kidneys.
    o Increased creatinine clearance. Related to decreased perfusion of the kidneys.
- Monitor for embolism:
    o Hematuria (blood in urine)
    o Decreased mentation
    o Cough or painful breathing
- Monitor for heart failure:
    o Weight gain. Related to fluid retention.
    o Dependent edema. Related to fluid retention.
    o Jugular vein distention. Related to fluid overload.
    o Crackles. Related to build-up of fluids in the lungs.
    o Shortness of breath (dyspnea). Related to decreased oxygen in the blood.
    o Tachycardia. The body's attempts to increase oxygen flow to the heart.
- Blood culture and sensitivity test 3 times, one hour apart. Identifies the microorganism and treatment.
- Administer antibiotics as ordered.

Congestive Heart Failure (CHF)

Ventricles cannot contract to full capacity resulting in decreased circulation. Right-side heart failure occurs when the right ventricles are unable to fully contract resulting in blood backing up in the circulatory system leading to edema, especially in peripheral areas. Left-side congestive heart failure occurs when the left ventricles are unable to fully contract resulting in blood backing up in the lungs.

Classic Signs
Early Signs:
- Fatigue. Related to increased cardiac workload.
- Nocturia (waking up from sleep to urinate). Related to increased fluid volume.
- Shortness of breath (dyspnea) on exertion. Related to decreased oxygen in the blood.
- Bilateral crackles. Related to build-up of fluids in the lungs

Advanced Signs:
- Shortness of breath lying down (orthopnea). Related to fluids in the lungs.
- Enlarged heart (cardiomegaly). Related to overworking of the heart or underlying cardiac disease.
- Enlarged liver (hepatomegaly). Related to the backup of blood in the circulatory system.
- Frothy or pink sputum. Related to fluids in the lungs.
- Decreased hemoglobin.
- Decreased hematocrit (three times less than hemoglobin).
- High BUN. Related to decreased perfusion of the kidneys.
- High Creatinine clearance. Related to decreased perfusion of the kidneys.
- Decreased urine output. Related to decreased perfusion of the kidneys. Normal is 1 ml per kg per hour. Critical is < 0.5 ml per kg per hour.

Interventions
- Place patient in high Fowler's position. Decreases cardiac workload.
- Measure weight daily. Weight increase indicates fluid retention.
- Monitor vital signs.
- Measure fluid intake and output. Assess for renal output and renal perfusion. Normal is 1 ml per kg per hour. Critical is < 0.5 ml per kg per hour.
- Raise legs. Decreases dependent edema.
- Administer as ordered:
    o 2 to 4 liters 100% oxygen. Use a non-rebreather face mask to increase oxygen supply to the patient.
    o Diuretics. Decreases fluid volume.
    o ACE inhibitors. Decreases pressure in the left ventricle.
    o Beta-adrenergic blockers. Decreases cardiac contractions.
    o Inotropic medication. Strengthens cardiac contractions.
    o Vasodilator. Dilates blood vessels and decreases cardiac workload.
    o Anticoagulant. Decreases blood coagulation.

Hypertensive Crisis

A sudden spike in blood pressure to 180/120 or higher.

Classic Signs
— Dizziness. Related to decreased oxygen to the brain.
— Confusion. Related to decreased oxygen to the brain.
— Irritability. Related to decreased oxygen to the brain.
— Nausea/vomiting. Related to decreased oxygen in the blood.
— Short of breath on exertion. Related to decreased oxygen in the blood.
— Blurred vision. Related to decreased oxygen in the blood.
— Seizure. Related to decreased oxygen in the blood.
— Decreased level of consciousness. Related to decreased oxygen to the brain.

Interventions
— Provide quiet, low-lit environment.
— Monitor blood pressure every fifteen minutes. Blood pressure should decrease no more than 25% of Mean arterial pressure (MAP) within the first two hours of treatment.
— Monitor ECG continuously.
— Monitor urine output. Normal is 1 ml per kg per hour. Critical is < 0.5 ml per kg per hour.
— Monitor pulse oximetry (arterial oxygen saturation). 95 to 100% is normal on room air without chronic pulmonary disease. A lower value is normal for a patient with chronic pulmonary disease.
— Administer as ordered:
    o 2 to 4 liters 100% oxygen. Use a non-rebreather face mask to increase oxygen supply to the patient.
    o Vasodilator. Dilates blood vessels and decreases cardiac workload.

Hypovolemic Shock

Decreased intravascular volume related to decreased circulation of blood, plasma, and other body fluids leading to inadequate organ perfusion.

Classic Signs
- Tachycardia. Related to decreased blood volume.
- Agitation. Related to decreased oxygen to the brain.
- Hypotension. Related to decreased blood volume.
- Decreased skin temperature. Related to decreased circulation.
- Decreased blood pressure. Related decreased blood volume.
- Urine output less than 25 ml/hour. Related to decreased kidney perfusion. Normal is 1 ml per kg per hour. Critical is < 0.5 ml per kg per hour.
- Decreased hemoglobin. Related to decreased blood volume.
- Decreased hematocrit. Related to decreased blood volume.
- High BUN. Related to decreased perfusion of the kidneys.
- High Creatinine clearance. Related to decreased perfusion of the kidneys.
- Arterial Blood Gas.
    - Decrease pH
    - Increase pCO_2
    - Decrease pO_2

Interventions
- Monitor vital signs every 15 minutes.
- Monitor for bilateral crackles. Related to build up of fluids in the lungs as a result of treatment.
- Measure urine output hourly using indwelling urinary catheter.
- Increase fluid intake if urine output is less than 30 ml/hour.
- Insert large IV catheter (18G).
- Administer as ordered:
    - 2 to 4 liters 100% oxygen. Use a non-rebreather face mask to increase oxygen supply to the patient. Increase oxygen if less than 80 mmHg systolic
    - Catecholamines. Increases blood pressure.
    - Inotropic medication. Increases blood pressure.
    - Crystalloid solutions. Expands intravascular and extravascular fluid volume.
    - Fresh frozen plasma. Increases clotting.
    - Blood replacement (Type O negative, universal donor).

Myocarditis

Inflamed cardiac muscle due to infection.

Classic Signs
- Shortness of breath (dyspnea) on exertion. Related to decreased oxygen in the blood.
- Chest pain. Related to necrosis of cardiac muscle as a result of infection and inflammation.
- Fever. Related to increased circulation related to the inflammation process.
- Tachycardia. Related to increased cardiac workload.
- Increased CK-MB. Related to necrosis of cardiac muscle.
- Increased troponins. Related to necrosis of cardiac muscle.

Interventions
- Bed rest without bathroom privileges. Decreases cardiac workload.
- Place patient in high Fowler's position. Decreases cardiac workload.
- Monitor vital signs.
- Gradually return to normal activities.
- Administer as ordered:
    o   Antiarrhythmics. Controls cardiac arrhythmias.

Pericarditis

Inflammation of the pericardium from infection. Acute pericarditis is typically caused by a viral infection. Chronic pericarditis is typically caused by disease or medication reaction.

Classic Signs
- Anxiety. Related to pain and changes in respiratory function.
- Sharp pain over the precordium radiating to the neck, shoulders, back, and arm relieved by leaning forward or sitting up. Related to inflammation affecting a common nerve.
- Pain in the teeth or muscles. Related to inflammation affecting a common nerve.
- Arrhythmias. Related to irritability of cardiac muscle from inflammation.

- Difficulty breathing (dyspnea). Related to decreased oxygen from decreased cardiac output caused by inflammation.
- Tachypnea. Related to increased cardiac workload.
- Fever. Related to inflammation.
- Increased AST. Related to necrosis of liver cells.
- Increased LST. Related to necrosis of liver cells.
- Increased CK-MB. Related to necrosis of cardiac muscle.
- Increased WBC. Related to inflammation.
- Increased SED rate. Related to inflammation.

Interventions
- Bed rest without bathroom privileges. Decreases cardiac workload.
- Place patient in high Fowler's position. Decreases cardiac workload.
- Coughing, deep breathing exercises. Expands lungs and decreases discomfort
- Monitor vital signs.
- Administer as ordered:
    o Corticosteroids. Decreases inflammation.
    o Nonsteroidal Anti-inflammatory Drugs (NSAIDs). Decreases inflammation.

Pulmonary Edema

Fluid buildup in lungs as a result from decreased contractions by the left ventricle.

Classic Signs
- Frothy or pink sputum. Related to fluids in the lungs.
- Bilateral Crackles. Related to build-up of fluids in the lungs.
- Tachycardia. The body's attempts to increase oxygen flow to the heart.
- Jugular vein distention. Related to fluid overload.
- Cyanosis. Related to poor perfusion.
- Clammy, pale skin. Related to decreased circulation.
- Restlessness. Related to decreased oxygen to the brain.
- Difficulty breathing (dyspnea) when sitting upright. Related to fluid in the lungs.
- Hypertension. Related to increased vascular pressure.
- Oxygen saturation. oxygen saturation is < 90%

Interventions
- Measure fluid intake and output. Assess for renal output and renal perfusion. Normal is 1 ml per kg per hour. Critical is < 0.5 ml per kg per hour.
- Place patient in high Fowler's position. Decreases cardiac workload.
- Monitor vital signs.
- Place on low sodium diet. Decreases fluid retention.
- Decrease fluid intake to avoid risk of fluid overload.
- Measure weight daily. Weight increase indicates fluid retention.
- Monitor capillary refill. Normal is < 3 seconds.
- Administer as ordered:
  - 2 to 4 liters 100% oxygen. Use a non-rebreather face mask to increase oxygen supply to the patient.
  - Vasodilator. Dilates blood vessels and decreases cardiac workload.
  - Inotropic medication. Strengthens cardiac contractions.
  - Diuretics. Decreases fluid volume.
  - Analgesic. Decreases cardiac workload and pain.
  - Bronchodilator. Dilates bronchiole tubes and decreases bronchospasms.

Thrombophlebitis

A blood clot (thrombus) in a vein resulting in inflammation caused by decreased circulation, trauma, medication side effect, or coagulation disorder.

Classic Signs
- Asymptomatic
- Cramps in effective area. Related to decreased blood flow.
- Positive Homans' sign. Calf pain when toes are pointed upwards (dorsiflexion).
- Warmth in affected area. Related to inflammation.
- Swelling in one leg (edema). Related to decreased blood flow.
- Clot moved to lungs:
  - Difficulty breathing not improved with oxygen. Related to blocked vessels in lungs.
  - Tachycardia. The body's attempts to increase oxygen flow to the heart.
  - Bilateral Crackles. Related to build-up of fluids in the lungs.

Interventions
- Elevate affected area to encourage circulation.
- Bed rest without bathroom privileges. Decreases cardiac workload.
- Apply warm, moist compresses on affected area to increase blood flow.
- Monitor for signs of clot moving to lungs.
- After clot resolves, tell the patient:
    - No crossing legs, this causes decreased circulation.
    - No oral contraceptives due to increase in clotting.
    - Wear support hose.
- Administer as ordered:
    - Nonsteroidal Anti-inflammatory Drugs (NSAIDs). Decreases inflammation.
    - Anticoagulant. Decreases blood coagulation.

Respiratory Assessment, Disorders, Interventions

Assessment
- Is the patient showing signs of problem breathing?
    - Agitation. Related to decreased oxygen levels.
    - Sweating. Related to increased stress from decreased oxygen levels.
    - Cyanotic nail beds, tip of the nose, and ear lobes. Related to decreased circulatory oxygenation.
    - Pale. Related to decreased circulation.
    - Elevated shoulders. Related to use of accessory muscles to supplement diaphragmatic breathing.

Stop the assessment if the patient becomes unstable and focus on stabilizing the patient.

Interview
- Keep questions simple that can be answered with yes or no. The patient is in distress.
- Initial Questions:
    - What makes you feeling that something is wrong?
    - What happen before you noticed this problem?
    - Have you recently undergone any medical procedure?

- Follow up questions:
  - o Do you have a cough?
  - o How long have you been coughing?
  - o Are there changes in your cough?
  - o What time of day do you cough?
  - o What aggravates or relieves the cough?
  - o Is the cough productive?
  - o Do you have shortness of breath (dyspnea)?
  - o Do you have shortness of breath when lying down (orthopnea)?
  - o How many pillows do you use when sleeping?
  - o What aggravates or relieves shortness of breath?
  - o Are you drowsy or irritable during the day (sign of sleep apnea)?
  - o Do you have allergies?
  - o Have you been recently exposure to an allergen?
  - o What happens when you are exposed to an allergen?
  - o Do you smoke?
  - o How many packs per day?
  - o How long have you been smoking?
  - o Are you exposed to second-hand smoke?
  - o Do you have a respiratory disease?
  - o What treatment are you receiving?
  - o Were you exposed to environmental conditions that may be associated with your respiratory complaint?

Inspection
- Count respiration. Normal is 10 to 20 respirations per minute
- Breathing patterns. Normal is even and unlabored.
- Abnormal:
  - o Biot's Respiration. Alternating shallow rapid breathing followed by sudden apnea. Related to central nervous system problems.
  - o Cheyne-Strokes. A cycle of shallow to deep breathing followed by up to 20 seconds of apnea. Normal during sleep. Abnormal if related to cardiac failure, kidney failure, or central nervous system problems.
- Cyanotic nail beds, tip of the nose, and ear lobes. Related to decreased circulatory oxygenation.
- Clubbing of fingers related to chronic deoxygenation of blood.
- Flaring nostrils. Related to respiratory distress.

– Pursing of lips. Related to effort by the patient to opening the airway longer to improve breathing.
– Asymmetrical chest movement. Related to uncoordinated respiration and the use of accessory muscles to breath.
– Displaced trachea. Related to collapsed lung.
– Agitation. Related to decreased oxygen levels.

Palpation
– Feel chest wall vibrations (*tactile fremitus*). Place hands lightly on patient's back. Have patient fold arms across chest. Ask the patient to say aloud "99."
  o Little vibration. Bronchial obstruction or fluid in pleural cavity (pleural effusion).
  o Less vibration. Pleural effusion, emphysema, or pneumothorax.
  o Intense vibration. Tissue consolidation.
– Feel separation of the frontal intercostal space. Place hands on the patient's chest with thumbs position in the second intercostal space. Ask patient to breath normally.
  o Thumbs separate equally. Normal.
  o Thumbs separating asymmetrically. Pleural effusion, pneumonia, pneumothorax, or atelectasis (collapsed lung).
  o Thumbs decrease separation. Emphysema, ascites (fluid), respiratory depression, paralysis of the diaphragm, obesity, atelectasis.

Percussion
– Place one finger on the patient's chest. Tap the finger to vibrate the lung fields:
  o Front: Begin at the upper right, then move left, down, and to the right to the end of the rib cage.
  o Back: Move along the shoulder lines then move upper right, across to the right, down and across to the left until the end of the rib cage.
– Hyperresonance. Indicates air in the lungs (asthma, emphysema, and pneumothorax)
– Hyporesonance (dull). Indicates decreased air in the lungs (atelectasis (partial collapse lung), pleural effusion, or tumor)

Auscultation
- Listen to air moving through bronchi with a stethoscope.
  - o Normal breath sounds:
    - ▪ Trachea: Harsh sound on inspiration and expiration
    - ▪ Bronchial (next to the trachea). High-pitched, loud, and discontinuous. Loudest on expiration.
    - ▪ Bronchovesicular (between scapulae and upper sternum). Medium-pitched, continuous on inspiration and expiration.
    - ▪ Vesicular (remaining lung area). Low-pitched, soft, prolonged on inspiration and short on expiration.
  - o Abnormal breath sounds:
    - ▪ Crackles. Crackling sound on inspiration. Related to air moving through secretions.
      - • Fine Crackles. Sounds like hair rubbing together.
      - • Coarse Crackles. Gurgling.
    - ▪ Wheezing. High-pitched sound on inspiration or expiration. Related to blocked airflow.
    - ▪ Rhonchi. Low-pitched sound (snoring) on expiration. Changes when the patient coughs.
    - ▪ Stridor. High-pitched wheezing during inspiration. Related to obstructed airway.
    - ▪ Pleural Friction Rub. Low-pitched grating sound on inspiration and expiration, painful.
- Voice sounds are chest vibrations when the patient speaks.
  - o Egophony: Ask the patient to say "E."
    - ▪ Normal: Muffled.
    - ▪ Abnormal: Sounds like "A." Lung area is dense (consolidated).
  - o Bronchophony: Ask the patient to say "99."
    - ▪ Normal: Muffled.
    - ▪ Abnormal: Loud, lung area is dense (consolidated).
  - o Whispered pectoriloquy: Ask the patient to whisper "1, 2, 3."
    - ▪ Normal: Unable to distinguish the numbers.
    - ▪ Abnormal: Loud and distinct, lung area is dense (consolidated).

Common Classic Signs
- Stridor (high-pitched wheezing) on inspiration:
  o Upper Airway Obstruction
  o Croup (children)
  o Aspiration of foreign body
- Stridor (high-pitched wheezing) on expiration:
  o Lower Airway Obstruction
  o Asthma
  o Bronchitis
- Rapid respiration rate and grunting:
  o Pneumonia
  o Pulmonary edema
- Disordered control over breathing:
  o Increased intracranial pressure
  o Medication overdose
  o Poisoning
  o Neuromuscular disorder
- Difficulty catching breath or working to breath:
  o Respiratory distress
  o Inadequate perfusion
  o Sepsis shock
- Change in voice:
  o Upper airway obstruction
- Inability to speak more than one word at a time:
  o Lower airway obstruction

Acute Respiratory Distress Syndrome (ARDS)

An inflammatory response from sepsis or shock leading to the buildup of fluid and protein in the alveoli causing the alveoli to collapse causing an impaired gas exchange.

Classic Signs
- Difficulty breathing (dyspnea). Related to decreased oxygen in the blood.
- Pulmonary edema. Related to fluid in the lungs.
- Tachypnea. The body's attempts to increase gas exchange.
- Crackles. Related to air moving through secretions.
- Hypoxemia. Related to decreased oxygen levels.

- Elevated shoulders. Related to use of accessory muscles to supplement diaphragmatic breathing.
- Decreased breath sounds. Related to blocked vessels in lungs.
- Cyanotic nail beds, tip of the nose, and ear lobes. Related to decreased circulatory oxygenation.
- Rhonchi. Related to secretions or obstruction of large airways.
- Anxiety. Related to decreased oxygen levels
- Tachycardia. The body's attempts to increase oxygen flow to the heart.
- Restlessness. Related to decreased oxygen levels.

Interventions
- Place patient in high Fowler's position. Decreases cardiac workload.
- Bed rest. Decreases cardiac workload.
- Measure weight daily. Weight increase indicates fluid retention.
- Monitor vital signs.
- Measure fluid intake and output. Assess for renal output and renal perfusion. Normal is 1 ml per kg per hour. Critical is < 0.5 ml per kg per hour.
- Coughing and deep-breathing exercises. Improves pulmonary gas exchange.
- Administer as ordered:
    o Analgesic. Decreases pain.
    o Diuretics. Decreases fluid volume.
    o Proton Pump Inhibitor. Decreases risk of aspiration and gastric stress ulcer.
    o Steroids. Decreases inflammation.
    o Exogenous surfactant. Decreases surface tension within alveoli that causes alveoli to collapse.

Asthma

A trigger (allergen or non-allergen) causes inflammation of the airway and bronchospasm leading to difficulty breathing.
- Atopic asthma (extrinsic) caused by allergens.
- Non-atopic asthma (intrinsic) caused by cold air, humidity, or other non-allergens.

Classic Signs
- Difficulty breathing (dyspnea). Related to decreased oxygen in the blood.

- Bronchoconstriction. Related to inflammation.
- Tachypnea. The body's attempts to increase gas exchange.
- Wheezing on inspiration or expiration. Related to blocked airflow.
- Cough. Related to removal of mucus and secretions that block the airways.
- Elevated shoulders. Related to use of accessory muscles to supplement diaphragmatic breathing.
- Tachycardia. The body's attempts to increase oxygen flow to the heart.
- Anxiety. Related to decreased oxygen levels
- Sweating (diaphoresis). Related to increased anxiety from decreased oxygen.
- Hyperresonance on percussion. Related to hyperinflation of lungs.

Interventions
- Remove trigger.
- Place patient in high Fowler's position. Decreases cardiac workload.
- Monitor pulse oximetry, arterial oxygen saturation. 95% to 100% is normal on room air.
- Monitor vital signs.
- Give patient three liters of fluid daily to liquefy secretions.
- Administer as ordered:
  - o Oxygen therapy 1 to 2 liters per minute.
  - o Bronchodilator. Dilates bronchiole tubes.
  - o Anticholinergic medication. Decreases bronchospasms.
  - o Leukotriene modulators. Decreases inflammation.
  - o Corticosteroids. Decreases inflammation.
  - o Mast cell stabilizer. Decreases inflammation.
  - o Proton pump inhibitor. Decreases acid reflux that leads to bronchoconstriction.

Atelectasis

Collapsed lung leading to decreased gas exchange. Common causes are airway obstruction, pleural space infusion, tumor, anesthesia, immobility, or no deep breathing exercise post-op.

Classic Signs
- Decreased breath. Related to collapsed lung.
- Sweating (diaphoresis). Related to increased anxiety from decreased oxygen to cardiac muscle.
- Difficulty breathing (dyspnea). Related to decreased oxygen.
- Hypoxemia. Related to decreased gas exchange.
- Tachypnea. The body's attempts to increase gas exchange.
- Tachycardia. The body's attempts to increase oxygen flow to the heart.
- Cyanotic nail beds, tip of the nose, and ear lobes. Related to decreased circulatory oxygenation.
- Anxiety. Related to decreased oxygen levels.
- Elevated shoulders. Use of accessory muscles indicating an increased attempt to increase air flow.

Interventions
- Provide humidified air to loosen secretions.
- Coughing, deep-breathing exercises. Expands lungs and decreases discomfort
- Use the incentive spirometer. Slow, deep breaths help lungs expand.
- Perform abdominal diaphragmatic breathing exercises with pursed-lip breathing. Helps lungs expand.
- Administer as ordered:
    - o 1 to 2 liters per minute 100% oxygen. Use a non-rebreather face mask to increase oxygen supply to the patient.
    - o Bronchodilator. Dilates bronchiole tubes.
    - o Mucolytics. Loosens secretions.

Bronchiectasis

Excessive mucus obstructs the bronchi and bronchioles caused by increased dilation of the bronchi and bronchioles related to inflammation.

Classic Signs
- Coughing up blood (hemoptysis). Related to inflammation.
- Difficulty breathing (dyspnea). Related to decreased oxygen associated with inflammation.

- Cyanotic nail beds, tip of the nose, and ear lobes. Related to decreased circulatory oxygenation.
- Cough when lying down. Related to infection.
- Foul smelling cough. Related to infection.
- Crackles on inspiration. Related to air moving through secretions.
- Rhonchi on inspiration. Related to secretions or obstruction of large airways.

Interventions
- Chest percussions. Loosens secretions in lungs.
- Postural drainage. Drain mucus from lungs to throat using gravity.
- Administer as ordered:
    o Oxygen therapy 1 to 2 liters per minute. Supplement oxygen to the patient.
    o Bronchodilator. Dilates bronchiole tubes.
    o Antibiotics to treat the infection.

Bronchitis

Increased mucus production in the lungs caused by infection that leads to airway blockage and decreased gas exchange.
- Acute bronchitis. Reversible within 10 days.
- Chronic bronchitis [Chronic Obstructive Pulmonary Disease (COPD)]. Not reversible.

Classic Signs
- Productive cough. Related to increased mucus production.
- Difficulty breathing (dyspnea). Related to decrease oxygen from increased mucus production.
- Wheezing on inspiration or expiration. Related to blocked airflow.
- Elevated shoulders. Related to use of accessory muscles to supplement diaphragmatic breathing.
- Fever. Related to infection.
- Weight gain. Related to decreased perfusion leading to fluid retention.
- Fatigue. Related to increased respiratory and cardiac workload.

Interventions
- Use incentive spirometer. Helps to expand lungs.
- High Fowler's position. Decreases respiratory and cardiac workload.
- Administer 3 liters of fluid daily. Helps to liquefy secretions.
- Weigh patient daily. A weight gain of 2 lbs. or more in a day indicates fluid retention.
- Measure fluid intake and output. Assess for renal output and renal perfusion. Normal is 1 ml per kg per hour. Critical is < 0.5 ml per kg per hour.
- Coughing, deep-breathing exercises. Expands lungs and decreases discomfort.
- Administer as ordered:
    o Oxygen therapy 1 to 2 liters per minute via nasal cannula.
    o Bronchodilator. Dilates bronchiole tubes.
    o Steroids. Decreases inflammation.
    o Diuretics. Decreases fluid volume.
    o Proton pump inhibitor. Decreases acid reflux that leads to bronchoconstriction.
    o Expectorant. Liquefies secretions.
    o Anticholinergic. Reduces bronchospasm.

Cor Pulmonale

Right-side heart failure leading to pulmonary hypertension and enlargement of the right ventricle resulting from chronic obstructive pulmonary disease (COPD).

Classic Signs
- Productive cough. Related to increased mucus production.
- Edema. Related to decreased perfusion leading to fluid retention.
- Weight gain. Related to decreased perfusion leading to fluid retention.
- Shortness of breath lying down (orthopnea). Related to fluids in the lungs.
- Difficulty breathing (dyspnea). Related to decreased oxygen from increased mucus production.
- Tachycardia. The body's attempts to increase oxygen flow to the heart.
- Cyanotic nail beds, tip of the nose, and ear lobes. Related to decreased circulatory oxygenation.
- Fatigue. Related to increased respiratory and cardiac workload.
- Tachypnea. The body's attempts to increase gas exchange.
- Wheezing on inspiration or expiration. Related to blocked airflow.

Interventions
- Bed rest. Decreases cardiac workload.
- Monitor vital signs.
- Weigh patient daily. A weight gain of 2 lbs. or more in a day indicates fluid retention.
- No overexertion. Decreases respiratory and cardiac workload.
- Limit fluid to 2 liters daily. Patient is retaining fluids.
- Place patient on a low-sodium diet to decrease fluid retention.
- Monitor pulse oximetry, arterial oxygen saturation. 95% to 100% is normal on room air without chronic pulmonary disease. A lower value is normal for a patient with chronic pulmonary disease.
- Administer as ordered:
    o Oxygen therapy 1 to 2 liters per minute via nasal cannula.
    o Calcium Channel Blockers. Dilates blood vessels decreasing blood pressure.
    o Potassium channel activator. Dilates blood vessels decreasing blood pressure.
    o Angiotensin-converting enzyme (ACE) inhibitor. Dilates blood vessels decreasing blood pressure.
    o Diuretics. Increases fluid excretion.
    o Cardiac glycoside. Strengthens cardiac contractions.

Emphysema

Chronic inflammation of lungs leading to decreased flexibility of the walls of the alveoli resulting in the distention of the alveolar walls and causing air to be trapped.

Classic Signs
- Difficulty breathing (dyspnea). Related to decreased oxygen from decreased cardiac output caused by inflammation.
- Elevated shoulders. Related to use of accessory muscles to supplement diaphragmatic breathing.
- Barrel chest. Results from the rib cage being partially expanded all the time caused by the chronic over-inflation of the lungs.
- Loss of weight. Related to increased caloric usage required by the increased respiratory workload. Chronically inflated lungs interfere with expansion of the stomach making it uncomfortable to eat.

- Diminished breath sounds. Related to the chronic hyperinflation of the lungs.
- Wheezing on expiration. Related to blocked airflow.
- Hyperresonance on percussion. Related to hyperinflation of lungs from trapped air in the alveoli.

Interventions
- Place patient in high Fowler's position. Decreases respiratory and cardiac workload.
- Measure fluid intake and output. Assess for renal output and renal perfusion. Normal is 1 ml per kg per hour. Critical is < 0.5 ml per kg per hour.
- Monitor vital signs.
- Monitor sputum changes for signs of infection.
- Use incentive spirometer. Helps to expand lungs.
- Administer 3 liters of fluid daily. Helps to liquefy secretions.
- Coughing, deep-breathing exercises. Expands lungs and decreases discomfort.
- Weigh patient daily. A weight gain of 2 lbs. or more in a day indicates fluid retention.
- Administer as ordered:
    o Oxygen therapy 1 to 2 liters per minute via nasal cannula. Do not use more than 2 liters/minute for COPD patients if the patient is not intubated. Decreased carbon dioxide levels can decrease the respiratory drive in COPD patients.
    o Bronchodilator. Dilates bronchiole tubes and decreases bronchospasms.
    o Diuretics. Increases fluid excretion.
    o Expectorant. Liquefies secretions
    o Anticholinergic. Reduces bronchospasm
    o Steroids. Decrease inflammation
    o Proton pump inhibitor. Decrease acid reflux that leads to bronchoconstriction

Pleural Effusion

Lung expansion is restricted because the pleural sac fills with blood hemothorax), pus (empyema), or fluid impeding gas exchange.

Classic Signs
- Difficulty breathing (dyspnea). Related to decreased oxygen caused by restricted lung expansion.
- Decreased breath sounds. Related to restricted lung expansion.
- Tachypnea. The body's attempts to increase gas exchange.
- Tachycardia. The body's attempts to increase oxygen flow to the heart.
- Decreased blood pressure (in hemothorax). Related to decreased blood volume.
- Fever. Related to infection.
- Dullness on percussion over the affected area of the lung. Related to fluid in the pleural sac.
- Coughing. Related to attempts to open the airways.
- Pleural friction rub. Grating sounds related to the lining of the plural sac rubbing together as a result of fluid.

Interventions
- Monitor vital signs.
- Coughing, deep-breathing exercises. Expands lungs and decreases discomfort.
- Make sure chest drainage tube (post-thoracentesis) is patent.
- Administer as ordered:
  - o   2 to 4 liters per minute 100% oxygen. Use a non-rebreather face mask to increase oxygen supply to the patient.
  - o   Antibiotics. Decreases infection.

Pneumonia

A lung infection that leads to the inflammation process and results in increased mucus production and thickening of alveolar fluid causing decreased gas exchange.

Classic Signs
- Difficulty breathing (dyspnea). Related to inflammation.
- Crackles. Related to air moving through secretions.
- Blood-tinged sputum. Related to infection.
- Coughing. Related to attempts to open the airways.
- Fever. Related to the inflammation response.

- Chills. Rapid muscle contraction and relaxation to increase the body temperature as part of the inflammation response in addressing the infection.
- Pain on respiration. Related to inflammation.
- Tachypnea. The body's attempts to increase gas exchange.
- Tachycardia. The body's attempts to increase oxygen flow to the heart related to decreased gas exchange.
- Hypoxemia. Related to decreased oxygen levels.
- Sweating (diaphoresis). Related to the body's attempts to maintain an appropriate temperature. The body is cooling.
- Wheezing on inspiration or expiration. Related to blocked airflow.

Interventions
- Monitor vital signs.
- Bed rest. Decreases respiratory and cardiac workload.
- Increase fluid. Helps to liquefy secretions.
- Place patient in high Fowler's position. Decreases respiratory and cardiac workload.
- Use incentive spirometer every 2 hours. Helps to expand lungs.
- Measure fluid intake and output. Assess for renal output and renal perfusion. Normal is 1 ml per kg per hour. Critical is < 0.5 ml per kg per hour.
- Monitor sputum characteristics. Related to infection.
- Monitor pulse oximetry, arterial oxygen saturation. 95% to 100% is normal on room air without chronic pulmonary disease. A lower value is normal for a patient with chronic pulmonary disease.
- Administer as ordered:
    o 2 to 4 liters per minute 100% oxygen. Use a non-rebreather face mask to increase oxygen supply to the patient.
    o Antibiotics. Decreases infection.
    o Bronchodilator. Dilates bronchiole tubes and decreases bronchospasms.
    o Antipyretic. Decreases fever.

Pneumothorax

Partially or completely collapse of the lung related to air entering the pleural space from an opening in the chest or lung. Types include:
- Open pneumothorax. Caused by penetrating chest wound.
- Closed pneumothorax. Caused by blunt trauma.

- Spontaneous pneumothorax. Caused by disease such as emphysema.
- Tension pneumothorax. Air in the pleural space is under pressure causing the lungs to compress.

Classic Signs
- Tachypnea. Attempt to increase gas exchange.
- Tachycardia. Attempt to increase oxygen flow to the heart related to decreased gas exchange.
- Tracheal deviation toward the unaffected side (tension pneumothorax). Related to pressure in the pleural space.
- Absent breath sounds over the affected area. Related to collapsed lung.
- Sharp chest pain aggravated by coughing. Related to inflammation of pleura.
- Interventions
- Monitor pulse oximetry, arterial oxygen saturation. 95% to 100% is normal on room air without chronic pulmonary disease. A lower value is normal for a patient with chronic pulmonary disease.
- Monitor vital signs. Identify changes in the patient status.
- Place patient in high Fowler's position. Decreases respiratory and cardiac workload.
- Bed rest. Decreases respiratory and cardiac workload.
- Make sure chest drainage tube is patent.
- Coughing, deep-breathing exercises. Expands lungs and decreases discomfort.
- Administer as ordered:
  - o 2 to 4 liters per minute 100% oxygen. Use a non-rebreather face mask to increase oxygen supply to the patient.
  - o Analgesic. Decreases pain.
  - o Bronchodilator. Dilates bronchiole tubes and decreases bronchospasms.
  - o Antipyretic. Decreases fever.

Respiratory Acidosis

Decreased ventilation (hypoventilation) increases the level of carbon dioxide (acid) in the blood (acidosis).

Classic Signs
- Difficulty breathing (dyspnea). Related to decreased oxygen.

- Hypoxemia. Related to decreased oxygen levels.
- Headache. Related to decreased oxygen to the brain.
- Irritability. Related to decreased oxygen to the brain.
- Confusion. Related to decreased oxygen to the brain.
- Cardiac arrhythmia. Related to decreased oxygen to the heart.

Interventions
- Monitor pulse oximetry, arterial oxygen saturation. 95% to 100% is normal on room air without chronic pulmonary disease. A lower value is normal for a patient with chronic pulmonary disease.
- Coughing, deep-breathing exercises. Expands lungs.
- Monitor vitals.
- Administer as ordered:
    - o   2 to 4 liters per minute 100% oxygen. Use a non-rebreather face mask to increase oxygen supply to the patient.
    - o   Bronchodilator. Dilates bronchiole tubes and decreases bronchospasms.

Tuberculosis

An airborne bacterial infection of the lung. Primary tuberculosis is when the patient is initially infected. Secondary tuberculosis is when the bacteria become reactivated if the patient had been previously infected. Latent tuberculosis results in positive test results and no symptoms.

Classic Signs
- Blood-tinged sputum (hemoptysis). Related to the infection.
- Productive cough persists for two weeks. The body's attempts to clear the airways.
- Low grade fever. Related to the inflammation process.
- Chills. Rapid muscle contraction and relaxation to increase the body temperature as part of the inflammation response in addressing the infection.
- Difficulty breathing (dyspnea). Related to decreased oxygen in the blood.
- Night sweats. Related to the inflammation response in addressing the infection.
- Fatigue. Related to increased metabolism associated with the increased inflammation process.

- Weight loss. Related to increased metabolism associated with the increased inflammation process.

Interventions
- Isolate the patient. Related to airborne infection.
- Monitor vitals. Identify changes in patient status.
- Monitor fluid intake and output. Identify fluid retention.
- Increase fluid. Helps to liquefy secretions.
- Bed rest. Decreases respiratory and cardiac workload.
- Increase carbohydrate, protein, Vitamin C in diet. Related to weight loss.
- Administer as ordered:
  - o   Anti-tubercular antibiotic. Decreases infection.

Acute Respiratory Failure

There is insufficient ventilation to support adequate gas exchange in the lungs.

Classic Signs
- Difficulty breathing (dyspnea). Related to decreased oxygen in the blood.
- Shortness of breath lying down (orthopnea). Related to fluids in the lungs.
- Tachypnea. Attempts to increase gas exchange.
- Crackles. Related to air moving through secretions.
- Cyanotic nail beds, tip of the nose, and ear lobes. Related to decreased circulatory oxygenation.
- Rhonchi. Related to secretions or obstruction of large airways.
- Sweating (diaphoresis). Related to increased anxiety from decrease oxygen.
- Coughing up blood (hemoptysis). Related to inflammation.
- Diminished breath sounds. Related to decreased ventilation.
- Fatigue. Related to increased respiratory and cardiac workload.

Interventions
- Place patient in high Fowler's position. Decreases respiratory and cardiac workload.
- Coughing, deep-breathing exercises. Expands lungs.
- Monitor vitals. Identify changes in patient status.
- Monitor fluid intake and output. Identify fluid retention.
- Change patient position every two hours. Prevent pressure ulcers.

- Monitor pulse oximetry, arterial oxygen saturation. 95% to 100% is normal on room air without chronic pulmonary disease. A lower value is normal for a patient with chronic pulmonary disease.
- Administer as ordered:
    o 2 to 4 liters per minute 100% oxygen. Use a non-rebreather face mask to increase oxygen supply to the patient.
    o Bronchodilator. Dilates bronchiole tubes.
    o Anticholinergic. Decreases bronchospasms.
    o Steroid. Decreases inflammation.
    o Proton pump inhibitor. Decreases acid reflux that leads to bronchoconstriction.
    o Analgesic. Decreases pain and decreases cardiac oxygen demand.

Pulmonary Embolism

Blood flow is impaired by an obstruction (thrombus, air emboli, or fat emboli) resulting in alveoli collapse leading to impaired gas exchange. Most common is a thrombus from a deep vein in the leg or pelvis.

Classic Signs
- Sudden difficulty breathing (dyspnea). Related to obstruction.
- Chest pain. Related to decreased oxygen to the heart.
- Tachypnea. Attempts to increase gas exchange.
- Tachycardia. Attempts to increase oxygen flow to the heart related to decreased gas exchange.
- Crackles at site of emboli. Related to air moving through secretions.
- Coughing up blood (hemoptysis). Related to inflammation.
- Anxiety. Related to decreased oxygen levels.
- Decreased level of consciousness. Related to decreased oxygen levels.
- Hypotension. Related to decreased oxygen levels.
- Leg swelling. Related to thrombus.
- Leg pain. Related to thrombus.

Interventions
- Place patient in high Fowler's position. Decreases respiratory and cardiac workload.
- Bed rest. Decreases respiratory and cardiac workload.

- Coughing, deep-breathing exercises. Expands lungs.
- Monitor fluid intake and output. Identify fluid retention.
- Monitor pulse oximetry, arterial oxygen saturation. 95% to 100% is normal on room air without chronic pulmonary disease. A lower value is normal for a patient with chronic pulmonary disease.
- Administer as ordered:
    o 2 to 4 liters per minute 100% oxygen. Use a non-rebreather face mask to increase oxygen supply to the patient.
    o Anticoagulant. Decreases clot formation.
    o Analgesic. Decreases pain and decreases cardiac oxygen demand.
    o Thrombolytics. Removes clot within 3 to 12 hours of blockages.

Neurological Assessment, Disorders, Interventions

Assessment
There are two memory jogger acronyms that will help you remember how to assess for the causes of altered mental status.
- AEIOU
    o Alcohol, arrhythmia
    o Endocrine/exocrine, electrolytes, encephalopathy
    o Insulin
    o Oxygen, opiates
    o Uremia
- TIPS
    o Trauma, temperature disorders
    o Infection
    o Psychiatric, porphyria, poisons
    o Shock, seizures, stroke, subarachnoid hemorrhage, space occupying lesion
- Assess the patient's altered mental status:
    o Alert. Responds to stimuli with little or no delay.
    o Oriented. Oriented to time, person, and place.
    o Sleepy. Arousable to a normal level of awareness.
    o Lethargic. A global depression of awareness of the environment and of the patient himself.
    o Stupor. Is sleepy and can be aroused to a semi-normal level of awareness using noxious stimuli.
    o Coma. Cannot be aroused.

- o. Delirium. Acutely confused showing psychomotor excitement and impaired memory and perception. The patient may experience hallucination.
  - o Dementia. A gradual deterioration of mental function.
- Assess for mental impairment using the Abbreviated Mental Test Score (AMTS). Each correct answer is valued at 1 point. A score of 6 or less suggest mental impairment that requires further testing.
  - o What is your age?
  - o What is the time to the nearest hour?
  - o What year is this?
  - o What is the name of this hospital?
  - o Do you know who I am? Do you know who this person is? The patient is expected to recognize two people who are in the room by name or title.
  - o What is your date of birth?
  - o When was Pearl Harbor attacked? (Any important history event can be asked.)
  - o Who is the President of the United States?
  - o Count backwards from 20 to 1.
  - o Mention an address to the patient then ask the patient to repeat the address.

Common Classic Signs
- Changes in pupils:
  - o PERRLA. Pupils equal, round, and reactive to light and accommodation (normal)
  - o Pinpoint bilateral nonreactive to light indicates:
    - Lesion in the pons resulting from a hemorrhage
    - Drug intoxication (heroin, opiates)
  - o Dilated bilateral fixed nonreactive to light indicates:
    - Cerebral ischemia
    - Anticholinergic toxicity
    - Severe brain damage
    - Hypoxia
    - Drug (sympathomimetic) intoxication (cocaine, methamphetamine, amphetamines, ecstasy, bath salts, stimulants)
  - o Small unilateral nonreactive to light indicates:
    - Spinal cord lesion

- o Dilated, unilateral fixed nonreactive to light indicates:
  - Normal if patient has a history of severe eye injury
  - Increased intracranial pressure
- o Subdural hematoma or epidural hematoma
  - Brain stem compression
  - Brain herniation leading to oculomotor nerve damage
- o Midsize, bilateral, fixed, nonreactive indicates:
  - Contusion
  - Brain edema
  - Brain hemorrhage
  - Laceration of the brain
  - Infarction in the brain
- Motor function. Inability to perform this exercise quickly may indicate alcohol toxicity, cerebellar disorder, or stroke:
  - o Push against your hands. There should be equal pressure from both arms.
  - o Close eyes, then extend both arms, palms up, for 20 seconds. Both arms should remain in position without any drift.
  - o Sit at the edge of the bed and raise both legs against your hands. There should be equal pressure from both legs.
  - o Push feet against your hands. There should be equal pressure from both legs.
  - o Stand. The patient should stand without assistance or support.
  - o Sit. The patient should sit without assistance or support.
  - o Walk. The patient's gait should be steady.
    - Bias towards one side may indicate a cerebellar lesion on that side.
    - Unsteady gait may indicate abnormal cerebellar functioning.
  - o Touch nose with an extended finger one hand at a time. The patient should be able to perform this action without hesitation.
  - o Touch your extended finger as you move your finger. The patient should be able to perform this action without hesitation.
  - o Touch each finger with the thumb on his same hand. Perform the test on the other hand. The patient should be able to perform this action without hesitation.
- Reflexes
  - o Tactile stimulation. Stroke the patient's skin. The more you stroke, the less of a reflex response should be noticed.

        ○ Plantar Reflex. Use a tongue blade and slowly stroke from the patient's heel to the great toe. Toes should flex. The Babinski's reflex (fanning of the smaller toes and upward movement of the great toe) is abnormal unless the patient is 2 years of age or younger.

        ○ Abdominal reflex. Stroke one side of the abdomen with the handle of the reflex hammer. Abdominal muscles contract and the umbilicus should deviate toward the same side. Repeat this on the opposite side.

–   Cranial nerve assessment (Table 8.4):

Table 8.4: Cranial Nerve Assessment

Cranial Nerve	Function	Examine
I Olfactory	Smell	Test each nostril with scents such as peppermint, coffee, and vanilla.
II Optic	Vision	Test eyes with Snellen eye chart.
III Oculomotor	Eye movement Constricting pupils Raising eyelid	Pupil size Pupil shape Pupil response to light
IV Trochlear	Moving eyes down and in	Ask the patient to move his eyes down and in.
V Trigeminal	Sensation for face and scalp Chewing Corneal reflex	Ask the patient to look up and out. Touch a piece of cotton to the other side of the eye. Both eyes should blink. Ask patient close both eyes. Randomly press a sharp and blunt object on the patient's forehead, jaw, and cheek. Ask the patient if he feels anything and. If so, to describe the feeling as sharp or dull. Ask the patient to open his mouth and clench his teeth.
VI Abducens	Moving eyes laterally	Ask the patient to move eyes laterally.
VII Facial	Taste Moving mouth, eyes, and forehead to show expression. Tears (lacrimation), salivation.	Raise and lower eye brows Smile showing teeth Puff cheeks Wrinkle forehead
VIII Acoustic	Balance Hearing	Stand an arm's length away from the patient's ear and rub two fingers. Ask if the patient hears anything. Repeat the test on the other ear. Conduct the Weber test by placing a vibrating fork on top of the patient's head the asking, "Where do you hear sound coming from?" The response should be midline.

Cranial Nerve	Function	Examine
		Conduct the Rinne test. Place a vibrating fork on the mastoid bone behind the ear. Ask the patient when he stops hearing it. Then move the fork to the patient's ear so the patient can hear the tone. The patient should hear better with the fork by the ear rather than on the mastoid bone.
IX Glossopharyngeal	Taste Swallowing Gag Reflex Salivating	Ask patient to swallow
X Vagus	Gag reflex Swallowing Heart rate Peristalsis Talking Abdominal function Thoracic functions	Ask the patient to talk Check the gag reflex touching the back of the tongue with a tongue blade. Ask the patient to open his mouth and say "ah." Uvula should be midline and soft palate should upward symmetrically.
XI Accessory	Rotation of head Moving shoulder	Ask patient to shrug shoulders while you press down on them. The shrug should be bilaterally equal. Apply resistance to the side of the patient's head while the patient rotates his head against the resistance. Repeat on the other side of the head.
XII Hypoglossal	Moving tongue	Ask the patient to stick out his tongue. The tongue should be midline. Ask the patient to say, "Round the rugged rock that ragged rascal ran." The patient should show little problem articulating. Results are depended on the patient's cognitive ability. Ask the patient to push his tongue against his cheek. Apply resistance to the cheek. The tongue should be symmetrical.

Cerebral Hemorrhage

Bleeding within the brain, between the dura mater and the skull, or layers covering the brain during time of injury or up to days after an injury.

– Cerebral Contusion. Blunt force trauma thrusts the brain against the inside of the skull resulting in cerebral edema, cerebral hemorrhage, and loss of consciousness longer than that in a concussion.
– Cerebral Edema. Fluid within the skull moves to the third space resulting in increased cranial pressure.

- Concussion. Blunt force trauma thrusts the brain against the inside of the skull but does not result in bruising.
- Contrecoup Injury. Blunt force trauma causes the head to recoil thrusting the brain against the inside of the skull at a point opposite of the blunt force trauma.
- Coup Injury. Blunt force trauma thrusts the brain against the inside of the skull at the point of the blunt force trauma.
- Epidural hematoma. Bleeding from an artery with blood accumulating between the dura and skull.
- Intracerebral Hemorrhage. Bleeding within brain tissue caused by shearing or tearing of small vessels within the brain and between the cerebrum and brain stem.
- Subarachnoid Hemorrhage. Bleeding between the arachnoid mater and the pia mater, the location of cerebrospinal fluid.
- Subdural Hematoma. Bleeding from a vein in the area between the dura mater and the arachnoid mater resulting in slow, chronic bleeding.

Classic Signs
- Symptoms are related to the location of the bleed and the amount of tissue affected by the bleed:
    o Unequal pupil size. Related to increased intracranial pressure.
    o Diminished or absent pupil reaction. Related to optic nerve impairment.
    o Cognitive changes. Related to ineffective functioning of the frontal lobe and temporal lobe.
    o Speech changes. Related to ineffective functioning of the left frontal lobe (Broca's Area) of the brain.
    o Motor movement changes. Related to ineffective functioning of the cerebellum.
    o Decreased level of consciousness. Related to decreased oxygen supply to the brain.
    o Amnesia. Related to ineffective frontal and temporal lobes of the brain and the limbic system.
    o Unilateral paralysis (hemiplegia). Related to insufficient oxygen supply to a portion of the brain that controls movement of the paralyzed area.
    o Facial weakness or droop. Related to inflammation of the facial nerve.

- o Widening pulse pressure. Related to increased intracranial pressure.
- o Increased blood pressure. Related to increased intracranial pressure.
- o Slow pulse. Related to increased intracranial pressure.

Interventions
- Place patient in semi-Fowler's position. Decreases pressure on the brain by allowing drainage by gravity.
- Monitor vitals. Identify changes in patient status.
- Seizure precautions. Prevents injury if patient exhibits seizure.
- High protein, high calorie, high vitamin diet. Related to increased metabolism.
- Monitor for Diabetes Insipidus (drinking large amounts of water). Related to injury to the pituitary gland.
- Monitor neurologic status.
- Administer as ordered:
    - o Osmotic diuretics. Decreases cerebral edema.
    - o Loop diuretics. Decreases edema and circulating blood volume.
    - o Antihypertensive medication. Decreases blood pressure.
    - o Opioid. Decreases agitation and pain.

Bell's Palsy

Inflammation of the seventh cranial nerve causes facial paralysis leading to the inability to close eyelids, raise eyebrows, or smile. This self-resolves.

Classic Signs
- Unilateral facial paralysis. Related to inflamed nerve.
- Change in taste. Related to inflamed nerve.
- Ear and jaw pain. Related to inflamed nerve.

Interventions
- Monitor for eye irritation.
- Provide meals in private. Patient my feel self-conscious when eating.
- Administer as ordered:
    - o Artificial tears. Moistens eyes.
    - o Corticosteroid medication. Decreases inflammation.

Brain Abscess

An infection results in the accumulation of pus within the brain.

Classic Signs
- Seizures. Related to infection.
- Severe headache not relieved by medication. Increased blood flow related to the inflammation process.
- Drowsiness. Related to increased cranial pressure.
- Confusion. Related to effect on the cerebellum.
- Ataxia (loss of coordination). Related to effects on the cerebral cortex, basal ganglia, and cerebellum.
- Widened pulse pressure. Related to increased cranial pressure.
- Nystagmus (involuntary eye movement). Related to effects on the temporal lobes.
- Aphasia (inability to use or understand language). Related to effect on the cerebellum.

Interventions
- Monitor vital signs. Identify changes in patient status.
- Monitor mental status. Identify changes in the frontal lobe.
- Monitor fluid intake and output. Identify fluid retention.
- Monitor movement. Identify changes in the cerebral cortex, basal ganglia, and cerebellum
- Monitor senses. Identify changes in the parietal lobe.
- Administer as ordered:
    - Antibiotics. Decreases bacterial infection.
    - Corticosteroids. Reduces inflammation.
    - Anticonvulsants. Decreases the risk of seizures.
    - Osmotic diuretics. Decreases cerebral edema.

Brain Tumor

An abnormal growth of cells within the brain leading to increased intracranial pressure. Types of brain tumors are:
- Meningiomas: Benign tumors generated from the meninges.
- Gliomas: Malignant, rapidly-growing tumor generated from glial cells.

- Astrocytoma: Type of glioma.
- Oligodendroglioma: Slower growing glioma.
- Glioblastoma: Differentiated gliomas (a type of astrocytoma).

Classic Signs
- Parietal Lobe:
    o Visual field defect
    o Sensory loss
    o Seizures
- Frontal Lobe:
    o Anosmia (loss of sense of smell)
    o Personality changes
    o Expressive aphasia
    o Slowing of mental activity
- Occipital Lobe:
    o Prosopagnosia (face blindness)
    o Impaired vision
- Cerebellum or brain stem:
    o Ataxia
    o Lack of coordination
    o Hypotonia of limbs
- Temporal Lobe:
    o Receptive aphasia
    o Auditory hallucinations
    o Depersonalization
    o Seizures
    o Smell hallucinations
    o Emotional changes
    o Visual field defects

Interventions
- Monitor neurologic function. Identify changes in patient status.
- Seizure precautions. Prevents injury if patient exhibits seizure.
- Administer as ordered:
    o Glucocorticoid. Decreases inflammation.
    o Anticonvulsant. Decreases risk of seizures.
    o Osmotic diuretic. Reduces cerebral edema.
    o Proton Pump Inhibitors. Decreases gastric irritation.

Cerebral Aneurysm

Ballooning of a blood vessel wall in the brain that can rupture and lead to intracranial pressure.

Classic Signs
- Asymptomatic unless rupture occurs.
- Decreased level of consciousness. Related to decreased oxygen to the brain.
- Headache. Related to hemorrhage and increased intracranial pressure.

Interventions
- Elevate head of bed 30 degrees. Decreases intracranial pressure.
- Bed rest. Decreases demand for oxygen.
- Monitor level of consciousness. Identify changes in patient status.
- Monitor vital signs for indication of increased intracranial pressure (widened pulse pressure and bradycardia).
- Report headache immediately to the healthcare provider. Related to increased intracranial pressure.
- Administer as ordered:
    o Glucocorticoid. Decreases inflammation.
    o Anticonvulsant. Decreases risk of seizures.
    o Stool softener. Decreases pressure related to straining during bowel movement.

Encephalitis

Inflammation of the brain. Commonly caused by a virus but can be caused by bacteria, fungus, or protozoa.

Classic Signs
- Fever. Related to infection.
- Stiff neck. Related to infection.
- Headache. Related to increased inflammation process associated with the infection.
- Nausea and vomiting. Related to effects on the brain stem.
- Drowsiness. Related to increased cranial pressure.
- Lethargy. Related to increased cranial pressure.

– Seizure. Related to interruptions of normal brain function.

Interventions
– Monitor vital signs for indication of increased intracranial pressure.
– Monitor neurological changes. Assist in identifying the progress of the infection.
– Monitor fluid input and output. Identify fluid retention.
– Monitor electrolyte levels. Identify imbalance.
– Provide a quiet environment. Reduces stimulation.
– Range of motion exercises (active or passive). Maintains mobility.
– Turn and position patient every 2 hours. Reduces the risk for pressure ulcers.
– Administer as ordered:
    o Glucocorticoid. Decreases inflammation.
    o Anticonvulsant. Decreases risk of seizures.
    o Osmotic diuretic. Reduces cerebral edema.
    o Antipyretics. Reduces fever.

Guillain-Barré syndrome

An autoimmune disorder that damages the myelin surrounding the axons on the peripheral nerves resulting in an acute, progressive weakness and paralysis of muscles a few weeks following a viral infection, acute illness, or surgery. Damage may be permanent or temporary.
– Ascending Guillain-Barré. The damage begins at the distal lower extremities and move upwards.
– Descending Guillain-Barré: The damage begins with muscles in the face and throat and moves downward, paralyzing the diaphragm and intercostal muscles leading to respiratory compromise.

Classic Signs
– Acute illness or infection within the past several weeks. Identify primary cause of syndrome.
– Absence of deep tendon reflexes. Related to damaged myelin.
– Burning or prickling feeling (initial sign). Related to damaged myelin.
– Symmetrical weakness. Related to damaged myelin.
– Flaccid paralysis. Related to damaged myelin.
– Fluctuating blood pressure. Related to damaged myelin.

- Cardiac dysrhythmias. Related to damaged myelin.
- Facial weakness. Related to damaged myelin.
- Difficulty swallowing (dysphagia). Related to damaged myelin.

Interventions
- Monitor airway, breathing, and circulation.
- Monitor vital signs. Identify changes in patient status.
- Monitor for progression or change. Identify changes in patient status.
- Monitor gag reflex. Identify risk for aspiration. Insert NG tube if dysphagia present.
- Develop non-verbal communication method (call bell). Enables patient to communicate if unable to speak.
- Turn and position patient every two hours. Reduces the risk for pressure ulcers.
- Administer as ordered:
  - o Immunoglobulin. Strengthens the immune response.

Meningitis

Infection of the meningeal coverings of the brain and spinal cord commonly caused by bacteria but can also be caused by a virus, fungus, protozoa, or toxic exposure.

Classic Signs
- Fever. Related to infection.
- Nuchal rigidity (pain when flexing chin toward chest). Related to increased inflammation process associated with the infection.
- Stiff neck. Related to infection.
- Petechial rash on skin and mucus membranes. Related to infection.
- Photophobia (sensitivity to light). Related to infection.
- Headache. Related to increased inflammation process associated with the infection.
- Malaise. Related to infection.
- Fatigue. Related to increased metabolism associated with infection.
- Seizures. Related to interruptions of normal brain function.
- Nausea and vomiting. Related to effects on the brain stem.
- Myalgia (muscle aches). Related to infection.

- Chills. Related to attempts to cool the body.
- Altered level of conscience. Related to infection.

Interventions
- Isolation. Reduces risk of spreading the infection.
- Darken room. Reduces stimulation.
- Seizure precautions. Prevents injury if patient exhibits seizure.
- Bed rest. Reduces workload.
- Monitor fluid intake and output. Identify fluid retention.
- Monitor neurologic function every two hours. Identify changes in patient status.
- Administer as ordered:
  o Glucocorticoid. Decreases inflammation.
  o Anticonvulsant. Decreases risk of seizures.
  o Osmotic diuretic. Reduces cerebral edema.
  o Antipyretics. Reduces fever.
  o Antibiotics for bacterial meningitis.
  o Anti-fungal medication for fungal infection.

Spinal cord injury

Partial (incomplete) or entire thickness (complete) damage of the spinal cord. The level of damage to the spinal cord determines the degree of disability. Damage is assessed after inflammation related to trauma subsides.

Classic Signs
- Signs are related to incomplete or complete associated nerve damage.
- Tingling (paresthesia).
- Reduce sensation (hypoesthesia).
- Increased sensation (hyperesthesia).
- Weakness (flaccid paralysis).
- Absences of reflexes.
- Lack of bowel control.
- Loss of bladder control.
- Hypotension.
- Hypothermia.
- Bradycardia.
- Loss of motor control below the level of the injury.

Interventions
- Position flat on rotating bed. Stabilizes spine while providing a means to alternate pressure on the back.
- No flexion. Stabilizes spine.
- Immobilize spinal cord with traction. Decreases irritation.
- Monitor traction. Prevent skin irritation.
- Monitor for spinal shock. Loss of reflexes below injury, bradycardia, hypotension, paralytic ileus (intestinal obstruction), flaccid paralysis.
- Monitor vital signs. Identify changes in patient status.
- Monitor fluid intake and output. Identify fluid retention.
- Monitor mental status. Identify changes in patient status.
- Monitor neurologic status. Identify changes in patient status.
- Monitor skin for pressure ulcers. Reduces the risk for pressure ulcers.
- Care of cervical traction pin sites. Decreases irritation and inflammation at site.
- Administer as ordered:
    - Corticosteroid. Decreases inflammation.
    - Plasma expander. Increases circulation and oxygen to injured tissue.
    - H2 receptor antagonists. Protects from formation of stress ulcer.

Cerebrovascular Accident (CVA)

Interruption of blood supply to the brain resulting in necrosis in the affected tissue. Three types of cerebrovascular accidents are:
- Ischemic stroke (common, 88% of all strokes) is an interruption of arterial blood flow by an obstruction (clot) caused by a thrombus or embolus.
- Hemorrhagic stroke is an interruption of blood flow by rupture or leakage of a blood vessel into brain tissues and ventricles.
- Transient Ischemic Attack (TIA) is a temporary interruption of blood flow that resolves in a few hours with no permanent neurologic deficit.

Classic Signs
- Difficulty speaking (aphasia). Related to damage to the front lobe.
- Personality changes. Related to damage to the front lobe.
- Confusion. Related to decreased oxygen to the brain.
- Sensory changes. Related to damage to the parietal lobe.
- Numbness. Related to decreased oxygen to nerves.

- Severe headache. Related to hemorrhage and increased intracranial pressure.
- Seizure. Related to interruptions of normal brain function.
- Difficulty with gait and coordination. Related to damage to the cerebellum.
- Facial droop. Related to lack of oxygen or increased pressure on the brain.
- Altered vision. Related to damage to the occipital lobe.

Interventions
- Bed rest. Reduces the work load.
- Monitor vital signs. Identify changes in the patient status.
- Monitor neurological status. Identify changes in the patient status.
- Monitor for increased intracranial pressure. Identify decreased levels of consciousness, restlessness, confusion, headaches, nausea and vomiting.
- Develop non-verbal communication method (call bell). Related to inability to speak.
- Physical therapy. Maintains muscle tone
- Speech therapy. Assists swallowing and speech
- Occupational therapy. Regain independent living
- Administer as ordered:
  - Thrombolytic agent within three hours of onset of symptoms (ischemic).
  - Anticoagulants. To main therapeutic effect of thrombolytic agent (ischemic).
  - Anti-platelet medications. Decreases platelet adhesiveness (ischemic).
  - Corticosteroid. Decreases inflammation.

Seizure disorder

Sudden uncontrolled discharge of neurons in the brain resulting in abnormal behavior. Before the seizure (pre-ictal stage) the patient may experience alterations in sight, sound, or smell. After the seizure (post-ictal stage) the patient is fatigued, confused, and may not recall the seizure.

Classic Signs
- Tonic seizure. Limb rigidity, loss of consciousness.
- Clonic seizure. Sustained rhythmic jerking.

- Absence. Staring and brief loss of consciousness.
- Myoclonic. Brief rhythmic jerking.
- Atonic. Loss of muscle tone.
- Simple Partial. No loss of consciousness, unusual sensation, unusual movement, begins with aura.
- Complex Partial. Lip smacking, patting, picking, loss of consciousness.

Interventions
- Seizure precautions. Prevents injury if patient exhibits seizure.
- During seizure:
    o Place patient on side to decrease risk of aspiration.
    o Remove objects from around patient to prevent injury.
    o Note duration and patient's actions during seizure.
    o Monitor for status epilepticus (prolonged seizures or repeated seizures without recovery time between)
    o Do not insert anything in patient's mouth during seizure.
- Administer as ordered:
    o Anticonvulsant. Decreases risk of seizures.

Concussion

Head trauma causes the brain to move within the skull. There is no bruising of brain tissue. Full recovery occurs within 48 hours of the head trauma.

Classic Signs
- Signs are caused by neuronal dysfunction caused by functional abnormalities related to the concussion.
    o Vomiting
    o Lethargy
    o Unusual behavior
    o Headache
    o Temporary amnesia. Related to traumatic event.
    o Dizziness
    o Blurry vision
    o Confusion
    o Loss of consciousness for a few minutes but no more than six hours.

Interventions
– Monitor vital signs. Identify changes in patient status.
– Monitor neurological status. Identify changes in patient status.
– Monitor for increased intracranial pressure. Identify decrease level of consciousness, restlessness, confusion, headaches, nausea and vomiting.
– Administer as ordered:
  o Analgesic. Decreases pain.

Contusion

A bruise of the brain as a result of an acceleration-deceleration brain trauma. Two common contusions are:
– Coup injury. Bruising occurs at the site of the impact (blow to the head).
– Contrecoup injury. Bruising occurs at the opposite side of the impact (for example, head hits the windshield in a motor vehicle accident).

Classic Signs
– Signs are caused by neuronal dysfunction caused by functional abnormalities related to the trauma.
  o Difficulty breathing
  o Disorientation
  o Confusion
  o Loss of consciousness
  o Visible wound may or may not exist
  o Agitated
  o Unequal pupils
  o Drowsiness
  o Violent
  o Weakness on one side (hemiparesis)
  o Abnormal posturing
  o Nausea and/or vomiting
  o Visual disturbance
  o Difficulty speaking

Interventions
– Elevate head of bed. Decreases intracranial pressure.
– Monitor vital signs. Identify changes in patient status.

- Monitor neurological status. Identify changes in patient status.
- Monitor for increased intracranial pressure. Identify decreased level of consciousness, restlessness, confusion, headaches, nausea and vomiting.
- No physically or mentally demanding activities. Decreases workload.
- Administer as ordered:
    - o   Anticonvulsant. Decreases risk of seizures.
    - o   Osmotic diuretic. Reduces cerebral edema.

Subdural Hematoma

Blood (blood clot) that accumulates between the dura mater and arachnoid mater (called the subdural space) and has the highest mortality and morbidity rate of all hematomas. There are three classifications of subdural hematoma each of which can be bilateral or unilateral.
- Acute: Less than 72 hours old and considered a medical emergency requiring surgical intervention to prevent increased intracranial pressure from occurring.
- Subacute: 48 hours to two weeks following the acute injury.
- Chronic: 21 days or more following the acute injury.

Classic Signs
- Unequal pupils. Related to increased intracranial pressure.
- Severe headache that is worsening. Related to increased bleeding.
- Decreased level of consciousness (acute). Related to decreased oxygen to the brain.
- Confusion. Related to decreased oxygen to the brain.
- Weakness on one side of the body (hemiparesis) (acute). Related to damaged area of the brain.
- Fixed/dilated pupils (acute). Related to decreased level of consciousness.

Interventions
- Bed rest. Decreases workload.
- Monitor vital signs. Identify changes in patient status.
- Monitor neurological status. Identify changes in patient status.
- Monitor for increased intracranial pressure. Identify decreased level of consciousness, restlessness, confusion, headaches, nausea and vomiting.
- No aspirin. Risk for bleeding.

- No Anticoagulants. Risk for bleeding.
- Administer as ordered:
    - o Antiemetic. Decreases risk of nausea and vomiting.
    - o Osmotic diuretic. Reduces cerebral edema.

Diffuse Axonal Injury

A traumatic brain injury resulting in damage to white matter in the brain stem, cerebral hemispheres, and corpus callosum. The axon disconnects and swells. Diffuse axonal injuries are classified as:
- Mild: Return to baseline neurologic function within 24 hours of the injury.
- Moderate: Patient is in a coma for a few days.
- Severe: Patient is in a coma for weeks.

Classic Signs
- Signs are caused by neuronal dysfunction caused by functional abnormalities related to the injury.
    - o Loss of consciousness
    - o Abnormal posturing
    - o Coma
    - o Dysautonomia (dysfunction of the autonomic nervous system)

Interventions
- Bed rest. Decreases workload.
- Total care. Patient is unconscious.
- Monitor vital signs. Identify changes in patient status.
- Monitor neurological status. Identify changes in patient status.
- Administer as ordered:
    - o Corticosteroid. Decreases inflammation.
    - o Osmotic diuretic. Reduces cerebral edema.

Skull Fracture

A breakage of bones in the skull caused by blunt force head trauma. Common skull fractures are:

- Linear: Breakage transverse the thickness of the skull. No bone displacement occurs.
- Comminuted: Bone is crushed, broken, and splintered.
- Depressed: Breakage cause bone to be displaced inward leading to increased intracranial pressure.
- Basilar: Breakage occurs at the base of the skull.
- Diastatic: Breakage occurs at a suture line.
- Compound: Breakage causes the bone to tear the epidermis, meninges, paranasal sinuses or the middle ear.

Classic Signs
- Signs are caused by neuronal dysfunction caused by functional abnormalities related to the injury to the brain related by the traumatic event.
  - o Asymptomatic
  - o Bleeding from nose, ears, eyes, or site of wound.
  - o Pupils unequal and not reactive to light
  - o Visual disturbances
  - o Drainage of clear fluid (cerebral spinal fluid) from the ears or nose
  - o Bruising behind the ears (Battle's sign) or under the eyes (raccoon eyes).
  - o Loss of smell
  - o Confusion
  - o Irritability
  - o Nausea/vomiting
  - o Confusion
  - o Restlessness
  - o Headache
  - o Seizure

Interventions
- Bed rest. Decreases workload.
- Monitor vital signs. Identify changes in patient status.
- Monitor neurological status. Identify changes in patient status.
- Monitor for increased intracranial pressure. Identify decreased level of consciousness, restlessness, confusion, headaches, nausea and vomiting.
- No aspirin. Risk for bleeding.
- No anticoagulants. Risk for bleeding.

– Linear fractures: No treatment.
– Overnight observation. Identify changes in patient status.
– Do not probe wound. Disturbance may exacerbate condition.
– Stabilize head and neck. Reduces risk for further injury.
– Administer as ordered:
  o Corticosteroid. Decreases inflammation.
  o Osmotic diuretic. Reduces cerebral edema.
  o Antibiotic. Decreases bacterial infection in a compound fracture.
  o Anticonvulsant. Decreases risk of seizures.

Intracerebral Hematoma

Blood (blood clot) that accumulates in the cerebrum typically from veins leading to slow bleeding

Classic Signs
– Unequal pupils. Related to increased intracranial pressure.
– Severe headache that is worsening. Related to increased bleeding.
– Decreased level of consciousness. Related to decreased oxygen to brain.
– Confusion. Related to decreased oxygen to brain.
– Nausea/vomiting. Related to neuronal dysfunction caused by functional abnormalities related to the injury.
– Memory loss. Related to neuronal dysfunction caused by functional abnormalities related to the injury.
– Impaired language ability (aphasia). Related to neuronal dysfunction caused by functional abnormalities related to the injury.

Interventions
– Bed rest. Decreased workload.
– Monitor vital signs. Identify changes in patient status.
– Monitor neurological status. Identify changes in patient status.
– Monitor for increased intracranial pressure. Identify decreased level of consciousness, restlessness, confusion, headaches, nausea and vomiting
– No aspirin. Risk for bleeding.
– No anticoagulants. Risk for bleeding.
– Administer as ordered:

       ○   Antiemetic. Decreases nausea and vomiting.
       ○   Osmotic diuretic. Reduces cerebral edema.
       ○   Anticonvulsant. Decreases risk of seizures.

Subarachnoid Hemorrhage

Bleeding into the area between the arachnoid mater and the pia mater surrounding the brain called the subarachnoid space. Frequently caused by rupture of a cerebral aneurysm related to a fall with head injury.

Classic Signs
- Signs are caused by neuronal dysfunction caused by functional abnormalities related to the injury to the brain.
    - ○ Asymptomatic
    - ○ Thunderclap headache
    - ○ Low level of consciousness
    - ○ Vomiting
    - ○ Seizures
    - ○ Neck stiffness
    - ○ Drowsiness
    - ○ Coma
    - ○ Confusion
    - ○ Bleeding into the eyeball Terson Syndrome (intraocular hemorrhage)

Interventions
- Bed rest. Decreased workload.
- Monitor vital signs. Identify changes in patient status.
- Monitor neurological status. Identify changes in patient status.
- Monitor for increased intracranial pressure. Identify decreased level of consciousness, restlessness, confusion, headaches, nausea and vomiting.
- No aspirin. Risk for bleeding.
- No anticoagulants. Risk for bleeding.
- Administer as ordered:
    - ○ Antiemetic. Decreases nausea and vomiting.
    - ○ Osmotic diuretic. Reduces cerebral edema.
    - ○ Anticonvulsant. Decreases risk of seizures.

Gastrointestinal Assessment, Disorders, Interventions

Assessment

Be sure to follow the order of the gastrointestinal assessment:
- Inspection
- Auscultation
- Percussion
- Palpation

Interview
- Initial Questions:
    o What makes you feel that something is wrong?
    o Do you have allergies?
    o Have you taken any medications or herbal supplements recently?
    o Have you recently undergone any medical procedure?
    o What have you eaten recently?
    o What happen prior to noticing this problem?
    o Do you have irregular bowel movements?
    o Is there blood in your stool?
    o Have there been changes in the appearance of your stool?
    o Have you recently traveled out of the country?
- Follow up questions:
    o When did this problem start?
    o How long have you had this problem?
    o Can you describe the problem?
    o How bad does the problem bother you?
    o Where do you feel uncomfortable?
    o Is the problem spreading or does is the problem remaining in one place?
    o Does anything make the problem worse?
    o Does anything make the problem better?
- Lifestyle questions:
    o Do you drink alcohol?
    o Do you use recreational drugs?
    o Do you use laxatives?
    o Did you have any dental problems or problems chewing food?
    o Do you have any dietary restrictions?

- o Do you exercise?
- o Do you use tobacco?
- o Have you been diagnosed with any medical condition?
- Family history:
  - o Does anyone in your family have or had colon cancer?
  - o Does anyone in your family have or had Crohn's disease?
  - o Does anyone in your family have or had Ulcerative Colitis?

Inspection
- Eyes:
  - o Color of Sclera. Abnormal: Yellowing
- Mouth:
  - o Odor. Abnormal: acetone, unusual odor
  - o Jaw. Abnormal: asymmetrical, swelling
  - o Bite. Abnormal: over- or underbite
  - o Teeth. Abnormal: broken, missing
  - o Dentures. Abnormal: improper fitting
  - o Gums. Abnormal: swelling, bleeding, ulceration, exudate
  - o Lips. Abnormal: swelling, bleeding, ulceration, exudate
  - o Tongue. Abnormal: swelling, bleeding, ulceration
  - o Pharynx. Abnormal: lesions, uvular deviation, plaque, exudate, abnormal tonsils
- Abdomen:
  - o Skin. Abnormal: striate (pink, blue, silvery white), dilated veins, scars
  - o Surface. Abnormal: asymmetrical, masses, bulges, peristalsis waves, pulsation

Auscultation
- Abdomen:
  - o Turn off suction to abdominal tube or nasogastric tube before auscultating the abdomen.
  - o Listen for at least two minutes in each quadrant of the abdomen.
  - o Listen for bowel sounds (diaphragm of the stethoscope).
  - o Listen for vascular sounds (bell of the stethoscope).
  - o Normal: No vascular sounds should be heard

- o Right lower quadrant. Abnormal: hypoactive bowel sounds, hyperactive bowel sounds
- o Right upper quadrant. Abnormal: hypoactive bowel sounds, hyperactive bowel sounds
- o Left upper quadrant. Abnormal: hypoactive bowel sounds, hyperactive bowel sounds
- o Left lower quadrant. Abnormal: hypoactive bowel sounds, hyperactive bowel sounds

Percussion
- Abdomen:
    - o Don't percuss the abdomen if:
        - ▪ The patient received a transplanted abdominal organ.
        - ▪ You hear a bruit, venous hum, or friction rub over the abdomen.
    - o Direct percussion: Strike your finger over the abdomen.
    - o Indirect percussion: Rest your finger on the abdomen and strike the finger with the middle finger of your dominant hand
    - o Order of percussion:
        - ▪ Right lower quadrant
        - ▪ Right upper quadrant
        - ▪ Left upper quadrant
        - ▪ Left lower quadrant
    - o Determine the location and size of abdominal organs.
        - ▪ Tympany sound: Clear hollow sound indicates no organ or hollow organ.
        - ▪ Dull sound: Indicates organ or solid mass.
- Liver:
    - o Begin percussing below the umbilicus at the right mid-clavicular line.
    - o Initial sound in tympany.
    - o Move upward.
    - o Dullness indicates the edge of the liver.
    - o Move downward from above the nipple along the right mid-clavicular line
    - o The sound should be from tympany over the lungs to dullness near the fifth to seventh intercostal space.
    - o Measure the distance between these two positions to estimate the size of the liver.

Palpation
- Abdomen:
    - Light palpation: Press fingertips lightly into the abdomen ½ to ¾ inches
    - Deep palpation: Press fingertips of both hands into the abdomen 1½ inches moving in a circular motion over structures within the abdomen.
    - Rebound tenderness: May occur when fingertips are withdrawn from the abdomen.
    - Order of Palpation:
        - Right lower quadrant
        - Right upper quadrant
        - Left upper quadrant
        - Left lower quadrant
- Spleen:
    - A normal spleen is not palpable.
    - Stand on the patient's right side with the patient standing.
    - Place your hand on the back left of the patient's lower rib cage.
    - Ask the patient to take a deep breath.
    - Place your right hand on the patient's abdomen
    - Press your right hand up to the spleen
    - Stop palpating if you feel the spleen for risk of rupturing the spleen.
- Liver:
    - A normal liver is not palpable.
    - Begin at the lower left quadrant.
    - Ask the patient to take and hold a deep breath.
    - Ask the patient to exhale while you move your hands upward to the margin of the liver.

Common Classic Signs
- Rebound tenderness assessment. Pain is felt on removal rather than application of pressure. Related to aggravation of the parietal layer of the peritoneum by stretching or moving. Don't repeat assessment if rebound tenderness exists for risk of rupturing the appendix.
- Obturator Sign (Cope's obturator test). Related to irritation of the obturator interns muscle.
    - Place patient in the supine position
    - Flex right leg 90 degrees

- o   Hold leg at ankle and above the knee
- o   Rotate leg laterally
- o   Rotate leg medially.
- o   Pain in hypogastric region exists
— Iliopsoas Sign (Psoas Sign). Related to irritation to the iliopsoas group or hip flexors in the abdomen.
- o   Place patient in the left side position
- o   Keep legs straight
- o   Exert pressure as the patient raises his right leg
- o   Exert pressure as the patient raises his left leg
- o   Abdominal pain exists
— Vomiting. Related to purging associated with infection or poisoning.
— Projectile vomiting. Related to hypertrophic pyloric stenosis (pediatric).
— Diarrhea. 300g within 24 hours is related to infection or ulcerative colitis.
— Constipation
— Bleeding
- o   Vomiting red blood (hematemesis). Related to bleeding from gums/teeth or esophageal varices.
- o   Vomiting dark blood (coffee grounds). Related to peptic ulcer.
- o   Severe retching, coughing blood. Related to Mallory-Weiss Syndrome or gastro-esophageal laceration syndrome.
- o   Low blood pressure. Related to GI bleed.
- o   Rapid heart rate. Related to GI bleed as the heart compensates for the decreased blood volume.
- o   Black tarry stool (Melena). Related to GI bleed.
- o   Bloody stool (red). Related to hemorrhoids or ulcerative colitis.
— Jaundice
- o   Yellowing of sclera (white of the eye). Related to increase in bilirubin.
- o   Yellowing of skin. Related to increase in bilirubin.
- o   Pale stool. Decrease in the excretion of bilirubin.
- o   Dark urine. Decrease in the excretion of bilirubin.
— Tenderness. Related to inflammation.
— Abdominal pain:
- o   Sudden abdominal pain with rigidity and the pain subsidies. Related to perforation.
- o   Abdominal rigidity. Related to peritonitis.
- o   Acute right upper quadrant pain. Related to inflamed gallbladder (acute cholecystitis).

- o Colicky abdominal pain (starts and stops abruptly). Related to hernia, adhesion, or tumor.
- o Left iliac fossa pain. Related to constipation, acute diverticulitis, or irritable bowel syndrome.
- o Right iliac fossa pain. Related to appendicitis.
- Abdominal sounds:
  - o Vascular swishing sound (bruits). Related to arterial obstruction or arterial stenosis.
  - o Vascular hum. Related to cirrhosis.
  - o Vascular grating sound. Related to inflammation.
  - o Hypoactive or absent of sound. Related to peritonitis or paralytic ileus.
  - o High-pitched rushing sound with presentment of abdominal cramps. Related to intestinal obstruction.
  - o Hyperactive. Related to early intestinal obstruction, hunger, or diarrhea.
  - o High-pitched tinkling. Related to air or fluid in the intestine.
  - o Fever. Related to infection.
- Stool:
  - o Hard solid stool. Related to constipation.
  - o Loose stool. Related to viral infection or spastic bowel disorder.
  - o Pasty stool. Related to high fat content, pancreatic disorder or intestinal malabsorption disorder.
  - o Greasy stool. Related to high fat content, pancreatic disorder, or intestinal malabsorption disorder.
  - o Yellow stool. Related to prolonged diarrhea.
  - o Green stool. Related to prolonged diarrhea.
  - o Narrow, ribbon stool. Related to irritable bowel disorder, obstruction of the bowel or rectum, spastic bowel disorder.
  - o Black stool. Related to gastrointestinal bleed, iron supplement ingested.
  - o Red stool. Related to rectal bleeding related to hemorrhoids or side effect of drugs or foods.
  - o White stool. Related to blockage of hepatic or gallbladder duct, or cancer.
  - o Mucus-containing stool. Related to bacterial infection.
  - o Pus-containing stool. Related to colitis.

Appendicitis

Obstruction in the vermiform appendix leads to secretion of fluid by the mucosal lining of the appendix lead to increased pressure and decreased blood flow to the appendix resulting in gangrene.

Classic Signs
- Guarding of the abdomen. Related to abdominal pain.
- Abdominal pain from periumbilical region to right lower quadrant. Related to inflammation.
- Abdominal rigidity. Related to peritonitis.
- Rebound pain. Pain after pressing abdomen. Related to aggravation of the parietal layer of the peritoneum by stretching or moving.
- Right lower quadrant abdominal pain. Decreases with right hip flexing. Related to perforation.
- Loss of appetite. Related to infection.
- Fever. Related to infection.
- Nausea and vomiting. Related to purging associated with infection or poisoning.

Interventions
- NPO (*nil per os*). Nothing by mouth.
- Monitor vital signs. Identify changes in patient status.
- Monitor intake and output. Identify fluid retention.
- Monitor bowel sounds. Identify status of peristalsis.
- Assess pain level. Identify need for pain medication.
- Administer as ordered:
    o Analgesics. Decreases pain.
    o Antibiotics. Decreases bacterial infection.

Cholecystitis

Inflammation of the gallbladder related to cholelithiasis (gallstones) causing a blockage of the cystic duct and thus causing the gallbladder to become distended leading to obstructive jaundice and an increased risk of gangrene and perforation.

Classic Signs
- Pain in the upper right quadrant of the abdomen or epigastric area radiating to the right shoulder. Related to blockage of the cystic duct.
- Positive Murphy's sign. Upper right quadrant abdominal pain increases with palpation on inspiration resulting in the patient unable to take a deep breath.
- Increased flatulence. Related to bacterial infection.
- Increase eructation (belching). Related to ineffective digestion.
- Clay-colored stool. Related to decreased bile.
- Foamy, dark urine. Related to decreased bile.
- Nausea and vomiting following ingestion of fatty foods. Related to blockage of the cystic duct.
- Decreased appetite. Related to ineffective digestion.
- Fever. Related to infection.
- Yellowing of sclera of the eye (icterus). Related to the backup of bile.
- Pruritus (itching). Related to backup of bile.
- Jaundice. Related to blocked bile duct.
- Increased bilirubin direct (conjugated). Related to ineffective excretion of bile.
- Increased bilirubin indirect (unconjugated). Related to ineffective excretion of bile.
- Increased WBC. Related to infection.

Interventions
- Low fat diet. Related to the decreased availability of bile to digest fat.
- Monitor vital signs. Identify changes in patient status.
- Monitor bowel sounds. Identify status of peristalsis.
- Assess pain level. Identify need for pain medication.
- Administer as ordered:
    o Antiemetic. Decreases nausea and vomiting.
    o Analgesics. Decreases pain.
    o Antibiotics. Decreases bacterial infection.
    o Vitamins A, D, E, K. Replaces fat soluble vitamins.

Cirrhosis

Inflammation and necrosis of the liver leading to the formation of fibrosis and nodules resulting blockage of blood vessels and the bile duct causing increased portal vein pressure and enlarged liver, backup of venous blood to the spleen, and enlarged spleen, enlarged liver, and decreased liver function.

Classic Signs
- Asymptomatic
- Fatigue. Related to malnutrition.
- Weight loss. Related to malnutrition.
- Ecchymosis (bruises). Related to decreased Vitamin K absorption required for blood coagulation.
- Petechiae. Related to decrease blood flow in the portal vein.
- Pruritus (itching). Related to backup of bile.
- Spider veins. Related to decreased blood flow in the portal vein.
- Peripheral edema. Related to decreased blood flow in the portal vein.
- Portal hypertension. Related to decreased blood flow in the portal vein.
- Jaundice. Related to backup of bile.
- Hepatomegaly (enlarged liver). Related to increased scar tissue in the liver.
- Palmar Erythema (red palms). Related to decreased blood flow in the portal vein.
- Ascites (accumulation of fluid in peritoneum). Related to decreased blood flow in the portal vein.
- Dyspnea. Related to ascites.
- Glossitis (inflammation of the tongue)
- Encephalopathy. Asterixis (hand tremor), tremors, delirium, drowsiness, dysarthria (slurred speech), coma
- Increased:
  - Aspartate aminotransferase (AST). Related to increased rupture of liver cells.
  - Alanine aminotransferase (ALT). Related to increased rupture of liver cells.
  - Bilirubin direct (conjugated). Related to ineffective excretion of bile.
  - Bilirubin indirect (unconjugated). Related to ineffective excretion of bile.
  - Ammonia. Related to the decreased metabolism of ammonia by the liver.

Interventions
- Elevate head of bed 30 degrees or greater. Decreases intracranial pressure.

- Elevate feet. Reduces peripheral edema.
- Monitor signs of bleeding. Bruising.
- Monitor mental status. Identify change in patient status.
- Restrict fluid intake. Related to fluid retention.
- Monitor intake and output. Identify fluid retention.
- Monitor vital signs. Identify change in patient status.
- Daily Weight. Identify ascites.
- Measure abdominal girth. Identify ascites.
- Monitor for peripheral edema. Related to excess fluid.
- Monitor heart and lung sounds. Related to excess fluid.
- Low sodium diet. Related to decreased fluid retention.
- Administer as ordered:
    - Diuretics. Decreases fluids.
    - Vitamins. Related to decreased liver function.
    - Lactulose. Removes ammonia related to decreased liver function.
    - Antibiotics. Kills flora that produces ammonia.

Crohn's Disease

Inflammatory bowel disease that has periods of inflammation leading to strictures and fistulas.

Classic Signs
- Non-bloody diarrhea. Related to bowel spasm.
- Fatigue. Related to malabsorption.
- Weight loss. Related to malabsorption.
- Post-prandial bloating (after meals). Related to bowel spasm.
- Borborygmi (loud, frequent bowel sounds). Related to bowel spasm.
- Abdominal cramping. Related to bowel spasm.
- Pain in the right lower quadrant of the abdomen. Related to bowel spasm.
- Fever. Related to inflammation.
- Abdominal mass. Related to intestinal obstruction.
- Fistula formation. Related to tissue destruction and luminal bacterial infection.
- Vomiting. Related to gastroduodenal involvement.
- Abscesses. Related to infection.

Interventions
- Dietary restrictions. Reduce foods that irritate the intestines.
- Monitor intake and output. Identify fluid retention.
- Monitor vital signs. Identify patient status.
- Administer as ordered:
  - o Vitamins. Related to decreased absorption.
  - o Glucocorticoids. Decreases inflammation.
  - o Antidiarrheal medication. Decreases diarrhea.
  - o Aminosalicylates. Decreases inflammation.
  - o Purine. Decreases inflammation.
  - o Diphenoxylate hydrochloride and atropine sulfate. Decreases diarrhea.

Diverticulitis

Undigested food becomes trapped in outpouches (diverticula) along the large intestine leading the bacterial growth resulting in inflammation of the intestine.

Classic Signs
- Asymptomatic
- Bloating. Related to undigested food and bacterial infection.
- Rectal bleeding. Related to bleeding from pouching in the colon.
- Change in bowel habits. Related to increased stool weight and volume leading to increased bowel movements.
- Abdominal pain (most common symptom). Related to inflammation of the bowel.
- Fever. Related to infection.
- Nausea and vomiting. Related to infection.
- Lower left quadrant pain. Related to inflammation of the sigmoid colon.
- Fever. Related to infection.
- High WBC (leukocytosis). Related to infection.
- Constipation. Related to impacted fecal matter.

Interventions
- NPO. Rest bowel.
- Monitor vital signs. Identify changes in patient status.
- Monitor intake and output. Identify fluid retention.

- Assess abdomen for bowel sounds and distention. Identify intestinal activity.
- High fiber diet when asymptomatic. Encourages normal bowel movement.
- Low residue diet during acute inflammation. Decreases intestinal irritation.
- No lifting during acute inflammation. Lifting worsens pain.
- No laxatives. Decreases normal urge to defecate.
- No enemas. Decreases normal urge to defecate.
- Administer as ordered:
    - Antibiotics. Decreases bacterial infection.

Gastroenteritis

Inflammation of the gastrointestinal mucosa by a microorganism or exposure to a toxin.

Classic Signs
- Diarrhea. Related to bowel spasm.
- Abdominal pain. Related to bowel spasm.
- Nausea and vomiting. Related to infection.
- Fever. Related to infection.
- Malaise. Related to malabsorption.
- Headache. Related to infection.
- Dehydration. Related to diarrhea.
- Abdominal distention. Related to infection.
- Electrolyte imbalance. Related to diarrhea.
- Increased eosinophil count. Related to infection.
- Increased WBC. Related to infection.
- Stool positive for parasitic infection. Related to infection.

Interventions
- Monitor vital signs. Identify changes in the patient status.
- Monitor intake and output. Identify fluid balance.
- Assess for dehydration. Related to diarrhea.
- Replace fluids. Related to diarrhea.
- Allow for vomiting and diarrhea. Purges the microorganism.
- Administer as ordered:
    - Antiemetic medication. Decreases vomiting.
    - Antidiarrheal medication. Decreases diarrhea.

- Antimicrobial medication. Decreases infection.
- Intravenous fluid. Increases hydration.

Gastroesophageal reflux disease (GERD)

Contents (acid) of the stomach enters the esophagus causing pain (heartburn) resulting in damage to the mucosal layer of the esophagus. Scarring may occur leading to formation of strictures resulting in difficulty swallowing and a pre-malignant esophageal growth (Barrett's esophagus).

Classic Signs
- Sour taste. Related to the backflow of stomach acid and juices into the esophagus.
- Hoarseness. Related to acid reflux into the larynx.
- Epigastric burning. Related to acid reflux into the esophagus.
- Burping (eructation). Related to build up of pressure in the stomach.
- Cough. Related to regurgitation of food particles that are then aspirated.
- Nausea. Related to the backflow of stomach acid and juices into the esophagus.
- Bloating. Related to buildup of pressure in the stomach.
- Difficulty swallowing (dysphagia). Related to scar tissue forming in the esophagus.

Interventions
- Monitor vital signs. Identify changes in patient status.
- Elevate head of bed. Decreases the backflow of stomach acid and juices into the esophagus.
- Sleep on left side to reduce nighttime GERD. Helps stomach to empty and reduces acid reflux.
- Eat six small meals daily. Decreases the buildup of pressure in the stomach.
- No acidic foods. Citrus, vinegar, tomato, peppermint, caffeine, alcohol that increase stomach acid.
- Don't lie down after eating. Decreases the backflow of stomach acid and juices into the esophagus.
- No tight clothing at waist. Decreases pressure on the stomach.
- Administer as ordered:
    - o Antacids. Decreases acid.
    - o Proton Pump Inhibitor. Decreases acid production.

Gastrointestinal bleed

Upper or lower gastrointestinal tract bleeding leading to substantial blood loss.

Classic Signs
- Pallor. Related to decrease in circulation.
- Lightheadedness. Related to decreased oxygen to the brain.
- Orthostatic blood pressure. Related to decreased blood volume.
- Black, tarry stool (melena). Related to upper GI bleed and digested blood.
- Red or maroon rectal bleeding (hematochezia). Related to lower GI bleed.
- Vomiting maroon, coffee-ground blood (hematemesis). Related to upper GI blood and digested blood.
- Nausea. Related to blood in the digestive system.
- Tachycardia. The body's attempts to increase oxygen flow.
- Decreased hemoglobin. Related to decreased blood volume.
- Decreased hematocrit. Related to decreased blood volume.
- Decreased RBC. Related to decreased blood volume.

Interventions
- Monitor vital signs. Identify changes in patient status.
- Monitor intake and output. Identify fluid balance.
- Maintain large bore IV (16-18 gauge) access. Access for blood products.
- Administer as ordered:
    - o Isotonic IV fluids. Related to fluid replacement.
    - o Transfuse packed RBCs. Related to RBC replacement.
    - o Fresh frozen plasma. Related to plasma replacement.
    - o Albumin. Related to albumin replacement.

Gastritis

Inflammation of the stomach lining leading to malnutrition, gastric cancer, or lymphoma. Types of gastritis are:
- Erosive gastritis. Related to stress or medication (NSAIDs).
- Atrophic gastritis: Related to H. pylori bacteria, pernicious anemia, and alcohol use.

Classic Signs
- Vomiting maroon, coffee-ground blood (hematemesis). Related to digested blood (erosive gastritis).
- Nausea. Related to GI bleed (erosive gastritis).
- Black, tarry stool (melena). Related to upper GI bleed (erosive gastritis).
- Epigastric tenderness. Related to inflammation.
- Anemia. Related to GI bleed (erosive gastritis).
- Abdominal bloating. Related to GI bleed (erosive gastritis).
- Abdominal pain. Related to inflammation.
- Fecal Occult Blood Test positive. Related to GI bleed (erosive gastritis).
- Decreased hemoglobin. Related to GI bleed (erosive gastritis).
- Decreased hematocrit. Related to GI bleed (erosive gastritis).
- Decreased RBC. Related to GI bleed (erosive gastritis).
- Helicobacter pylori (H.pylori) positive. Related to bacterial infection.

Interventions
- Monitor stool for occult blood. Related to GI bleed (erosive gastritis).
- Monitor vital signs. Identify changes in patient status.
- Monitor intake and output. Identify changes in fluid balance.
- No alcohol, caffeine, acidic foods. Decreases irritation to stomach.
- No NSAIDs. Decreases irritation to stomach.
- No smoking. Decreases irritation to stomach.
- Administer as ordered:
    - Antacids. Decreases acid.
    - Proton Pump Inhibitor. Decreases acid production.
    - Sucralfate. Adheres to ulcer sites and provides protection from acids, enzymes, and bile salts.

Hepatitis

Inflammation of the liver commonly caused by a viral infection or exposure to drugs and toxins. Types of hepatitis:
- Hepatitis A: Transmitted orally, related to contaminated water or poor sanitation.
- Hepatitis B: Transmitted percutaneously, related to sexual contact, IV drug use, mother to neonate transmission, and transfusion.
- Hepatitis C: Transmitted percutaneously, related to IV drug use and sexual contact (less common).

- Hepatitis D: Transmitted percutaneously. Needs hepatitis B to spread.
- Hepatitis E: Transmitted orally, related to water contamination.
- Hepatitis G: Transmitted percutaneously, associated with chronic infection but not liver disease.

Classic Signs
- Blood Test:
  - Increased AST. Increased rupture of liver cells.
  - Increased ALT. Increased rupture of liver cells.
  - IgG anti-HBc. Positive. Past infection with Hepatitis B.
  - IgM anti-HBc. Positive. Acute or recent infection with Hepatitis B.
  - HBsAg. Positive. Current or past infection with Hepatitis B.
  - IgM anti-HAV. Positive. Acute or early convalescent stage of Hepatitis A.
  - IgG anti-HAV. Positive. Later convalescent stage of Hepatitis A.
  - HBeAg. Positive. Current viral replication of Hepatitis B and infectivity.
  - HBV DNA. Positive. Presence of Hepatitis B DNA (most sensitive).
  - Anti-HCV. Positive. Hepatitis C infection.
  - HCV RNA. Positive. Hepatitis C infection.
  - Anti HDV. Positive. Hepatitis D infection.
- Acute hepatitis
  - Tenderness in right upper quadrant of abdomen. Related to inflammation of the liver.
  - Jaundice. Related to backup of bile from liver failure.
  - Dark urine. Related to backup of bile from liver failure.
  - Hepatomegaly (enlarged liver). Related to increased scar tissue in the liver.
  - Diarrhea. Related to early stages of hepatitis.
  - Constipation. Related to insufficient bile secretion to lubricate the intestines and decrease in synthesis of proteins and vitamins that are necessary for intestinal motility.
  - Malaise. Related to malnutrition.
  - Low grade fever. Related to infection of the liver.
  - Anorexia. Related to malnutrition.
  - Muscle/joint pain. Related to inflammation.

- Chronic hepatitis
    o Asymptomatic
    o Bleeding. Related to decreased Vitamin K absorption required for blood coagulation.
    o Enlarged spleen. Related to decreased blood flow in the portal vein causing back pressure in the circulatory system.
    o Cirrhosis. Related to increased scar tissue in the liver.
    o Ascites. Related to decreased blood flow in the portal vein.
    o Esophageal varices. Related to decreased blood flow in the portal vein causing back pressure in the circulatory system.
    o Encephalopathy. Related to the decreased metabolism of ammonia by the liver.

Interventions
- Activity as tolerated. Related to malnutrition.
- Monitor vital signs. Identify changes in patient status.
- Monitor intake and output. Identify changes in fluid balance.
- Schedule rest periods (acute). Related to fatigue.
- High calorie diet. Related to malnutrition.
- Eat more at breakfast. Breakfast is tolerated more than other meals.
- No medications metabolized in the liver. Related to liver malfunction.
- No alcohol. Alcohol is metabolized by the liver and the liver has malfunctioned.
- Administer as ordered:
    o Interferon. For chronic Hepatitis B, Hepatitis C.
    o Prednisone. For autoimmune hepatitis.

Hiatal hernia (diaphragmatic hernia)

Protrusion of a portion of the stomach through the diaphragm into the chest near the esophagus. Types of hiatal hernia are:
- Rolling Hiatal Hernia. The upper portion of the stomach but not the lower esophageal sphincter moves through the diaphragm; no GERD.
- Sliding Hiatal Hernia. The upper portion of the stomach and the lower esophageal sphincter moves through the diaphragm; GERD.

Classic Signs
- Rolling hernia
    - o   Chest pain. Related to pressure in the chest cavity.
    - o   Palpitations. Related to irritation of the vagus nerve.
    - o   Fullness after eating. Related to pressure on the stomach.
    - o   Difficulty breathing after eating. Related to pressure on the diaphragm.
- Sliding hernia
    - o   Chest pain. Related to pressure in the chest cavity.
    - o   Palpitations. Related to irritation of the vagus nerve.
    - o   Heartburn. Related to pressure on the stomach.
    - o   Dysphagia (difficulty swallowing). Related to obstruction of the lower part of the esophagus causing a delaying in emptying the esophagus into the stomach.
    - o   Burping (eructation). Related to pressure on the stomach.

Interventions
- Elevate head of bed. Decreases the backflow of stomach acid and juices into the esophagus.
- Monitor vital signs. Identify changes in patient status.
- Small, frequent meals. Decreases the buildup of pressure in the stomach.
- No lying down after eating. Decreases the backflow of stomach acid and juices into the esophagus.
- No tight clothes at waist. Decreases pressure on the stomach.
- No acidic foods. Citrus, vinegar, tomato, peppermint, caffeine, alcohol that increase stomach acid.
- Administer as ordered:
    - o   Antacids. Decreases acid.
    - o   Proton Pump Inhibitor. Decreases acid production.

Intestinal obstruction and paralytic ileus

Block motility through the intestine. Commonly caused by an obstruction such as fecal impaction or tumor or caused by a paralytic ileus related to medication or illness such as sepsis.

Classic Signs
— Paralytic Ileus:
- o Diminished or absent bowel sounds. Related to decreased peristalsis.
  - ▪ Vomiting. Related to purging the backup of intestinal contents into the stomach.
  - ▪ Constant abdominal pain. Related to increased intestinal pressure.
  - ▪ Abdominal distention. Related to increased intestinal pressure.
— Obstruction:
- o Vomiting. Related to purging the backup of intestinal contents into the stomach.
- o Constipation. Related to a hard mass of stool and narrowing of the intestine.
- o High-pitched bowel sounds. Related to narrowing of intestine.
- o Abdominal tenderness. Related to increased intestinal pressure.
- o Abdominal cramping. Related to bowel spasm.
- o Abdominal distention. Related to increased intestinal pressure.

Interventions
— NPO. Inability of the gastrointestinal tract to process food.
— Insert NG tube. Suction stomach contents.
— Parenteral nutrition and vitamin supplements. Related to malabsorption.
— Monitor vital signs. Identify patient status.
— Monitor intake and output. Identify fluid balance.
— Assess bowel sounds. Identify peristalsis status.
— Administer as ordered:
- o Antiemetic. Decreases vomiting.
- o IV fluids. Replaces fluids.

Pancreatitis

Inflammation of the pancreas. Commonly caused by blockage of the pancreatic duct by gallstones or inflammation. There are two types of pancreatitis. These are:
— Acute. Autodigestion of the pancreas by pancreatic enzymes.
— Chronic. Fibrosis resulting in decreased pancreatic function.

Classic Signs
- Cullen's sign. Bluish-gray discoloration of periumbilical area and abdomen. Related to bleeding behind the peritoneum.
- Turner's sign. Bluish-gray discoloration of flank areas. Related to bruising of the flanks, between the last rib and the top of the hip. Can predict a severe attack of acute pancreatitis.
- Abdominal pain. Related to inflammation.
- Pain radiating to back or left shoulder (acute). Related to inflammation.
- Gnawing continuous pain (chronic). Related to inflammation.
- Epigastric pain. Related to inflammation.
- Knee-chest position reduces pain. Decreases the stretch of the pancreas.
- Nausea. Related to inflammation.
- Vomiting. Related to inflammation.
- Fatigue. Related to malnutrition.
- Hyperglycemia. Related to decreased production of insulin.
- Weight loss. Related to malnutrition.
- Fever. Related to infection.
- Blood Test:
    - o Increased:
        - ▪ Amylase. Related to rupture of pancreatic cells.
        - ▪ Lipase. Related to rupture of pancreatic cells.
        - ▪ WBC. Related to inflammation.
        - ▪ Glucose. Related to decrease insulin production.

Interventions
- NPO (acute). Decreases the need to produce pancreatic enzymes.
- NG tube. Suction stomach contents.
- Monitor vital signs. Identify changes in patient status.
- Monitor intake and output. Identify fluid balance.
- Monitor blood glucose. Related to decreased insulin production.
- Monitor lung sounds. Identify plural effusion.
- Assess abdomen for bowel sounds, tenderness, masses, ascites.
- Schedule rest periods. Decreases risk for fatigue.
- Take pancreatic enzymes with meals. Assists in digestion.
- No alcohol. Decreases inflammation of the pancreas.
- No caffeine. Decreases inflammation of the pancreas.
- Bland, low fat, high protein, high calorie diet. Decreases pancreatic enzyme production.
- Small frequent meals. Decreases pancreatic enzyme production.

– Administer as ordered:
   o No morphine. Causes spasm of the sphincter of Oddi.
   o IV fluids. Increases fluids.
   o Total parenteral nutrition. Bypasses the pancreas.
   o Vitamin supplements. Increases nutrition.
   o Analgesia. Decreases pain.
   o Insulin (chronic). Replaces decreased insulin production by pancreas.

Peritonitis

Acute inflammation of the peritoneum (lining of the abdominal cavity) that may lead to septicemia if the infection enters the bloodstream.

Classic Signs
– Abdominal rebound pain. Related to inflammation.
– Abdominal distention. Related to increased intestinal pressure.
– Rigid abdomen. Related to inflammation.
– Decreased bowel sounds. Related to decreased peristalsis.
– Fever. Related to infection.
– Tachycardia. Related to infection.
– Nausea. Related to infection.
– Vomiting. Related to infection.
– Decreased urine output. Related to progressive kidney failure.
– Increased WBC. Related to infection.

Interventions
– NPO. Inability of the gastrointestinal tract to process food.
– Elevate head of bed. Decreases the backflow of stomach acid and juices into the esophagus.
– Monitor vital signs. Identify patient status.
– Monitor intake and output. Identify fluid balance.
– Daily weight. Assess for fluid retention.
– Administer as ordered:
   o Antibiotic. Decreases infection.
   o IV fluids. Increases fluids.

Peptic Ulcer Disease (PUD)

Erosion of the mucosal layer of the stomach or duodenum. Stomach acid contacts epithelial tissues leading to bleeding, perforation, peritonitis, paralytic ileus, septicemia, shock, and ischemia or ulcerate. Two types of peptic ulcers are:
- Gastric Ulcer. Mucosal layer of the stomach is eroded, lessening the curvature of the stomach.
- Duodenal Ulcer. Mucosal layer of the duodenal is eroded resulting in penetration to the muscular layer.

Classic Signs
- Bloating. Related to pressure on the stomach.
- Loss of appetite. Food increases pain (gastric ulcer).
- Blood Test:
    o Decreased RBC. Related to bleeding.
    o Decreased hemoglobin. Related to bleeding.
    o Decreased hematocrit. Related to bleeding.
- Stool occult blood positive. Related to upper GI bleeding.
- Epigastric pain:
    o Worse after eating (gastric ulcer). Related to irritation of the stomach.
    o Worse 1 to 3 hours after eating or at night (duodenal ulcer). Related to irritation of the duodenum.
- Weight Change:
    o Loss (gastric ulcer). Related to food intake causing pain and patients avoiding eating.
    o Gain (duodenal ulcer). Related to food easing pain and patients increasing eating.
- Bleeding:
    o Vomiting red, maroon blood (hematemesis) (gastric ulcer). Related to upper GI bleed.
    o Coffee-ground emesis (gastric ulcer). Related to upper GI bleed and digested blood.
    o Tarry stool (melena) (duodenal ulcer). Related to upper GI bleed.
- Perforation:
    o Sudden, sharp pain relieved with knee-chest position which decreases the stretch of the stomach and duodenum.
    o Tender, rigid abdomen. Related to inflammation.
- Hypovolemic shock. Related to bleeding.

Interventions
- Monitor intake and output. Identify fluid balance.
- Monitor vital signs. Identify changes in patient status.
- Monitor bowel sounds. Identify peristalsis status.
- Monitor abdomen tenderness, rigidity. Assess inflammation.
- Small frequent meals. Decreases irritation to stomach.
- No caffeine. Related to irritation to stomach.
- No alcohol. Related to irritation to stomach.
- No acidic foods. Related to irritation to stomach.
- No NSAIDs medication. Related to irritation to stomach.
- No smoking. Related to irritation to stomach.
- Administer as ordered:
    - Antacids. Decreases stomach acid.
    - Proton pump inhibitors. Decreases production of stomach acid.
    - Sucralfate. Adheres to ulcer sites and provides protection from acids, enzymes, and bile salts.
    - Antibiotic. Decreases infection by H. pylori.

Ulcerative colitis

Inflammation of the mucosal layer of the large intestine leading to ulcerations and abscess formation. Risk for malabsorption, toxic megacolon, and perforation.

Classic Signs
- Chronic bloody diarrhea with pus. Related to infection.
- Tenesmus (spasms of the anal sphincter, feeling need to defecate with no stool present). Related to inflammation.
- Weight loss. Patients avoid eating to reduce symptoms.
- Abdominal pain. Related to inflammation.
- Blood Test:
    - Decreased RBC. Related to bleeding.
    - Decreased hemoglobin. Related to bleeding.
    - Decreased hematocrit. Related to bleeding.
    - Increased erythrocyte sedimentation rate. Related to inflammation.

Interventions
- NPO during exacerbations. Inability of the gastrointestinal tract to process food.
- Monitor intake and output. Identify fluid balance.
- Monitor stool output. Assess for bloody diarrhea with pus.
- Daily Weight. Assess changes in the patient's weight.
- Monitor for toxic megacolon. Distended, tender abdomen, fever, distended colon.
- Keep stool diary. Identify irritating foods.
- Low fiber, high protein, high calorie diet. Less irritating to the GI tract.
- Perianal skin care area:
    o Sitz bath.
    o Apply barrier cream to skin. Protects the skin.
    o Witch hazel. Soothes sensitive skin.
    o No fragranced products. Risks of irritating the skin.
- Administer as ordered:
    o Antidiarrheal medication. Decreases diarrhea.
    o Corticosteroids (during exacerbations). Decreases inflammation.
    o Anticholinergics. Decreases gastrointestinal cramps.
    o Salicylate. Decreases pain.

Musculoskeletal Assessment, Disorders, Interventions

Assessment
The five P's of musculoskeletal injury (head to toe):
- Pain
- Paralysis
- Paresthesia
- Pulse
- Pallor

Assess range of motion:
- Adduction: Moving the limb close to the body (adding to the body).
- Abduction: Moving the limb away from the body (subtracting from the body).

Interview
- Initial Questions:
    - o   What makes you feeling that something is wrong?
    - o   What happened prior to noticing this problem?
    - o   Have you recently undergone any medical procedure?
- Follow up questions:
    - o   When did this problem start?
    - o   How long have you had this problem?
    - o   Can you describe the problem?
    - o   How bad does the problem bother you?
    - o   Where do you feel uncomfortable?
    - o   Is the problem spreading or does is the problem remain in one place?
    - o   Does anything make the problem worse?
    - o   Does anything make the problem better?
    - o   Did you have this problem or a similar problem in the past?
    - o   Have you been diagnosed with any medical condition?
    - o   What medications do you use?
    - o   Do you use an assistive device?
    - o   Do you have you recently fallen?
    - o   Do you have a history of falling?
    - o   Do you have any vision problems?
- Lifestyle questions:
    - o   What is your occupation?
    - o   Do you perform repetitive actions?
    - o   Do you or did you exercise?
    - o   Do you or did you play sports?
    - o   Do you consume caffeine?
    - o   Do you drink alcohol?
    - o   Do you use recreational drugs or prescription drugs that are not prescribed to you?
    - o   Do you use tobacco?
- Family history:
    - o   Does anyone in your family have or had osteoarthritis?
    - o   Does anyone in your family have or had rheumatoid arthritis?
    - o   Does anyone in your family have or had osteoporosis?
    - o   Does anyone in your family have or had spondyloarthropa-thies?
    - o   Does anyone in your family have or had cancer?

Inspection
- Assess the patient's gait.
- Does the patient have difficulty bearing weight?
- Is the patient guarding the site of the injury?
- Does the patient have pain during movement or at rest (assess facial expression)?
- Muscles:
  - o Weakness
  - o Swelling
  - o Bruising
- Bone:
  - o Skin breakage
  - o Deformed skeleton
  - o Impaired range of motion. Never force range of motion movement.
- Range of Motion Assessment:
  - o Temporomandibular Joint (TMJ):
    - ▪ Place first two fingers on patient's ear.
    - ▪ Ask patient to open and close his mouth.
    - ▪ Place fingers into the depression over the joint.
    - ▪ Ask patient to open and close his mouth.
    - ▪ The patient should easily open and close his mouth without pain or discomfort.
- Neck:
  - o If there is no suspected neck or spinal injury, ask the patient to:
    - ▪ Touch right ear to right shoulder.
    - ▪ Touch left ear to left shoulder.
    - ▪ Touch chin to chest (45 degrees is normal).
    - ▪ Tilt head back and look at the ceiling (55 degrees is normal).
    - ▪ Turn head to each side.
    - ▪ Move head in a circle (70 degrees is normal).
- Spine:
  - o If there is no suspected neck or spinal injury, ask the patient to:
    - ▪ Bend at the waist.
    - ▪ Let arms hang at sides.
  - o Palpate the spine with your fingers.
  - o Palpate the spine with the side of your hands.

       o The spine should be symmetrical with no tenderness or swelling.

– Shoulders:

       o Shoulders should be symmetric and not deformed.

       o Palpate the:
- Bony landmarks with your fingers
- Shoulder muscles with your hand
  - Muscles should be firm and symmetrical
- Elbow and ulna

       o Ask the patient to:
- Extend his arms straight at the side (neutral position).
- Lift arms straight to shoulder level.
- Bend elbows at 90 degrees.
- Extend arms out parallel to the floor, palms down and fingers extended.
- Extend forearms up with fingers pointed to the ceiling. Forearms should move 90 degrees.
- Extend forearms down with fingers pointing to the floor. Forearms should move 90 degrees.
- Extend arms straight at the side (neutral position).
- Move arms forward and up over head.
- Extend arms straight at the side (neutral position).
- Move arms as far back as possible. Arms should bend 30 degrees.
- Extend arms straight at the side (neutral position).
- Move arms away from body (abduction). Arms should move 180 degrees.
- Extend arms straight at the side (neutral position).
- Move arms across the front of the body (adduction). Arms should move 50 degrees.
- Extend arms straight at the side (neutral position).
- Flex elbows. Elbows should flex 90 degrees.
- Place the side of the hand (thumbs facing up) on a flat surface.
- Rotate the palm of hand down to the surface (pronation). The elbow should rotate 90 degrees.
- Rotate the palm of hand upward from the surface (supination). The elbow should rotate 90 degrees.

- Wrists and hands:
  - ○ Examine the hands. Look for:
    - ▪ Deformities
    - ▪ Swelling
  - ○ Feel bones in the fingers and wrist. Look for tenderness.
  - ○ Ask the patient to:
    - ▪ Rotate the wrist in a waxing motion. There should be 55 degrees of movement away from the body (lateral movement) and 20 degrees of movement towards the body (medial movement).
    - ▪ Move the wrist backward with fingers pointing upward. The wrist should move 70 degrees.
    - ▪ Move the wrist downward with fingers pointing to the floor. The wrist should move 90 degrees.
    - ▪ Move only the fingers to the ceiling (extension). Fingers should move 30 degrees.
    - ▪ Move only the fingers towards the floor (flexion). Finger should move 90 degrees.
    - ▪ Touch little finger with thumb.
    - ▪ Form a fist (adduction).
    - ▪ Spread fingers (abduction).
    - ▪ Compare the length of the patient's arms. There should be no more than 1 cm difference in length.
- Hips:
  - ○ Examine the hips. Look for symmetry.
  - ○ Palpate the hips and note any tenderness.
  - ○ Assess the patient's hip:
    - ▪ Flexion. Place your hand under the lumbar spine. Ask the patient to raise knee to chest. The patient's lumbar spine should touch your hand. The opposite thigh and hip should remain flat. Repeat the test with the other hip.
    - ▪ Abduction. Press the superior iliac spine. Move the patient's leg by the ankle away from the other leg. You should feel movement of the iliac spine. The leg should move 45 degrees.
    - ▪ Adduction. Press the superior iliac spine. Move the patient's leg by the ankle toward the other leg. You

should feel movement of the iliac spine. The leg should move 30 degrees.

- Extension. Ask the patient to lie face down. Ask the patient to raise the thigh upwards. Repeat the test with the other hip.
- Internal and external rotation. Ask the patient to lie on his or her back and raise one leg while keeping the knee straight. Turn the patient's leg away from the other leg (external rotation) and then turn the patient's leg towards the other leg (internal rotation). The leg should turn 45 degrees.

o Repeat the test with the other hip.

— Knees:

o Ask the patient to stand.

o Examine the knees. Look for:
- Deformities
- Swelling
- Tenderness

o Ask the patient to bring the heel to:
- Buttocks (flexion). The leg should move 120 degrees. If the patient is unable to stand, then ask the patient to lie down on his or her back and raise knee to chest. The thigh should touch the calf.
- The floor.

— Ankles and feet:

o Examine the ankles and feet. Look for:
- Deformities
- Swelling

o Feel bones in the feet and ankle. Look for tenderness.

o Ask the patient to:
- Sit.
- Point toes towards the floor (plantar flexion). The toes should move 45 degrees.
- Point toes to the ceiling (dorsiflexion). The toes should move 20 degrees.
- Turn feet inward (inversion). The feet should move 45 degrees.
- Turn feet outward (eversion). The feet should move 20 degrees.

- Clench and release toes (metatarsophalangeal joints). Toes should move freely without tenderness.
  - Compare the length of the patient's legs. There should be no more than 1 cm difference in length.
- Muscles:
  - Measure the circumference of the same muscle on each side of the body. They should have relatively the same measurement.
  - Repeat the range of motion assessment (see above) except *you* move the limb (passive range of motion). You should feel slight resistance to the motion (muscle tone).
  - The limb should return easily to the neutral position when you finish the range of motion assessment.
  - Ask the patient to extend arms with palms up for 30 seconds (strength of shoulder girdle).
  - Place your hands on the patient's palm and press down. You should feel resistance.
  - Ask the patient to:
    - Bend the arm. Pull down on the patient's arm (bicep strength). You should feel resistance.
    - Bend the arm and then try to straighten the arm as you push the forearm upward (triceps strength). You should feel resistance.
    - Flex the wrist, then push against it. You should feel resistance.
    - Extend the wrist then push down on it. You should feel resistance.
    - Squeeze your hand. You should feel resistance.
    - Have the patient lie on his or her back.
      - Raise both legs simultaneously. Both legs should raise to the same distance at the same time.
      - Lower legs.
      - Raise each leg as you push down on the leg (quadriceps strength). You should feel resistance.
      - Bend knees and place feet on the bed.
  - Pull the patient's leg forward (lower leg strength). You should feel resistance.
  - Ask the patient to:

- Bend the knee as you push against it. You should feel resistance.
- Push foot down against your hand as you push the foot up (ankle strength). You should feel resistance.
- Pull foot up as you push the foot down. You should feel resistance.
    - o Measure muscle strength by using the muscle grade (Table 8.5).

Table 8.5: Muscle Grade

Grade	Description
0	No muscle contraction
1	Muscle contraction is felt but joint does not move
2	Complete range of motion with assistance (passive ROM)
3	Complete range of motion against gravity
4	Complete range of motion against gravity with moderate resistance
5	Complete range of motion against gravity with full resistance

Auscultation
- Listen for abnormal sounds during the range of motion inspection.
    - o Clicking
    - o Crunching
    - o Grating

Common Classic Signs
- Unsteady gait
- Swelling (edema)
- Pain or tenderness, especially during movement
- Discoloration of skin
    - o Pale (neurovascular problem)
    - o Purple bruising (ecchymosis)
- Skin temperature cool at site (neurovascular problem)
- Unstable joint(s)
- Difficulty with range of motion
- Loss of sensation (paresthesia) or abnormal sensation (neurovascular problem)
- Decrease or absence of pulse (reduced blood supply to site)

- Asymmetric skeletal structure
- Misaligned skeletal structure

Carpal Tunnel Syndrome

The median nerve that passes through the carpal tunnel in the anterior wrist is compressed causing pain and numbness to fingers and is related to repetitive hand movement.

Classic Signs
- Weakness and pain in the hand. Related to nerve compression.
- Paresthesia in the hand. Related to nerve compression.
- Tingling in the hand. Related to nerve compression.
- Numbness in the hand. Related to nerve compression.
- Positive Tinel's sign. Tapping over the carpal tunnel area causes tingling, numbness, or pain in the hand.
- Inflating the blood pressure cuff on the upper arm causes pain, tingling, and burning sensation in the wrist and hand. Related to nerve compression.

Interventions
- Physical therapy. Maintains mobility.
- Administer as ordered:
    - Anti-inflammatory. Decreases inflammation.
    - Corticosteroids. Decreases inflammation.

Dislocations

Two or more bones in an articulated joint move out of anatomical alignment resulting in injury to nerves, soft tissue, and circulation. Common sites of dislocation are:
- Shoulder. Resulting from a fall with the arm extended.
- Acromioclavicular separation. Resulting from blunt force trauma to the shoulder.
- Elbow. Resulting from a fall with the arm extended.
- Wrist. Resulting from a fall with the hand extended.

- Finger. Resulting from blunt force trauma to the fingertip or a fall with the hand extended.
- Hip. Resulting from blunt force trauma to a bent knee (for example, knee hitting the dashboard in a motor vehicle accident).
- Knee. Resulting from blunt force trauma to the knee (for example, sports injury).
- Patella. Resulting from twisting the leg with the foot planted on the ground or blunt force trauma to the knee.
- Ankle. Resulting from blunt force trauma to the foot (for example, pushing the brake pedal in a motor vehicle accident.)

Classic Signs
- Pain or tenderness in the joint. Related to pressure on nerves.
- Deformity at the joint. Related to the dislocation.
- Reduced range of motion. Related to the dislocation.
- Swelling. Related to inflammation.
- Enlargement of joint. Related to inflammation.

Interventions
- Pain management. Decreases pain.
- Immobilize the site. Decreases pain and tissue damage.
- Administer as ordered:
    o Anti-inflammatory. Decreases inflammation.
    o Analgesics. Decreases pain.

Fractures

Break in a bone resulting in hemorrhage, edema, and local muscle and tissue damage. Types of fractures include:
- Incomplete fracture: The fracture is not complete through the bone.
- Complete fracture: The fracture is completely through the bone. Types include greenstick, spiral, comminuted, transverse, oblique, and impacted.
- Open fracture: The fracture penetrates the skin.
- Closed fracture: The fracture does not penetrate the skin.

Classic Signs
- Edema. Related to inflammation.
- Abnormal range of motion. Related to obstruction to range of motion.

- Local bleeding. Related to damage to blood vessels.
- Muscle spasms. Related to involuntary contraction of muscles.

Interventions
- Monitor vital signs. Identify changes in patient status.
- Monitor circulation in area of the fracture. Identify decreased circulation at site.
- Monitor signs of bleeding. Increased pulse, increased respiration, decreased blood pressure.
- Perform range of motion exercises. Maintains muscle tone.
- Complications:
    - Fat embolism. Yellow bone marrow releases fat into the blood stream resulting in emboli.
    - Delayed union. A fracture that is not joined within 6 months.
    - Compartment syndrome. Nerves, blood vessels and muscles are compressed leading to tissue necrosis.
    - Deep vein thrombosis (DVT). Clots form as a result of immobility from fracture.
    - Misalignment. Bone pieces are not anatomically aligned.
    - Muscle wasting. Deterioration of muscle as a result of immobilization related to the fracture.

Contusion

A hemorrhage beneath the skin resulting in discoloration and discomfort at the site of the injury.

Classic Signs
- Dark "black-and-blue" mark beneath the skin. Related to bleeding.
- Yellow-green color at the site 48 hours after the bleeding. Related to metabolism of blood.
- Swelling. Related to inflammation.
- Discomfort when the site is touched or with movement. Related to inflammation.

Interventions
- Assess if the patient is on anticoagulant therapy. Anticoagulant therapy increases bleeding time.
- Assess if bleeding has stopped. Circle site of contusion. If "black and blue" color moves beyond the circled site, then bleeding has not stopped.
- Administer as ordered:
    - o Analgesics. Decreases pain.
    - o NSAIDs. Decreases inflammation.

Gout

Purine-based proteins are not adequately metabolized resulting in uric acid crystals accumulating in joints (big toe) and crystallization of uric acid in the kidneys leading to kidney stones.

Classic Signs
- Swollen joint. Uric acid crystals deposited in the joint.
- Red, tender joint. Uric acid crystals deposited in the joint.
- Joint pain especially at night. Uric acid crystals deposited in the joint.
- Kidney stones (nephrolithiasis) Uric acid crystals deposited in the kidneys.

Interventions
- Monitor serum uric acid levels. Identify increased uric acid levels.
- Immobilize the joint. Reduces pain.
- Don't touch joint. Reduces pain.
- Increase daily fluids (3 liters) of fluid. Decreases crystallization of uric acid.
- Avoid fructose sweetened drinks. Decreases crystallization of uric acid.
- Low fat, low cholesterol diet. Decreases uric acid production.
- Avoid foods that are high in purine proteins. Turkey, organ meats, sardines, smelts, mackerel, anchovies, herring, and bacon. Increases uric acid production.
- Avoid alcohol. Inhibits renal excretion of uric acid.
- No aspirin. Aspirin retains uric acid.
- Administer as ordered:
    - o Xanthine oxidase inhibitor. Decreases uric acid level.
    - o Anti-inflammatory. Decreases inflammation.
    - o Uricosuric. Decreases uric acid level.

Compartment Syndrome

Decreased circulation to a body part caused by increase pressure resulting in damage to nerves, capillaries, and muscles at the site of the fracture. Classifications of compartment syndrome:
- Internal. Caused by the pressure of a build-up of blood in muscle or beneath the skin (contusion), frostbite, infiltration of an IV, snake bite, or by a fracture.
- External. Caused by the pressure of an immobilization device such as a cast or dressing.

Classic Signs
- Swelling. Related to inflammation.
- Decreased pulse or pulselessness. Related to decreased circulation.
- Decreased temperature at site. Related to inflammation.
- Numbness or tingling (paresthesia). Related to nerve compression.
- Pain disproportionate to the underlying injury. Related to inflammation.
- Pallor. Related to decreased circulation.
- Paralysis. Related to nerve compression.

Interventions
- Remove immobilizing device. Returns circulation to site.
- Stabilize site. Prevents tissue damage.
- Apply ice to the site 20 minutes on, 20 minutes off. Decreases inflammation.
- Administer as ordered:
    o Analgesics. Decreases pain.

Osteoarthritis

A degenerative joint disease resulting in the destruction of the articular cartilage that causes bones to rub together and injuring bone tissue leading to bone spurs (regrowth of bone tissue). This places pressure on joints and soft tissue resulting in pain when the joint is moved.

Classic Signs
- Crepitus (grating sound or sensation). Friction between bone and cartilage or bone and bone.

– Joint pain on movement relieved with rest. Related to bone on bone contact on movement of the joint.
– Stiff joints for a short time in morning, usually 15 minutes or less. Related to immobility.
– Heberden's nodes (enlargement of joint). Related to calcific spurs.
– Enlargement of joint.

Interventions
– Exercise. Maintains mobility.
– Reduce weight. Decreases stress on joints.
– Administer as ordered:
  o Analgesics. Decreases pain.
  o Anti-inflammatory. Decreases inflammation.

Osteomyelitis

A bone infection commonly caused by Staphylococcus aureus bacteria secondary to an acute infection.

Classic Signs
– Pain. Related to inflammation.
– Malaise. Related to infection.
– Fever. Related to infection.
– Chills. Related to attempts to cool the body.
– Increased WBC. Related to infection.

Interventions
– Monitor vital signs. Identify changes in patient status.
– Administer as ordered:
  o Analgesics. Decreases pain.
  o Antibiotics. Decreases bacterial infection.

Osteoporosis

Decreased bone density when the rate of bone replacement is exceeded by bone reabsorption, resulting in brittle bones and increased risk of fractures.

Classic Signs
- Asymptomatic
- Decreased height. Related to spinal compression.
- Kyphosis (hunchback appearance). Related to spinal compression.
- Unexplained fractures. Related to decreased bone density.
- Back pain. Related to spinal fractures.

Interventions
- Perform weight-bearing activity. Reduces bone reabsorption.
- Perform range of motion exercises. Maintains mobility.
- Administer as ordered:
    - o Bisphosphonate. Inhibits bone reabsorption.
    - o Forteo (teriparatide). Stimulates collagenous bone growth
    - o Calcium. Increases availability of calcium
    - o Vitamin D. Enhances absorption of calcium.

Sprain and Strain

A sprain is injury caused by stretching ligaments (connecting bone to bone) in a joint. A strain is injury caused by a muscular tear. A sprain and strain are classified by degree (see Table 8.6).

Table 8.6: Classification of sprains and strains

Degree	Sprain	Strain
First	Ligament stretches without tearing. Joint stable and functional.	Over-stretched muscle.
Second	Ligament stretches and tears. Slight joint instability and limited functionality.	Partial tear of the muscle.
Third	Ligament stretches and tears leading to trauma to the tendon. The joint is unstable and functionality is severely lost.	Complete tear of the muscle.

Classic Signs
- Swelling. Related to inflammation.
- Bruising (ecchymosis). Related to ruptured blood vessels.
- Pain caused by movement. Related to inflammation.
- Spasms. Related to involuntary muscle movement.
- Loss of function (third degree). Related to ligament stretches and tears.
- Protrusion at the trauma site (third degree). Related to ligament stretches and tears.
- Unstable joint (third degree). Related to ligament stretches and tears.

Interventions
- Apply ice 20 minutes on and 20 minutes off for the first 24 hours. Reduces swelling.
- Apply heat 20 minutes on and 20 minutes off for the second 24 hours to enhance the inflammation process repairing the tissue. Increases inflammation response.
- Elevate trauma site. Reduces swelling.
- Rest. Decreases pain and encourages healing.
- Immobilize site (second and third degree). Reduces pain and injury.
- Keep site free from any binding such as jewelry. Inhibits circulation when the site is swollen.
- Gradually reuse the muscle. Regain range of motion.
- Administer as ordered:
    o Analgesics. Decreases pain.
    o Anti-inflammatory. Decreases inflammation.

Genitourinary and Gynecologic Assessment, Disorders, Interventions

Assessment
Assess the patient's urinary system first (least sensitive to discuss).
- Kidneys
- Ureters
- Bladder
- Urethra

Assess the patient's reproductive system last (most sensitive to discuss).
- Male:
  - Penis
  - Scrotum
  - Testicles
  - Epididymis
  - Vas deferens
  - Seminal vesicles
  - Prostate gland
- Female:
  - Vagina
  - Uterus
  - Ovaries
  - Fallopian tubes
  - Vulva
  - Labia majora
  - Labia minora
  - Clitoris
  - Urethral meatus
  - Skene's Glands
  - Bartholin's Glands

Interview
- Initial Questions:
  - Why did you come to the hospital today?
  - What makes you feeling that something is wrong?
  - What happened prior to noticing this problem?
  - Have you recently undergone any medical procedure?
- Follow up questions
  - When did this problem start?
  - How long have you had this problem?
  - Can you describe the problem?
  - How bad does the problem bother you?
  - Where do you feel uncomfortable?
  - Is the problem spreading or does the problem remain in one place?
  - Does anything make the problem worse?
  - Does anything make the problem better?
  - Did you have this problem or a similar problem in the past?

- o   Have you been diagnosed with any medical condition?
- o   What medications do you use?
- Urinary system questions:
    - o   Have there been any recent changes in your urination?
    - o   How often do you urinate?
    - o   Do you experience any burning during urination?
    - o   What color is your urine?
    - o   Does your urine have an odor?
- Reproductive system questions:
    - o   How many sexual partners have you had?
    - o   Do you have risk-taking behaviors?
    - o   What is your sexual preference?
    - o   Have you ever had or do you have a sexually transmitted disease (STD)?
    - o   Do you know your HIV status?
    - o   Do you use birth control?
    - o   Males:
        - ▪   Is there any discharge from your penis?
        - ▪   Do you experience any tenderness in your genitals?
        - ▪   Did you notice any lumps or growths in your genitals?
        - ▪   Do you experience any itching (pruritus) in your genitals?
    - o   Females:
        - ▪   When was your last menstrual period?
        - ▪   Do you experience vaginal dryness?
        - ▪   Do you experience vaginal itching?
        - ▪   Do you have hot flashes?
        - ▪   Do you experience flushing?
        - ▪   Do you have mood swings?
        - ▪   Describe your menstrual cycle.
        - ▪   Do you spot between menstruation cycles?
        - ▪   What is the length of your menstrual cycle?
        - ▪   When was your first menstrual period?
        - ▪   Do you use tampons?
        - ▪   Is there any vaginal discharge?
        - ▪   Do you experience any unusual uterine bleeding?
        - ▪   Do you experience any vaginal itching (pruritus)?
        - ▪   Do you experience pain with intercourse?
        - ▪   When was your last intercourse?

- When was your last Pap (Papanicolaou) test?
- What was the result of your last Pap test?
- Do you go for routine gynecological examinations?
- Family History.
  - Does anyone in your family have or had diabetes?
  - Does anyone in your family have or had hypertension?
  - Does anyone in your family have or had cardiovascular disease?
  - Does anyone in your family have or had kidney stones?

Inspection
- Snow crystals on the skin (uremic frost). Related to increased retention of metabolic waste caused by decreased renal function.
- Pale skin. Related to decreased hemoglobin caused by decreased renal function.
- The normal abdomen:
  - Symmetrical when the patient lies on back.
  - Has no discolorations.
  - Has no silvery streaks (striae). Silvery streaks indicate ascites related to nephrotic syndrome.
- Normal genitalia:
  - Has no discharge.
  - Does not appear inflamed.

Auscultation
- Listen for abnormal sounds in the renal arteries.
  - A turbulent sound (bruits). Related to a disruption in blood flow in the renal artery.

Percussion
- Percuss the kidneys:
  - The patient sits upright on the edge of the bed.
  - Place the ball of one hand on the patient's back over the kidney at the twelfth rib.
  - Strike your hand with your other hand. You should hear a thud.
  - Repeat the percussion on the other kidney.
    - Normal: Hearing a thud with no tenderness.
    - Abnormal: Tenderness related to kidney infection.

- Percuss the bladder:
    - o Have the patient urinate immediately before the examination.
    - o Ask the patient to lie on his or her back.
    - o Place a hand on the abdomen.
    - o Tap the middle finger with your other hand.
    - o Start at the symphysis pubis and move up over the bladder.
        - ▪ Normal: Hear tympany.
        - ▪ Abnormal: Dull sound related to urine retention or a mass.

Palpation
- Palpate the kidneys:
    - o Ask the patient to lie on his or her back.
    - o Place one hand under the patient below the kidney.
    - o Place the other hand above the patient by the kidney.
    - o The patient inhales.
    - o Press your hands together.
    - o Repeat this process on the other kidney.
        - ▪ Normal: Should not feel the kidney.
        - ▪ Abnormal: Feel kidney related to enlarged kidney.

Common Classic Signs

Urinary System
- Not urinating (anuria)
- Excessive urinating (polyuria)
- Producing small amount of urine (oliguria)
- Painful urination (dysuria)
- Hesitancy
- Involuntary urination (incontinence)
- Getting up from sleep to urinate (nocturia)
- Odor from urine (bacterial infection)
- Cloudy urine (bacterial infection)
- Blood in urine (hematuria)
- Clear urine (over-hydrated)
- Dark urine (dehydrated)

Reproductive System
- Males:
    - Itchy (pruritus)
    - Penile discharge
    - Mass on genitals
    - Tenderness on genitals
- Females:
    - Vaginal discharge
    - Vaginal odor
    - Uterine bleeding
    - Vaginal itching (pruritus)
    - Cramps
    - Infrequent menstrual periods (oligomenorrhea)
    - Short menstrual periods (hypomenorrhea)
    - Painful menstrual periods (dysmenorrhea)
    - No menstrual periods (amenorrhea)
    - Frequent menstrual periods (polymenorrhea)
    - Spotting (metrorrhagia)
    - Long menstrual periods (hypermenorrhea)

Testicular Torsion

The spermatic cord twists resulting in strangulation of the testis resulting in testicular infarction and disruption of blood flow to the testis. Necrosis occurs after 12 hours. Types of testicular torsion:
- Intravaginal torsion: Within the tissue covering the testicles. Testis is free to rotate.
- Extravaginal torsion: Outside the tissue covering the testicles. Spermatic cord twists above the testis.

Classic Signs
- Scrotal swelling not relieved by elevation of the scrotum. Related to inflammation.
- Severe pain in the scrotum. Related to nerve compression.
- Positive Prehn's Sign:
    - Elevate scrotum to symphysis pubis.
    - Positive Prehn's Sign. Increased pain.

    o   Negative Prehn's Sign. Decreased pain related to inflammation of testis (epididymitis).

Interventions
- Monitor vital signs. Identify changes in patient status.
- Administer as ordered:
  - o   Analgesics. Decreases pain.

Acute Glomerulonephritis (acute nephritic syndrome)

Kidney infection secondary to an ascending urinary infection or other infection.

Classic Signs
- Oliguria. Related to inflammation and infection.
- Hematuria. Related to RBC passing through the glomerulus.
- Peripheral edema. Related to buildup of fluids and salts.
- Increased blood pressure. Related to buildup of fluids and salts.
- Increase BUN. Related to the inability of the kidneys to excrete urea nitrogen in urine.
- Decreased albumin. Related to albumin passing through the glomerulus.
- Decreased glomerular filtration rate. Related to infection reducing the filtering capacity of the kidneys.

Interventions
- Monitor vital signs. Identify changes in patient status.
- Monitor intake and output. Identify if patient is retaining fluid.
- Weigh daily. Identify if patient is retaining fluid.
- Monitor extremities for edema. Identify if patient is retaining fluid.
- Decrease fluid intake. Due to risk of patient retaining fluid.
- Administer as ordered:
  - o   Antibiotics. Decreases bacterial infection.
  - o   Analgesics. Decreases pain.
  - o   Diuretic. Decreases fluid retention.

Kidney stones (Renal Calculi, nephrolithiasis)

Formation of crystals from calcium, uric acid, cysteine, or struvite related to slow urine flow and resulting in blockage of the ureter leading to swelling of the kidneys (hydronephrosis).

Classic Signs
- Unilateral extreme flank pain (renal colic). Related to kidney stones.
- Hematuria. Related to irritation of the kidney or ureter.

Interventions
- Monitor intake and output. Identify fluid imbalance.
- Strain urine. Identify passed kidney stone.
- Increase fluid intake. Increase passage of kidney stone.
- Dietary modification based on makeup of stone. Decreases formation of kidney stone.
- Administer as ordered:
    - Analgesics. Decreases pain.

Pyelonephritis

Infection of the kidneys secondary to ascending urinary tract infection.

Classic Signs
- Flank pain. Related to inflammation.
- Fever. Related to infection.
- Chills. Related to attempts to cool the body.
- Urinary frequency. Related to infection.
- Urinary urgency. Related to infection.
- Costovertebral angle (CVA) tenderness. Percussion in the area of the back over the kidney causes pain.
- Nausea. Related to infection.
- Vomiting. Related to infection.
- Diarrhea. Related to infection.

Interventions
- Monitor vital signs. Identify changes in patient status.
- Monitor intake and output. Identify fluid imbalance.
- Increase fluid intake. Flush kidneys.
- Administer as ordered:
    - Analgesics. Decreases pain.
        - Phenazopyridine. Local analgesic. Turns urine orange.
    - Antibiotics. Decreases bacterial infection.
    - Antipyretics. Decreases fever.

Renal Failure

Decreased renal function. Types of renal failure are:
- Acute. Sudden decrease in renal function.
- Prerenal. Diminished renal perfusion.
- Hypovolemia. Blood or fluid loss.
- Postrenal. Urinary tract obstruction.
- Chronic. Progressive decrease in renal function related to irreversible renal disease.

Classic Signs
- Decrease urinary output. Related to decreased kidney function.
- Peripheral edema. Related to backup of fluids.
- Abdominal bruit. Related to renal artery stenosis.
- Weight loss. Related to loss of appetite.
- Uremic pruritus. Related to excessive urea in the blood.
- Elevated BUN. Related to the inability of the kidneys excrete urea nitrogen in urine.
- Elevated creatinine. Related to the inability of the kidneys excrete creatinine in urine.
- Decreased creatinine clearance. Related to the inability of the kidneys excrete creatinine in urine.
- Decreased RBC. Related to insufficient production of erythropoietin (EPO) by the kidneys.
- Decreased hemoglobin. Related to insufficient production of erythropoietin (EPO) by the kidneys.
- Proteinuria. Related to albumin passing through the glomerulus.
- Decreased glomerular filtration rate. Related to decreased kidney function.

Interventions
- Monitor vital signs. Identify changes in patient status.
- Monitor intake and output. Identify if patient is retaining fluid.
- No contrast dye tests. Kidneys unable to excrete dye.
- Restrict potassium, phosphate, sodium, protein in diet. Related to decreased kidney function to filter and excrete urine.
- Administer as ordered:
  - Antibiotics. Decreases bacterial infection.
  - Antipyretics. Decreases fever.
  - Phosphate binders. Decreases phosphate levels.
  - Sodium polystyrene sulfonate. Decreases potassium levels.
  - Erythropoietin. Replaces the erythropoietin hormone normally produced by the kidney to form red blood cells.

Urinary tract infection

An infection of the urinary tract commonly caused by E. coli bacteria.

Classic Signs
- Dysuria. Related to infection.
- Low back pain. Related to infection.
- Feeling of fullness in suprapubic area. Related to infection.
- Urinary frequency. Related to infection.
- Urinary urgency. Related to infection.
- Increase leukocytes (WBC) in urine. Related to infection.

Interventions
- Increase fluid intake. Flushes infection.
- Monitor vital signs. Identify changes in patient status.
- Monitor fluid intake and output. Identify if patient is retaining fluid.
- Administer as ordered:
  - Analgesics. Decreases pain.
    - Phenazopyridine. Local analgesic. Turns urine orange.
  - Antibiotics. Decreases bacterial infection.

Ectopic Pregnancy

A fertilized egg implants in the fallopian tube risking that the fallopian tube will burst resulting in hemorrhage.

Classic Signs
- Sharp, darting pain in the lower pelvic area. Related to growth of fertilized egg.
- Backache. Related to growth of fertilized egg.
- Vaginal bleeding. Related to ruptured fallopian tube.
- Absence of menstruation (amenorrhea). Related to pregnancy.
- Beta hCG elevated but lower than if pregnant. Related to implanting of fertilized egg in the fallopian tube.

Interventions
- Monitor vital signs. Identify changes in patient status.
- Monitor bowel sounds. Assess for vascular bruit.
- Monitor abdominal distention. Assess risk of ruptured fallopian tube.
- Monitor vaginal bleeding. Assess risk of ruptured fallopian tube.

Ovarian Cysts

A sac (fluid, semi-fluid, solid) that forms on the ovary resulting from an abnormal dissolving of the corpus luteum. Many ovarian cysts are self-resolving.
Types of ovarian cysts:
- Endometrioma. Formed when tissue from uterine lining attaches to the ovaries.
- Dermoid. Cysts containing hair, skin, and other tissue.
- Polycystic Ovarian Disease (POD). A buildup of follicles causing enlarged ovaries with thick outer covering.
- Functional. Self-resolving within three menstrual cycles.
- Cystadenoma. Developed from the surface of the ovaries.

Classic Signs
- Asymptomatic
- Menstrual changes. Related to growth of ovarian cysts.
- Pelvic pain (unilateral, sharp). Related to growth of ovarian cysts.

Interventions
- Monitor vital signs. Identify changes in patient status.
- Rest. Decreases pain.
- Administer as ordered:
    - o Anti-inflammatory. Decreases inflammation.
    - o Low-dose hormonal contraceptive.
    - o Clomiphene citrate (Clomid). Induces ovulation (POD).

Pelvic Inflammatory Disease

Inflammation of the uterus, fallopian tubes, or other reproductive organs leading to ectopic pregnancy, abscess, chronic pelvic pain, and infertility.

Classic Signs
- Vaginal discharge. Related to infection.
- Fever. Related to infection.
- Painful sexual intercourse (dyspareunia). Related to inflammation.
- Cervical motion tenderness. Related to inflammation.
- Chlamydia test positive. Related to infection.
- Gonorrhea test positive. Related to infection.
- VDRL test positive (syphilis). Related to infection.
- RPR test positive (syphilis). Related to infection.
- Elevated WBC. Related to infection.

Interventions
- Administer as ordered:
    - o Antibiotics. Decreases bacterial infection.

Preeclampsia and Eclampsia

Preeclampsia (toxemia). High blood pressure, elevated urine protein, swollen hands and feet in second or third trimester of pregnancy.
- Eclampsia. Untreated preeclampsia leads to seizures, coma, and death during or after birth.

Classic Signs
- Decreased RBC. Related to RBC breakdown.
- Increased proteinuria > 300 mg/24 hours. Related to kidney dysfunction.
- Increased creatinine. Related to kidney dysfunction.
- Preeclampsia:
  - o Asymptomatic
  - o Blood pressure > 140/90. Related to pregnancy.
  - o Headache. Related to hypertension.
  - o Weight gain (rapid). Related to edema.
  - o Edema. Related to decreased urine output.
  - o Decreased urine output. Related to kidney dysfunction.
- Eclampsia:
  - o Seizure. Related to periods of disturbed brain activity.
  - o Asymptomatic
  - o Blood pressure > 140/90. Related to pregnancy.
  - o Headache. Related to hypertension.
  - o Weight gain (rapid). Related to edema.
  - o Edema. Related to decreased urine output.
  - o Decreased urine output. Related to kidney dysfunction.

Interventions
- Bed rest. Decreased workload.
- Monitor vital signs. Identify changes in patient status.
- Monitor fluid intake and output. Identify if patient is retaining fluid.
- Low salt diet. Decreases hypertension.
- Administer as ordered:
  - o Antihypertensive medication. Decreases blood pressure.
  - o Anti-seizure medication. Decreases the risk of seizure.

Index

A

Abdomen 147, 177, 179, 242, 243, 244, 245, 247, 248, 250, 252, 256, 260, 261, 262

Abdominal distention 252, 259, 261, 289

Abdominal pain 245, 246, 247, 248, 251, 252, 255, 259, 260, 263

Abduction 264, 267, 268

Abilities 17, 24, 34, 49, 50, 52, 55, 79, 131, 182

Abnormal 202, 204, 242, 243, 282, 283

Abuse 109, 164

– substance 68, 69

Accessory muscles 171, 201, 203, 206, 207, 208, 209, 211

Accidents 100, 112

ACE (Angiotensin-converting enzyme), 153, 211

Acid reflux 207, 210, 212, 218, 253

ACLS (Advanced Cardiac Life Support), 100, 119

Acute Glomerulonephritis 285, 287, 289, 291

Acute Respiratory Distress Syndrome. *See* ARDS

Adduction 264, 267, 268

Administering 89, 136, 142, 145, 149, 150, 151, 155

Administering medications 23, 32, 50, 146, 149, 150, 151

Administration 102, 103, 112, 136, 149

– healthcare facility's 111

– levels of 101, 102

Admissions 89, 90, 175, 176

Advantages 94, 98, 99, 101, 102, 104, 105, 107, 108, 109, 110, 111, 112, 113, 114

Age 17, 57, 112, 123, 124, 131, 175, 176, 177, 180, 220, 222

Agency 69, 92, 93, 94, 95

– home healthcare 96, 97

Agency fee 7

Agency nurse 92, 93, 94

– local 95

Agency nursing 92, 93, 94

Agreement union security 7

Air 100, 146, 171, 203, 204, 205, 209, 211, 213, 214, 215, 216, 217, 218, 246

Airways 129, 171, 203, 206, 207, 213

Albumin 140, 178, 179, 254

Alcohol 147, 148, 159, 219, 253, 255, 257, 258, 260, 263, 275

Allergen 202, 206

Alveoli 171, 205, 206, 211, 212, 218

American Heart Association 49, 51, 75

American Nurses Credentialing Center 24

American Nurses' Credentials Center (ANCC), 5, 24

Ammonia 249, 250

Analgesics 163, 190, 191, 218, 219, 247, 248, 273, 275, 276, 277, 285, 286, 287, 288

ANCC (American Nurses' Credentials Center), 5, 24

Angiotensin-converting enzyme (ACE), 153, 211

Ankles 171, 188, 245, 268, 269, 273

Answer medication questions 165

Answers 13, 39, 40, 53, 54, 80, 117, 124, 129, 130, 131, 135, 136, 137, 180

– correct 39, 128, 129, 131, 220

– patient-centered 131

Antacids 253, 255, 258, 263

Antibiotics 159, 160, 161, 213, 214, 247, 248, 250, 252, 261, 263, 285, 287, 288, 290

– broad-spectrum 159

Anticoagulants 195, 201, 219, 233, 237, 238, 239, 240

Anticonvulsant 164, 226, 227, 228, 229, 231, 234, 236, 239, 240

Antiemetic 237, 240, 248, 259

Antipyretics 214, 215, 229, 231, 287, 288

Anxiety

– increased 189, 190, 192, 207, 208, 217

– patient's 185, 186

APACHE (Acute Physiology and Chronic Health Evaluation), 176

Aphasia 180, 182, 226, 232, 239

Appendix 244, 247

Applicants 5, 22, 28, 30, 48, 70, 71, 76, 77, 138

Application tracking system (ATS), 10, 11, 22, 27, 28, 29, 30, 48, 51, 70, 72, 73, 74, 76, 78

Application tracking system selection process 70

Applications 10, 11, 21, 22, 26, 27, 28, 29, 31, 56, 67, 70, 72, 79, 81
– computer 71
– resume and job 42, 47, 48, 49, 60
– resume/job 48

Applying In-house 9

ARDS (Acute Respiratory Distress Syndrome), 205, 207, 209, 211, 213, 215, 217

Arms 32, 148, 172, 177, 181, 188, 189, 190, 198, 221, 267, 270, 272

Ascites 203, 249, 250, 257, 260, 282

Aspirin 190, 191, 236, 238, 239, 240, 275

Assessments 14, 49, 50, 96, 124, 129, 172, 173, 175, 177, 183, 184, 185, 187, 201
– baseline 177
– physical 170

Ativan 138, 164

Attitude 120

Attorneys 108, 109

Auscultation 179, 204, 241, 242, 271, 282

Authorities regulatory 14, 18, 104

Average patient 169

B

Bachelor's degree in Nursing 49

Backflow of stomach acid and juices 253, 258, 261

Background 15, 16, 17, 32, 33, 34, 35, 36, 48, 52, 70, 72, 79, 119, 120
– criminal 16, 34
– non-nursing 46

Background Check Anxiety 32, 33, 35

Background report 17, 33, 34

Bacteria 159, 160, 161, 167, 168, 216, 228, 230

Bacterial infection 160, 167, 168, 169, 246, 247, 248, 251, 252, 255, 283, 285, 287, 288, 290

Bargaining agreement 7, 12, 20, 72
– collective 7, 8

Bargaining unit 7, 20, 65, 72, 90, 91, 127

Basic Life Support Certified 49, 51, 75

Bathroom privileges 191, 198, 199, 201

Beats 188, 190, 191, 192

Bed rest 191, 193, 194, 198, 199, 201, 214, 215, 217, 218, 236, 237, 238, 239, 240

Benefits 6, 7, 15, 16, 18, 27, 52, 61, 93, 95, 99, 103, 107, 108, 125

Benefits package 6

Beta-adrenergic blocker 190, 191, 192, 195

Bilateral crackles 195, 197, 199, 200

Bile
– backup of 248, 249, 256
– ineffective excretion of 248, 249

Bleeding 223, 224, 236, 237, 238, 239, 240, 242, 245, 250, 251, 262, 263, 274, 275

Blockage 191, 219, 246, 247, 248, 259, 286

Blocked airflow 204, 207, 209, 210, 212, 214

Blood 167, 168, 171, 188, 189, 191, 192, 194, 195, 196, 205, 206, 217, 254, 287
– digested 254, 255, 262

Blood clots 130, 180, 191, 200, 236, 239

Blood flow 153, 189, 193, 201, 218, 232, 249, 282, 284
– decreased 200, 247, 249, 257

Blood glucose 155, 157, 159

Blood glucose levels 155, 156, 157, 158, 159, 172
– normal 157, 158

Blood pressure 136, 139, 152, 154, 155, 162, 177, 184, 191, 193, 196, 197, 225, 274, 291
– increased 153, 154, 225, 285
– low 155, 245

– patient's 136, 152, 155
– systolic 175, 183, 190, 191, 192
Blood Test 172, 256, 260, 262, 263
Blood vessels 141, 146, 148, 153, 154, 158, 232, 248, 274
Bloodstream 139, 140, 141, 147, 261
Body 139, 140, 143, 155, 158, 167, 168, 171, 207, 208, 213, 214, 264, 267, 268
– patient's 167, 168, 171, 174, 184
Bones 237, 238, 266, 268, 269, 272, 273, 274, 276, 277, 278
Boss 61, 80, 90, 91
Bowel spasm 250, 252, 259
Bradycardia 228, 231, 232
Brain 163, 171, 190, 196, 216, 221, 223, 224, 226, 228, 232, 233, 236, 239, 240
Brain stem 224, 227, 228, 230, 237
Brain tissues 224, 232, 234
Breath shortness of 155, 171, 188, 189, 191, 192, 194, 195, 198, 202, 210, 217
Breathing 129, 130, 162, 172, 188, 189, 203, 205, 206, 208, 218, 230
Bronchodilator 200, 207, 208, 209, 210, 212, 214, 215, 216, 218
Bronchospasms 206, 207, 210, 212, 214, 215, 216, 218
Bruising 224, 234, 235, 238, 250, 260, 266, 279
BSN (Bachelor of Science in Nursing), 5, 24, 51, 52, 74, 75, 77, 87, 88, 105, 106
Business 52, 65, 99, 110, 113, 114

C
Caffeine 154, 253, 255, 258, 260, 263, 265
Call 13, 21, 22, 28, 29, 35, 43, 44, 55, 57, 80, 82, 94, 125, 169
Campus 52, 125
Candidates 4, 5, 8, 10, 11, 12, 14, 22, 24, 25, 27, 55, 72, 81, 122
– employers pressure 35
– experienced 80
– good 11, 12, 53, 72, 82, 88
– ideal 4, 66, 89, 117, 136

– internal 8, 71
– interviewing 25
– perfect 60, 77, 80, 81
– potential nursing 39
– qualified 10, 21, 28, 29, 36, 81
– selected 25, 81
– unqualified 21, 137
Cardiac contractions 193, 195, 200, 211
Cardiac muscle
– decreased oxygen to 190, 192, 208
– necrosis of 190, 198, 199
Cardiac workload 190, 191, 192, 193, 194, 195, 198, 199, 200, 201, 206, 210, 211, 217, 218
– increased 171, 190, 194, 195, 198, 199
Cardiovascular Assessment 187, 189, 191, 193, 195, 197, 199
Care 3, 4, 42, 47, 49, 73, 75, 96, 97, 100, 105, 108, 109, 110, 112
– effective patient-centered 73, 74, 75, 76
– inpatient hospice 103
Care nurses critical 100
Care plan 49, 50, 96
Care providers 97, 98
Career 54, 56, 57, 80, 85
– previous 56, 57, 87
Career goals 80, 85
Career path 85, 86, 87
Career plan 85
Caregivers 73
Case management 97
Case managers work 98
Cells 153, 157, 171, 226
Cerebellum 224, 226, 227, 233
Cerebral edema 223, 225, 226, 227, 229, 231, 236, 237, 239, 240
Cerebrovascular Accident (CVA), 232, 286
Certification 74, 87, 100, 101
Certified nursing assistant. See CNA
Challenges 20, 58, 59, 65, 69, 70, 72, 88, 91, 112, 185
Challenges of Recruiting Nurses 21
Changing jobs 6, 61, 88
Changing Nursing Specialty 88, 89
Chest patient's 203
Chest pain 189, 198, 218, 258
– episodes of 190, 191

Chronic obstructive pulmonary disease
(COPD), 171, 209, 210
Chronic pulmonary disease 196, 211,
214, 215, 216, 218, 219
Circulation 129, 130, 141, 188, 201, 230,
232, 254, 272, 276, 279
Classes 18, 19, 40, 57, 63, 107, 112, 142,
160
Classic Signs 189, 190, 192, 193, 195,
196, 198, 208, 213, 215, 228, 273,
276, 286, 289
Clients attorneys interview 108
Clinical ladder 59, 60, 90
Clinical policy 74, 75
Clinical rotations 39, 40, 41, 42, 46, 49,
50, 51, 52, 53, 54, 57, 107, 108
Clinical situations 60, 86, 136
Clinical staff 39, 101, 102, 107
CNA (certified nursing assistant), 8, 9, 41,
43, 50, 71, 96
Colleagues 20, 22, 24, 26, 54, 55, 61, 62,
67, 68, 69, 77, 90, 91, 124
Commissioned officers 45, 105, 106
Communication 122, 182
Compensation 15, 24, 34, 36, 60, 61, 93,
108, 114, 122, 125, 126
– physiological 167, 169
Complaints patient's 173
Concussion 223, 224, 234
Conflicts 23, 25, 26, 71, 90, 105, 118,
126, 128
Confusion 153, 155, 193, 196, 216, 226,
232, 233, 234, 235, 236, 238, 239,
240
Consciousness loss of 223, 233, 234,
235, 237
Consolidated organization 66
Consolidation 65, 66, 114
Constipation 165, 245, 246, 251, 256,
259
Contact network 39, 40, 41, 42
Contacts 11, 17, 21, 27, 32, 39, 40, 41,
44, 45, 67, 69, 78, 98, 102
Contract 19, 20, 65, 92, 93, 94, 95, 113,
127, 194
– healthcare facility's 93, 127

Conversation 13, 24, 31, 40, 53, 61, 69,
78, 79, 121, 123, 172, 182
Conviction criminal 33, 34
COPD (chronic obstructive pulmonary dis-
ease), 171, 209, 210
COPD patients 212
Corticosteroids 199, 207, 226, 232, 233,
237, 239, 264, 272
Cough 171, 194, 202, 207, 209, 253
Coughing 199, 202, 208, 210, 212, 213,
215, 216, 217, 218, 219
Courses non-nursing 39
Crackles 193, 194, 204, 205, 209, 213,
217, 218
Cruise ship nurse 113
Cruise Ship Nursing 113
Culture 15, 20, 23, 65, 66, 117, 122, 159
– healthcare facility's 53, 117
Current Nursing Career 87
Curriculum 106
Customers previous 77
CVA (Cerebrovascular Accident), 232, 286
Cyanotic nail beds 201, 202, 206, 208,
209, 210, 217

D
Dates 15, 19, 29, 34, 48, 61, 64, 71, 73,
127, 143, 144, 149, 151, 220
Days 5, 6, 7, 19, 22, 27, 28, 47, 62, 63,
76, 96, 97, 119, 202
Decision 9, 12, 22, 25, 35, 55, 56, 61, 70,
83, 85, 114, 122, 124, 125
– hiring nurse manager's 35
Decreased blood volume 152, 197, 245,
254
Decreased hematocrit 195, 197, 254,
255, 262, 263
Decreased hemoglobin 195, 197, 254,
255, 262, 263, 282, 287
Decreased oxygen 190, 191, 192, 193,
194, 195, 196, 197, 198, 199, 208,
216, 232, 236, 239
Decreased oxygen levels 201, 203, 205,
206, 207, 208, 214, 216, 218
Decreased perfusion 194, 195, 197, 209,
210

Decreased RBC   254, 255, 262, 263, 287, 291
Decreased workload   239, 240, 291
Deep vein thrombosis (DVT), 187, 274
Deep-breathing exercises   206, 208, 210, 212, 213, 215, 216, 217, 219
Deformities   268, 269, 273
Degree RNs   88
Degrees   24, 87, 92, 96, 106, 181, 228, 231, 244, 249, 266, 267, 268, 269, 278
– third   279
Diabetes   155, 156, 157, 158, 159, 282
Diabetic medications   132, 152, 155, 156, 157, 159
Diagnosis   49, 50, 97, 129, 170, 172
Diarrhea   159, 160, 161, 245, 246, 251, 252, 256, 264, 286
Difficulty breathing   199, 200, 205, 206, 208, 209, 210, 211, 213, 215, 216, 217, 235, 258
Dilates blood vessels   190, 191, 193, 195, 196, 200, 211
Dilates bronchiole tubes   200, 207, 208, 209, 210, 212, 214, 215, 216, 218
Disability   17, 123, 124, 125, 126, 231
Disadvantages   95, 97, 98, 101, 102, 103, 104, 106, 107, 109, 110, 111, 112, 113, 114
Discharges   6, 89, 90, 97, 281, 282
Disciplinary action   9, 12, 64, 68, 106
Discretion   20, 125, 127
Disorders   167, 168, 169, 170, 185, 187, 189, 191, 201, 219, 241, 263, 264, 265, 279
– substance abuse   68
DNP (Doctor of Nursing Practice), 92
Doctor of Nursing Practice (DNP), 92
Dose   68, 99, 138, 139, 141, 142, 149, 151, 153, 163
Dreaded Application Tracking System   3, 27, 29, 44, 48, 55, 72, 81
DVT (Deep vein thrombosis), 187, 274
Dysfunction   neuronal   234, 235, 237, 238, 239, 240

Dyspnea   191, 192, 194, 195, 198, 199, 205, 206, 208, 209, 210, 211, 213, 215, 216

E
Ear lobes   188, 201, 202, 206, 208, 209, 210, 217
Eating   158, 189, 225, 253, 258, 262, 263
Eclampsia   290, 291
Edema   peripheral   249, 250, 285, 287
Education   24, 29, 30, 33, 45, 48, 51, 54, 73, 74, 75, 80, 87, 103, 106
Education department   clinical   18
Effort   65, 94, 96, 181, 184, 203
Electronic medical record (EMR), 24, 49, 50, 67, 101, 102
Elevated shoulders   201, 206, 207, 208, 209, 211
Email   30, 31, 32, 40, 41, 44, 46, 47, 50, 51, 52, 55, 56, 81, 83
Email address   nurse recruiter's   44
Email nurse managers   46
Employee Health   15, 25, 32
Employees   7, 8, 16, 19, 27, 71, 89, 93, 95, 125, 127
– current   8, 22, 63
Employer   16, 17, 35, 66, 87, 104, 117, 121
– current   6, 15
– former   17, 34, 36, 77, 78
– present   80, 88
– previous   16, 17, 77
– prospective   64, 117
Employer's name   29, 48, 73
Employer's tuition reimbursement policy   88
Employment   7, 15, 20, 35, 44, 71, 88, 108, 119, 122, 123, 127, 128, 137
– conditions of   7, 15
– dates of   15, 17, 34, 121
– gaps in   79, 118
– minimum terms of   127, 128
– short periods of   79, 118
– short-term   117
– terminate   6
– terminating   20
– verifying   34
Employment benefits   6

Employment contract   19
Employment eligibility verification   33
Employment gaps   117
Employment letter   127
Employment opportu   114
Employment opportunities   40
– new   88
Employment physicals   22
Employment record   33
Employment terminates   127
EMR. *See* electronic medical record
EMR system   67, 101, 102, 103
EMR system problems   102
Enlisted nurses   106
Entries   3, 48, 73
Environment   stable working   90
Errors   17, 30, 95, 104
Esophagus   253, 257, 258, 261
Evidence   16, 109, 117
Exam
– exit   137, 138
– pre-employment health   13, 15
Examination   pre-employment health   16
Exertion   189, 195, 196, 198
Expect During   52, 53, 57, 78, 79
Expense   91, 93, 94, 100, 105, 113
Experience   42, 43, 53, 54, 59, 60, 78, 79,
    86, 89, 94, 120, 121, 159, 281
– bedside patient care   111
– five years of   59, 66
– non-nursing   43, 48, 87
– required   49, 60, 121
Experience interviewing   82
Experienced Nurse Interview   59, 60, 62,
    64, 66, 68, 70, 72, 74, 76, 78, 80, 82
Expert nurse   58, 86, 89, 94
– novice nurse to   85, 86
Expiration   204, 205, 207, 209, 210, 212,
    214
Eyes   11, 29, 144, 177, 180, 181, 222, 238,
    242, 245, 248

F
Facebook   16, 35
Facility   8, 19, 44, 52, 78, 80, 92, 93, 100,
    104, 118, 182
– nurse manager's   40

Family   17, 49, 50, 69, 88, 95, 97, 103,
    106, 113, 130, 186, 242, 265, 282
– patient's   98, 103, 177
Fatigue   192, 194, 195, 209, 210, 216,
    217, 230, 249, 250, 257, 260
Federal agencies   49, 50
Federal regulators   90
Fever   198, 199, 213, 214, 215, 228, 229,
    230, 231, 246, 247, 248, 250, 251, 252
Fingers   181, 188, 202, 203, 221, 222,
    243, 266, 267, 268, 272, 273
First nursing job   36, 39, 41, 44, 45, 46,
    52, 54, 56, 57, 66, 79, 85
First responders   101, 104, 184
Fit   13, 53, 54, 61, 62, 63, 64, 65, 70, 79,
    82, 89, 117, 122, 128
– good   11, 20, 25, 36, 53, 54, 61, 80, 83
Flight transport nurses   100, 101
Float pool nurses   19, 27
Flow of Interviews   25
Fluid balance   178, 252, 254, 255, 257,
    259, 260, 261, 263, 264
Fluid intake   197, 200, 250, 285, 286,
    287, 288
Fluid overload   192, 194, 199, 200
Fluid retention   193, 194, 195, 200, 206,
    209, 210, 211, 217, 219, 229, 231,
    232, 250, 251
Fluid volume   195, 197, 200, 206, 210
Fluids   192, 193, 194, 195, 199, 200, 203,
    210, 211, 212, 213, 214, 217, 246, 261
– buildup of   186, 199, 205, 285
– retaining   211, 285, 288, 291
Focus   4, 13, 114, 118, 121, 124, 128, 129,
    130, 131, 135, 170, 172, 186, 187
Food   106, 130, 141, 142, 146, 157, 158,
    159, 241, 246, 251, 262, 275
Forearms   267, 270
Forensic nurses work   109, 110
Fourth Career   56, 57
Fractures   130, 273, 274, 276, 277
Free medication   141
Frontal lobe   224, 226, 227
FTEs (full-time equivalent), 6
Full-time equivalent (FTEs), 6
Functional abnormalities   234, 235, 237,
    238, 239, 240

G

Gaps 4, 53, 79, 95, 97, 118

Gas exchange 171, 205, 207, 208, 210, 213, 214, 215, 217, 218

– decreased 171, 207, 208, 209, 213, 214

Gastrointestinal Assessment 241, 243, 245, 247, 249, 251, 253, 255, 257, 259, 261, 263

Genitourinary 279, 281, 283

GI 245, 255

Glasgow Coma Scale 169, 175, 176, 179, 180, 183

Glucocorticoid 227, 228, 229, 231, 251

Goal 14, 15, 31, 32, 40, 41, 85, 86, 96, 97, 110, 111, 117, 118, 170

Grads new 42, 43, 44, 45, 47, 48, 56, 57, 58, 59, 60, 61, 66, 94, 96

Graduate 49, 53, 74, 137, 138

– new 3, 8, 9, 51

Graduate nurse 8, 43, 49, 59

Graduation 5, 9, 39, 40, 43, 45, 46, 85

Gravity 178, 181, 209, 225, 271

Group interview 26

Gynecologic Assessment 279, 281, 283

H

Head 36, 130, 145, 172, 174, 177, 223, 224, 235, 264, 267

Headaches 155, 169, 216, 226, 228, 230, 233, 234, 235, 236, 238, 239, 240, 252, 291

Health patient's 96

Health care workers 45

Health insurance

– current employer's 6

– patient's 99

Health insurance benefits 81

Health insurers 110, 111

Health Stroke Scale 180, 181, 182

Healthcare facilities outof-state 56

Healthcare facilities report 137

Healthcare facilities stop 7

Healthcare facility 4, 6, 7, 17, 32, 62, 63, 71, 92, 93, 95, 98, 102, 107, 138

– current 8, 9, 35, 87, 88

– former 64

– good 62

– military 105

– nearest 87

– new 61, 69, 95

– primary 98

Healthcare facility administrators 42, 110

Healthcare facility culture 11

Healthcare facility help 10

Healthcare facility's policies 8, 33, 72, 92, 99, 127

Healthcare team 96

Heart 171, 172, 188, 189, 190, 192, 193, 194, 195, 199, 200, 206, 207, 208, 218

– patient's 129

Heart failure 152, 194

Heart rate 154, 167, 168, 171, 175, 176, 177, 190, 191, 192, 193, 223

Hepatitis 255, 256, 257

High Fowler's position 195, 198, 199, 200, 206, 207, 210, 212, 214, 215, 217, 218

Hiring manager 3, 9, 10, 11, 25, 26, 69, 70

Hiring nurse manager 12, 21, 22, 25, 26, 28, 29, 56, 57, 60, 70, 78, 81, 82, 83

Hiring nurse manager conducts 122

Hiring nurse manager time 12

Hiring nurse manager's office 26

Holidays 6, 47, 62, 93, 95, 97, 98, 107, 108, 111, 112, 119

Home 55, 56, 61, 80, 87, 94, 96, 97, 98, 102, 103, 111, 119, 123, 126

Home healthcare 69, 96, 97

Home healthcare nurse 96, 97

Home healthcare nurse works 96

Homework 79, 127

Hospice nurse cares 103

Hospital administrators 65

Hospital mergers 65

Hospital policies 124, 151, 159

Hospital protocol 149

Hospitals 23, 24, 41, 43, 50, 65, 66, 74, 75, 85, 100, 101, 110, 160, 170

– local 44, 45

Hours 5, 6, 155, 156, 175, 186, 190, 191, 193, 195, 196, 197, 214, 234, 236

Human resource rules 18
Human Resources 9, 10, 11, 13, 14, 25,
    26, 27, 28, 33, 34, 35, 44, 64, 71
– alert 10, 11
– call 21
– contact 8
– locating 78
Human Resources and Employee Health
    25
Human Resources and management 89
Human Resources Interview 11
Human Resources' objections of failure
    12
Hurdles 3, 13, 80
Hypertension 152, 153, 154, 184, 188,
    199, 282, 291
Hypertensive Medications 152, 154
Hypoglycemia 157, 158, 159

I

Immune system 160, 167, 168, 179
Inability 205, 221, 225, 226, 233, 259,
    261, 264, 285, 287
Increased intracranial pressure 205,
    221, 224, 225, 226, 228, 229, 233,
    235, 236, 238, 239, 240
Inexperienced nurse managers 13
Infection 104, 209, 213, 214, 216, 230,
    247, 251, 252, 256, 261, 285, 286,
    288, 290
– ear 160, 161
– kidney 282, 285
Infection control nurse 104
Inflammation 198, 199, 200, 206, 207,
    208, 218, 251, 255, 260, 263, 273,
    276, 279, 290
– acute 252, 261
Inflammation process 163, 198, 213, 216,
    226, 230, 279
Inflammation response 169, 213, 214,
    216, 279
Information 16, 17, 22, 26, 29, 30, 45,
    48, 82, 83, 121, 136, 138, 184, 185
– do not ask 123
Inject 146, 147, 148
Injection sites 147, 148

Injury 164, 223, 225, 231, 232, 234, 237,
    238, 239, 240, 266, 272, 274, 278,
    279
Inotropic medication 195, 197, 200
In-service training 106, 107
Inspiration 189, 192, 204, 205, 207, 209,
    210, 214, 248
Insulin 139, 147, 155, 156, 157, 158, 159,
    219, 260, 261
Insulin injections 112, 157, 158
Insurers 96, 97, 98, 110, 112
Interruptions 40, 139, 229, 230, 232,
    233
Interventions 75, 129, 191, 193, 195, 197,
    199, 201, 217, 225, 235, 251, 275,
    277, 279
Interview 13, 22, 25, 26, 36, 37, 55, 56,
    78, 81, 82, 117, 118, 120, 122
– coordinate 21
– courtesy 70
– face-to-face 11
– first 78
– formal 12
– initial 12, 35, 127, 128
– in-person 11
– last 81
– long 12
– longer 11
– the New Grad Nursing 11
– next 119
– passing 25
– phone 11
– pre-employment 117, 123, 149, 152,
    159, 161, 162
– short 11, 12
– technical 131
– telephone 11
Interview changes 126
Interview process 3, 11, 13, 55, 57, 137
Interview sets expectations 78
Interview stoppers 31
Interview winds 121
Interviewer 12, 36, 118, 120, 123, 124,
    131, 135
– good 36
Interviewing 3, 11, 23, 56, 82, 85, 123
– likely 81

Interviewing hurdles   3
Interviewing process   9, 11, 78, 80, 122
Intracranial pressure   228, 235, 238, 249
– vital signs for indication of increased
   228, 229
Irritation   232, 244, 245, 255, 258, 262,
   263, 286

J
Job   3, 11, 15, 17, 23, 31, 32, 36, 37, 61,
   63, 64, 80, 124, 128
– change   61
– new   17, 61, 89, 128
– night-shift   27
– nurse recruiter's   21, 48, 79
– present   71, 90
Job application   24, 42, 47, 48, 49, 60
Job description   4, 5, 23, 28, 29, 30, 46,
   47, 48, 50, 60, 73, 76
Job fairs   31, 67
Job orientation   135
Job postings   8, 10, 27, 44, 46, 48, 49,
   50, 51, 56, 72, 74, 80, 87, 119
Job requirements   4, 11, 12, 47, 48, 71,
   72, 73, 79, 81, 82, 117, 119, 126, 127
– healthcare facility's   30
– list of   48
– sample   49, 73
Job requirements set   72
Job Responsibilities   49
Joint Commission and state and federal
   regulators   90
Jones   Mary   50, 52, 74, 77
Juices   253, 258, 261

K
Kidney dysfunction   291
Kidney stones   275, 282, 286
Kidneys   140, 141, 152, 153, 168, 194, 195,
   197, 275, 282, 283, 285, 286, 287,
   288
Knowledge   3, 14, 50, 60, 102, 104, 130,
   135

L
Layoffs   65, 114
Leadership roles   24, 87

Legal nurse consultant   108, 109
– independent   108, 109
Legal Nurse Consulting   108
Legs   171, 178, 181, 188, 195, 200, 218,
   221, 245, 268, 269, 270, 273
– patient's   268, 269, 270
Length   11, 20, 30, 68, 71, 126, 147, 148,
   149, 268, 270, 281
Letter   15, 24, 34, 51, 58, 76, 122, 127
– adverse action   34
Level   9, 22, 54, 59, 96, 101, 130, 131,
   140, 146, 160, 182, 215, 231, 235
– decreased   233, 236, 238, 239, 240
License   9, 33, 34, 44, 51, 74, 75, 87, 90,
   99
– current registered nurse   51
– nurse's   68
License Professional Registered Nurse
   51, 75
Licensing boards   43, 53, 54, 58
– passed   99
Licensing requirements   86, 95
– meeting state   95
Life   101, 103, 124, 184
Liquid Medication   142
List   4, 5, 16, 23, 26, 41, 64, 72, 77, 87,
   119, 121, 125, 127, 131
– do-not-rehire   64, 77
List job requirements and match   48
Liters   190, 191, 192, 193, 195, 196, 197,
   207, 208, 209, 210, 211, 212, 213, 214
Liver   140, 156, 157, 168, 243, 244, 248,
   249, 255, 256, 257
Liver cells   increased rupture of   249,
   256
Local chapters   41
Loss   172, 181, 182, 185, 226, 227, 231,
   232, 234, 238, 247, 262, 271, 279,
   287
– sensory   181, 227
LPN   87, 88
Lungs   171, 189, 194, 195, 199, 200, 203,
   208, 209, 210, 211, 212, 213, 214, 217
– collapsed   203, 207, 208, 215

M

Malnutrition   178, 249, 254, 256, 257, 260

Management   7, 8, 20, 88, 89, 90, 91, 99

Manager   9, 10, 11, 20, 24, 26, 82, 89, 91, 93, 97, 98, 107, 110, 111

– case   97, 98, 104

– nurse recruiter and nurse   20, 34, 36, 62

MAP (mean arterial pressure), 168, 176, 177, 196

Mask   190, 191, 192, 193, 195, 196, 197, 200, 208, 213, 214, 215, 216, 218, 219

Massage   147, 148

Meals   155, 156, 157, 225, 250, 257, 260

Measure fluid intake   190, 193, 195, 200, 206, 210, 212, 214

Medical care

– first-line   113

– providing first-line   109

Medical Sales Representative   114, 115

Medication administration   14, 18, 130, 132, 135, 139

– safe   49, 50, 132, 152

Medication administration test, pre-employment   25, 135

Medication errors   151, 152

Medication order   149, 151

Medication Questions   135, 136, 137, 138, 140, 142, 144, 146, 148, 150, 152, 154, 156, 164, 165

Medications   135, 136, 139, 140, 141, 142, 143, 145, 148, 149, 150, 151, 152, 155, 164

– antihypertensive   152, 153, 155, 225, 291

– controlled   69

– intravenous   141

– metabolism of   141

– non-narcotic   163

– withdrawing   151

Members   7, 41, 42, 46, 69, 96, 103

Methicillin-resistant Staphylococcus aureus (MRSA), 160, 161

Military   45, 105, 106

Military nurses work in military hospitals   105

Mind   29, 67, 72, 74, 76, 79, 117, 131, 135, 137, 140, 162, 163, 165, 184

Minutes   11, 21, 36, 144, 145, 146, 156, 158, 196, 197, 234, 242, 276, 277, 279

Mistakes   42, 43, 47

MmHg   168, 169, 175, 192, 197

MOF (Multiple Organ Failure), 174

Monitor   194, 197, 225, 226, 229, 230, 232, 233, 235, 236, 237, 238, 239, 250, 289

Monitor fluid intake and output   217, 219, 226, 231, 232, 288, 291

Monitor for increased intracranial pressure   233, 235, 236, 238, 239, 240

Monitor intake and output   250, 251, 252, 254, 255, 257, 259, 260, 261, 263, 264, 285, 286, 287, 288

Monitor pulse oximetry   196, 207, 211, 214, 215, 216, 218, 219

Mortality   patient's   174, 175

Mortality Probability Model (MPM), 175

Motion   177, 178, 264, 266, 270, 271, 273, 279

Move   3, 4, 57, 58, 86, 88, 115, 203, 221, 234, 243, 267, 268, 269, 270

Move arms   267

Movement   180, 181, 224, 266, 268, 269, 271, 274, 277, 279

MPM (Mortality Probability Model), 175

MRSA (methicillin-resistant Staphylococcus aureus), 160, 161

MSN degree   24, 91, 102

Mucosal layer   253, 262, 263

Mucus production, increased   209, 210, 213

Multiple Organ Failure (MOF), 174

Muscles   141, 148, 153, 157, 198, 229, 266, 267, 270, 274, 276, 278, 279

Musculoskeletal Assessment   264, 265, 267, 269, 271, 273, 275, 277

N

National Institutes   180, 181, 182

National Labor Relations Act (NLRA)   7

Nausea 163, 228, 230, 235, 247, 248, 251, 252, 253, 254, 255, 260, 261, 286

Nausea and vomiting 228, 230, 233, 235, 236, 237, 238, 239, 240, 247, 248, 251, 252

NCLEX questions 13, 135, 136

Needle 147, 148, 149, 151

Negative situations 121

Nerve compression 272, 276, 284

Network 41, 45, 46, 69, 70, 146

Network time 46

Networking 10, 69

Neurological Assessment 219, 221, 223, 225, 227, 229, 231, 233, 235, 237, 239

Neutral position 267, 270

New Grad Nursing Interview 39, 40, 42, 44, 46, 48, 50, 52, 54, 56, 58

New grad programs 43, 44, 56

New nurse graduates 19

Nightshift 60, 128

NJ State Professional Registered Nurse License 74

NLRA (National Labor Relations Act), 7

Non-medication techniques 162, 163

Non-rebreather 190, 191, 192, 193, 195, 196, 197, 200, 208, 213, 214, 215, 216, 218, 219

Nonsteroidal Anti-inflammatory Drugs. *See* NSAIDs

Normal 181, 182, 193, 195, 196, 197, 200, 202, 203, 204, 206, 210, 212, 282, 283

Nose 145, 146, 171, 188, 201, 202, 206, 208, 209, 210, 217, 238

NPO 247, 251, 259, 260, 261, 264

NSAIDs (Nonsteroidal Anti-inflammatory Drugs), 163, 199, 201, 254, 255, 275

Nurse aboard 113

Nurse case manager 98

Nurse Clinician II 59

Nurse Clinician IV 59, 60

Nurse educators 55, 106, 107
– clinical 18, 19

Nurse educators in healthcare facilities 107

Nurse executives 4, 68

Nurse experience 59

Nurse Job Description 4

Nurse management 90, 91, 92, 108

Nurse manager 5, 12, 13, 20, 25, 26, 39, 40, 61, 71, 82, 91, 122, 135, 136
– experienced 13, 123
– multiple 26
– new 61, 63

Nurse manager feedback 40

Nurse manager interviews 12, 13, 27
– pre-employment 185

Nurse manager sifts 26

Nurse manager steps 25

Nurse managers and nurse recruiters 22

Nurse managers categorize 5

Nurse manager's expectations 126

Nurse manager's office 39, 40
– previous unit 40

Nurse manager's position 91

Nurse position 8, 21, 23
– clinical 108
– evening 77
– full-time medical-surgical 66
– medical-surgical 13, 76
– night-shift float pool 27

Nurse practitioner 86, 99, 100

Nurse practitioner compensation 100

Nurse practitioner programs 100

Nurse practitioner's position 159

Nurse recruiter 11, 12, 21, 22, 31, 43, 53, 55, 70, 76, 78, 79, 80, 81, 120
– good 123

Nurse recruiter listing 81

Nurse recruiter Mary Smith's email address 44

Nurse recruiter matches 48, 79, 117

Nurse recruiter prioritize 44

Nurse recruiter schedules 22

Nurse recruiter works 22

Nurse recruiters and nurse managers 77

Nurse recruiter's definition 23

Nurse Recruiters Look 46

Nurse recruiter's name 51, 76

Nurse recruiter's response 125, 126

Nurse school 165
– completing 39

Nurse specialty 88
Nurse works 99
– forensic 109
Nurses 4, 14, 24, 42, 53, 59, 60, 65, 66, 68, 94, 99, 105, 106, 114
– active-duty 105
– bedside 96, 100
– charge 28, 59, 91, 152
– competent 3, 14, 24, 54, 58, 115
– current 4, 43, 107, 108
– degree 88
– diem 14, 19
– educating 106
– elderly 135
– excellent 69, 131
– executive 24
– expensive 42
– experienced 14, 41, 42, 53, 56, 59, 60, 63, 69, 73, 76, 82, 83, 91, 137
– float 27, 62
– forensic 109, 110
– full-time 6, 93
– good 42, 54, 62, 77
– graduated 52
– hospice 103, 104
– inexperienced 95, 131
– informatics 101, 102
– interviewing 26
– licensed 41, 71, 85
– medical-surgical 60, 66, 77
– med-surg 14, 120
– military 105, 106
– new 25, 45, 52, 58
– novice 85, 86
– part-time 5, 6, 14, 67, 105
– primary 74, 75, 76, 124
– proficient 58, 86
– qualified 4, 22
– registered 9, 51
– reserve-status 105
– school 112
– super 13, 77
– telehealth 111
– triage 111
– underperforming 20
Nurse's assessment 96, 108
Nurses complaining 26

Nurse's role 99, 131
Nursing 41, 53, 54, 56, 57, 66, 67, 68, 69, 85, 86, 87, 106, 107, 108
– bedside 86, 91, 99, 110, 114
– home healthcare 96
– legal 85, 86, 108
– military 105, 106
Nursing assistants 21
Nursing associations 41
Nursing board exams 39, 79
Nursing boards 39, 68, 85, 135
Nursing care 105
Nursing career 42, 66, 83, 85, 87, 88, 91
Nursing community 68
Nursing courses 56
Nursing duties 41, 86
Nursing education 87, 105, 106
Nursing education department 17
Nursing experience 42, 43, 48, 59, 60, 82, 86, 87, 95
Nursing homes 41, 56, 59
Nursing informatics 85, 86, 101, 102
Nursing informatics nurse documents 101
Nursing interventions 185
Nursing Interview Process 3, 4, 6, 8, 10, 12, 14, 16, 18, 20, 21, 22, 24, 26, 28
Nursing job opportunity 4
Nursing jobs 3, 4, 5, 23, 34, 45, 56, 57, 61, 62, 65, 66, 68, 69, 70
– present 62, 63
Nursing knowledge 63, 66, 131, 185
Nursing license 32, 34, 37, 43, 44, 45, 46, 54, 67, 68, 92
– civilian 106
– current 24
– new 42
– valid 34
Nursing office 26
Nursing operations 87
Nursing opportunities 65, 85
Nursing orientation 18
Nursing peers 73
Nursing positions 4, 6, 8, 9, 10, 13, 14, 21, 60, 62, 65, 66, 68, 72, 77
– current 63
– full-time 27, 63

– part-time 5
– per diem 14
Nursing practice 18, 41, 43, 59, 60
– common 131
Nursing procedures 131
Nursing process 73, 74, 75, 129, 130
– standard 130
Nursing quiz 167
Nursing schools 39, 41, 42, 44, 51, 54,
    56, 57, 58, 60, 85, 86, 106, 107, 108
Nursing schools set 138
Nursing skills 13, 18, 23, 43, 47, 54, 58,
    60, 66, 67, 96, 107, 108, 132, 136
– bedside 91, 104, 111, 112
Nursing Specialty 85, 86, 88, 90, 92, 94,
    96, 98, 100, 102, 104, 106, 108, 114,
    115
Nursing staff 17, 18, 40, 46, 54, 65
Nursing students 39, 41, 46, 60, 108
Nutrition 178, 187, 261

O
Obstruction 218, 232, 247, 258, 259, 273
Odor 242, 281, 283
Older nurses 66
On-call 97, 100, 104, 110, 111, 113
On-call for home hospice patients 103
Online 8, 10, 11, 32, 41, 48, 70, 72, 106
Online applications 26, 52, 70
Online courses 9, 17, 106
Online medication administration tests
    128, 135, 137, 138
Online Medication Tests 137
Online Pre-Employment Tests 128, 129
Open positions 22, 27, 28, 30, 41, 46,
    47, 62, 70, 72, 78, 82, 85, 88, 122
Oral medication 141, 142
Order 99, 114, 138, 149, 150, 153, 159,
    163, 165, 190, 191, 241
Organization 4, 7, 8, 16, 17, 22, 23, 62,
    63, 64, 65, 70, 88, 89, 92
Organs 141, 155, 168, 243
Orientation 13, 14, 15, 17, 18, 19, 20, 27,
    42, 60, 61, 63, 125, 126, 128
– clinical 18, 63
Orientation process 17, 18
– healthcare facility's 92

Orientee 18, 19
Osmotic diuretic 225, 226, 227, 229,
    231, 236, 237, 239, 240
OTC medications 170
Output 217, 231, 232, 250, 251, 252, 254,
    255, 259, 260, 261, 263, 264, 285,
    288
– decreased cardiac 188, 191, 192, 199,
    211
– renal 190, 193, 195, 200, 206, 210,
    212, 214
Oxygen 189, 190, 191, 192, 193, 195, 196,
    197, 200, 208, 209, 213, 214, 215,
    219
Oxygen flow 189, 190, 192, 193, 194,
    199, 200, 206, 207, 208, 210, 213,
    214, 215, 218
Oxygen saturation arterial 196, 207,
    211, 214, 215, 216, 218, 219
Oxygen supply 190, 191, 192, 193, 195,
    196, 197, 200, 208, 213, 214, 215,
    216, 218, 219
Oxygen therapy 207, 209, 210, 211, 212

P
Pain 142, 161, 162, 163, 173, 174, 187,
    189, 262, 272, 273, 275, 276, 277,
    279
– burning 189
Pain level 161, 162, 247, 248
Pain medication 132, 142, 152, 154, 161,
    163, 164, 165, 247, 248
– administered 165
– daughter 124
– non-narcotic 163
Pain medication administrations 162
Pain signal 163
Palpate 266, 267, 268, 283
Pancreas 156, 157, 179, 259, 260, 261
Paperwork 21, 51, 97
Paralytic ileus 232, 258, 259, 262
Pass 14, 15, 16, 25, 32, 39, 57, 58, 103,
    105, 131, 135, 137, 138, 165
– first 140, 141
Passing 14, 15, 25, 39, 57, 58, 66, 131
Passing grade 14, 39, 57, 131, 136, 138
Patent 146, 177, 178, 213, 215

Patient   96, 97, 98, 103, 111, 146, 150,
   155, 158, 159, 170, 184, 185, 186, 223
– geriatric   103, 141
– hospice   103
– right   130, 135, 149
– stable   100, 184
Patient and family   49, 103, 186
Patient assessment   49, 50, 100, 172, 173
– ongoing   73, 77
Patient care   52, 60, 73, 91, 92, 98, 103,
   108, 111, 114, 115
– implemented individualized   75
– minimal   107, 108
Patient care situations   changing   59
Patient care unit   5, 6, 13, 14, 15, 19, 23,
   25, 26, 110
Patient care unit works   26
Patient education   152, 159
Patient safety   129, 131, 135, 136, 152,
   159, 167
Patient status   215, 233, 251, 252, 259,
   261
– changes in   217, 225, 226, 227, 230,
   232, 235, 236, 237, 238, 239, 240,
   250, 285, 288
Patient's assessment   49, 50
Payers   third-party   65, 97, 98, 110, 111
Payment   95, 110
Per diem nurse positions   63
Per diem nurses   5, 6, 63
Percussion   179, 189, 203, 207, 212, 213,
   241, 243, 282, 286
Perforation   245, 247, 262
Performance   8, 17, 19, 61, 63, 69, 77, 92,
   114
Performance improvement plan   18, 20,
   61, 63
Performance level   70, 71
Perfusion   renal   190, 193, 195, 200,
   206, 210, 212, 214
Pericardium   192, 198
Peritoneum   244, 247, 249, 260, 261
Peritonitis   245, 246, 247, 261, 262
Permission   16, 32
Person   4, 10, 11, 12, 27, 36, 52, 53, 77,
   79, 110, 111, 112, 219, 220
Phone   15, 50, 74, 99, 111

Phrases   28, 29, 30, 48, 49, 50, 73, 74,
   76, 118, 128
Physicians   73, 99, 100
Physiological reserves   167, 168, 170,
   171, 174, 176
Place   145, 146, 203, 223, 244, 266, 267,
   268, 270, 282, 283
Place patient   190, 191, 193, 211, 244,
   245
Place patient in high Fowler's position
   195, 198, 199, 200, 206, 207, 212,
   214, 215, 217, 218
Plan   28, 47, 55, 57, 73, 74, 77, 85, 90,
   119, 121, 126, 127, 128
Planning   25, 28, 42, 90, 129
Pleural effusion   189, 203, 212
Position patient   229, 230
Practice
– nurse practitioner's   99
– ongoing evidence-based   74, 75, 76
Practitioner   15, 16, 67, 98, 99, 100, 114,
   124, 129, 150, 153, 155, 160, 163, 170
– proficient   59
Preceptor   18, 19, 42, 49, 85, 87
Pre-employment medication test   138,
   139, 152
Pre-employment nursing tests   66
Pre-employment online nursing test   167
Pre-employment period   128
Pre-employment process   120, 127, 128,
   135, 155, 160, 167
Pre-employment technical tests   13, 15
Pre-employment tests   25, 63, 131, 161,
   167, 185
Pregnancy   289, 290, 291
Prepping for Medication Questions   14
Prepping for the Interview   14
Pressure   64, 189, 195, 215, 225, 228,
   232, 244, 245, 253, 257, 258, 262,
   273, 276
– increased cranial   223, 226, 228
– increased intestinal   259, 261
Pressure ulcers   217, 229, 232
Prevents injury   225, 227, 231, 234
Prioritize   40, 73, 129, 130
PRN medications   142, 151, 163
Probabilities   173, 174, 175

Probation period 56, 59, 60, 92, 119, 120, 128
Probationary period 6, 15, 19, 20, 92
Problem 9, 35, 36, 91, 101, 102, 103, 121, 137, 170, 173, 187, 241, 265, 280
– current 172
– kidney 152
– patient's 185
– underlying 171, 172
Professional nurse 55, 85
– registered 49, 50, 76
Program 34, 43, 44, 56, 57, 68, 69, 100, 101
– healthcare facility's orientation 47
Proton Pump Inhibitor 206, 207, 210, 212, 218, 227, 253, 255, 258, 263
Pruritus 248, 249, 281, 284
Purging 245, 247, 259

Q
Quadrant right lower 243, 244, 247, 250
Qualifications 11, 12, 22, 48, 57, 122, 127
Quality 90, 114, 173, 174
Quality care 54, 88, 96, 98
Quality patient care 13, 52, 54, 77, 88, 92, 94, 98
Questions
– list of 119, 124, 125
– nurse manager's 136
– open-ended 53, 79, 120

R
Range 135, 177, 178, 182, 186, 187, 229, 264, 266, 270, 271, 273, 274, 278
Reapplying 77
Reason 4, 17, 22, 36, 37, 40, 53, 56, 61, 64, 77, 81, 121, 142, 163
Recovery program 68, 69
Recruiter 11, 22, 30, 31, 53, 55, 106
Registered Nurse. *See* RN
Reimbursements 110, 111
Report 15, 17, 33, 35, 68, 127
Requirements 4, 5, 11, 12, 24, 46, 48, 51, 72, 76, 79, 87, 89, 117, 119
– background compliments 55
– basic 24

– preferred 5
– required 5
Requirements list 24
Resign 15, 63, 64
Resistance 157, 161, 223, 270, 271
Response 21, 35, 44, 53, 54, 55, 56, 57, 80, 118, 120, 121, 128, 129, 180
– patient's 74, 75, 182
Responsibilities 13, 49, 59, 85, 91, 92, 99, 107, 121
Restlessness 162, 192, 199, 206, 233, 235, 236, 238, 239, 240
Resume 10, 11, 12, 28, 29, 30, 31, 47, 48, 50, 51, 72, 73, 74, 121
– enclosed 76
– generic 72
– misspelled 29
– sample 74
– simple 49
Resume quizzing 120
Resume scores 28
Resume/application 48
Return 40, 61, 62, 67, 68, 77, 91, 157, 170, 183, 186, 198, 237, 270
Review 10, 16, 28, 29, 30, 61, 71, 78, 81, 132, 135, 149, 152, 160, 167
Revisiting 142, 143, 145, 147
Rights 7, 17, 33, 90, 130
Risk 61, 62, 88, 163, 164, 165, 168, 169, 187, 230, 237, 238, 239, 240, 244
Risk of low cardiac output 190, 191, 192
Risks of Changing Jobs 61
RN (Registered Nurse), 9, 49, 50, 51, 74, 75, 88, 106
Room air 196, 207, 211, 214, 215, 216, 218, 219
Rotation 39, 40
Rupture 228, 232, 240, 260

S
Saturdays 128
Schedule 22, 24, 26, 36, 78, 80, 93, 94, 96, 112, 119, 123, 153, 159, 164
Schools 34, 44, 51, 54, 57, 58, 62, 87, 88, 90, 112
– local nursing 44, 45, 138

Schools of nursing and healthcare facilities 106
Sciousness 233, 235, 236, 238, 239, 240
Score 28, 30, 176, 180, 183, 220
Script 118, 119, 120, 121, 122, 123, 125, 127
Searches 8, 16, 29, 30, 33, 43, 44, 46, 56, 80
Seconds 181, 188, 200, 202, 221, 270
Secretions 204, 205, 206, 207, 209, 213, 217, 218, 247
– liquefy 207, 210, 212, 214, 217
Seizure precautions 225, 227, 231, 234
Seizures 155, 158, 219, 225, 226, 227, 229, 230, 231, 233, 234, 238, 240, 290, 291
– risk of 226, 227, 228, 229, 231, 234, 236, 239, 240, 291
Seniority 12, 56, 65, 71, 81, 125
Sensitivity test 159, 194
Services 7, 64, 65, 68, 92, 97, 101, 103, 109
– healthcare facility's home healthcare 97
Shifts 18, 19, 26, 27, 47, 61, 62, 63, 75, 76, 80, 89, 91, 119, 125
Shoes new 89, 90
Shoulders 198, 267, 272
Showstoppers 125, 127
Sick days 93, 95, 119, 126
Side effects 140, 150, 160, 246
Signs 32, 127, 129, 170, 172, 173, 188, 201, 202, 231, 234, 235, 237, 238, 240
– abnormal 172, 179
– vital 186, 190, 191, 192, 193, 197, 198, 199, 200, 206, 207, 235, 251, 285, 288
Signs and symptoms 129, 150, 172, 173
Site 143, 147, 148, 149, 157, 163, 171, 232, 235, 266, 271, 273, 274, 276, 279
Situations 11, 13, 20, 40, 43, 91, 97, 120, 121, 122, 123, 124, 126, 128, 184
– abnormal 167, 168
– stressful 167

Skin 140, 143, 144, 146, 147, 148, 177, 178, 242, 245, 264, 271, 273, 274, 276
Soldiers 105, 106
Specialty 41, 42, 45, 53, 66, 89, 90, 93, 95, 99, 106, 115, 152, 167, 170
– changing 90
– new 62, 85, 88, 89, 90, 115
Speech 180, 182, 233
Spinal cord 230, 231, 232
Staff 17, 24, 26, 39, 40, 41, 54, 90, 91, 92, 93, 102, 104, 112, 113
– in-house 108, 109
Staff Nurse Clinical Level II 74, 75
Staff nurse experience 108
Staff nurses 91, 92, 93, 102, 104, 109
– experienced 42
Staffing 4, 5, 18, 27, 92
State 7, 8, 34, 35, 44, 45, 46, 49, 50, 51, 74, 75, 76, 90, 95
State Board of Nursing 68, 69
State licensing board certifies 47
State nursing boards 67, 68
Statement 130, 131
Status 22, 56, 80, 81, 83, 106, 183
– current 87, 150
– neurological 233, 235, 236, 237, 238, 239, 240
– patient's 185, 186
Stethoscope 179, 204, 242
Stimuli painful 180
Stomach 86, 146, 156, 159, 161, 163, 211, 253, 255, 257, 258, 259, 262, 263
Stomach acid 253, 258, 261, 263
Stroke 180, 219, 221, 222, 232
Support 13, 31, 32, 64, 65, 90, 96, 97, 103, 107, 112, 181, 217, 221
Surgery 97, 130, 186, 229
Swelling 149, 153, 163, 200, 242, 266, 267, 268, 269, 271, 273, 274, 276, 279, 286
Symptoms 129, 150, 151, 159, 169, 170, 171, 172, 173, 184, 185, 191, 216, 224, 233
Syndrome acute nephritic 285, 287, 289, 291
Syringes 68, 114, 146, 147, 148, 151, 157

Systems 26, 30, 31, 67, 74, 101, 103, 135, 168, 172, 185
– circulatory 129, 194, 195, 257

T

Table 29, 179, 180, 181, 182, 183, 222, 271, 278
Tablets 138, 142, 163
Tachycardia 189, 190, 192, 193, 194, 197, 198, 199, 200, 206, 207, 208, 213, 214, 215
Tachypnea 171, 199, 205, 207, 208, 210, 213, 214, 215, 217, 218
Tasks 15, 18, 19, 22, 60, 85, 92, 96, 100, 120, 171, 180
Teaching 106, 107
Team 3, 13, 24, 25, 54, 77, 82, 83, 102, 121
– clinical 101, 102, 103
– interdisciplinary 49, 51, 73, 74, 75
Team player 23, 47, 77, 82
Telehealth Nursing 111
Tenderness 245, 260, 267, 268, 269, 270, 271, 273, 281, 282, 284, 286
Termination 17, 18, 20, 62, 64, 77, 88, 114
Terms 7, 19, 20, 44, 57, 76, 93, 122, 127
– ideal 127, 128
Test 13, 14, 16, 18, 25, 57, 63, 131, 137, 138, 146, 221, 222, 268, 269
Testis 284, 285
Therapeutic effect 139, 140, 141, 142, 150, 233
Thumbs 148, 203, 221, 267, 268
Tissue 140, 143, 144, 193, 224, 232, 279, 284, 289
Tongue 140, 143, 160, 223, 242, 249
Topical Medication 144
Topics 3, 130, 133, 135
Touch 12, 40, 41, 123, 144, 145, 221, 222, 266, 268, 269, 275
Tract infections, urinary 160, 161, 286, 288
Training 18, 93, 94, 99, 107, 120
Training program 49
Transfer 8, 9, 12, 62, 63, 65, 70, 71, 88, 89, 90, 91, 119

Transfer application 9, 70, 71
Trauma blunt force 224, 272, 273
Treatment 49, 50, 93, 110, 163, 170, 174, 177, 182, 184, 194, 196, 197, 202, 239
Treatment team 110, 111
Triage Revised Trauma Score (TRTS), 183
TRST Score 183
TRTS (Triage Revised Trauma Score), 183
Turn and position patient 229, 230

U

Understanding 3, 82
Union 7, 20, 127
Unit 39, 40, 46, 60, 69, 82, 89, 90, 91, 92, 94, 122, 125, 126, 127
– clinical 102, 107
– intensive care 59, 60, 175
– step-down 19, 75
Unit clerk 71
United States 105, 123, 124, 164, 220
Upper GI 254, 255, 262
Urine 158, 169, 178, 187, 281, 283, 285, 287, 288
Urine output 175, 179, 191, 193, 197
– decreased 194, 195, 261, 291
Use 29, 45, 147, 148, 149, 190, 191, 192, 193, 195, 196, 197, 208, 213, 214
Utilization review nurse 110, 111
Utilization review nurse monitors 110

V

Vacations 47, 63, 105, 108, 119, 125
Value 28, 66, 161, 168, 169
– lower 196, 211, 214, 215, 216, 218, 219
Vasodilator 154, 193, 195, 196, 200
Vendors 16, 17, 32, 33, 34, 101, 102, 104, 135, 137, 138
Verbal intervention 183
Viable candidate 14, 55, 56, 80, 81, 121, 122, 123
Victims 33, 109
Vomiting 233, 234, 235, 236, 237, 238, 239, 240, 245, 247, 248, 250, 251, 252, 259

W, X, Y, Z
WBC (white blood cell), 167, 169, 175, 176, 179, 260, 288
Weaknesses 47, 54, 58, 87, 88, 118, 127, 231, 235, 236, 266, 272
Website healthcare facility's 10, 29, 44, 47, 76, 81
Weekends 11, 15, 31, 62, 98, 105, 107, 108, 112, 127, 128
Weight gain 194, 209, 210, 211, 212, 291
Weight loss 217, 249, 250, 260, 263, 287
Wheezing 171, 204, 207, 209, 210, 212, 214
Wong-Baker FACES Pain Rating Scale 161, 162
Words 3, 23, 28, 29, 30, 44, 53, 126, 128, 129, 180, 182, 205
Words and phrases 28, 48, 49, 50, 73, 74, 118
Work 19, 23, 42, 45, 62, 69, 89, 92, 93, 95, 102, 109, 111, 112, 121
– cardiac 195, 196

Work attire 36
Work environment hostile 95
Work ethic 8, 52
– good 43, 47
Work experience 29, 30, 42, 43, 48, 49, 50, 73, 74
Work history 23, 48, 64, 117
– stable 23
Work overtime 124
Work performance 35, 88
Work rules 61, 91
Work schedule 24, 31, 108, 119, 125
Work weekends 97, 111
Worker good 41, 117
Workflows 26, 101
– clinical 101, 102
Workload 117, 153, 214, 215, 231, 236, 237, 238
– increased respiratory 171, 211